Preface

Mammalian sociobiology is a rapidly advancing field which has made enormous strides in the last ten years. The last major monograph on the subject (Ewer, 1968) was published sixteen years ago, and there is a need for this information to be examined in terms of modern sociobiological theory.

My approach throughout is evolutionary and is therefore directed strongly towards research which throws light on the ways in which mammals behave in their natural environments. I have tried to cover as wide a range of mammalian species as possible, although, in some cases, the only data available were obtained from captive individuals. The coverage of this book is not a reflection of the volume of literature published on different species, as I have tried to avoid undue emphasis on the social behaviour of primates and laboratory rodents.

I have made scrupulous efforts throughout to avoid an anthropomorphic approach to mammalian behaviour. Terms such as 'strategy', 'evaluation' or 'choice' do not therefore imply conscious planning, but are used neutrally in the way in which they would be applied to a chess-playing computer. In the case of mammals, the programmer was natural selection. While I am fully aware that human beings are mammals, any detailed consideration of human social behaviour lies outside the scope of this book. However, the book may provide a complementary text to those interested in that subject.

A glossary of technical terms likely to be unfamiliar to general readers is included towards the back of the book, together with an outline classification of the Mammalia which covers those species mentioned in the text.

I am grateful to a number of people for helpful and stimulating discussions. They include Pat Bateson, Brian Bertram, Warren Brockelman, Alan Dixson, Robin Dunbar, Sian Evans, Peter Gortvai, Keith Kendricks, Morris Gosling and Bob Martin, but I take full responsibility for the views I have expressed. I must also thank Pat Bateson, Robin Dunbar, Morris Gosling and Miranda Stevenson for allowing me to quote from review papers in the press.

I must express my appreciation to the University College of Wales for granting me study leave, which enabled me to visit other institutions, both to take advantage of library facilities and to discuss the subject matter with other workers in the field. I am particularly grateful to Pat Bateson for providing me with facilities to work at the Sub-Department of Animal Behaviour, University of Cambridge, and to John Hearn and the Zoological Society of London for awarding me an Honorary Research Fellowship which enabled me to complete my writing under ideal conditions.

Last, but not least, I must thank Helen for encouraging me to write this book and for bearing with me during its two-year gestation period.

T. B. P.

Contents

CHAPTER ONE

INTRODUCTION

Social behaviour is any action directed by an individual towards a member of its own species. It includes both competitive behaviour, such as fighting, threat and submission, and co-operative interactions such as parental care and mating. All mammals show social behaviour, however infrequent their contact with other members of their own species, because internal fertilization necessitates mating and lactation involves an intimate relationship between mother and unweaned young.

1.1 Mammalian classification

Living mammals form a discrete group, distinguished by the possession of hair and mammary glands. The three surviving subclasses are quite distinct and can be assumed to have long independent evolutionary histories, because they differ fundamentally in their reproductive physiology.

Members of the subclass Prototheria, with a single order Monotremata, are egg-laying mammals, represented by three genera, all confined to Australia and New Guinea: the spiny anteaters or echidnas (*Zaglossus* and *Tachyglossus*) and the platypus (*Ornithorhynchus*). Members of the second subclass of mammals, the Metatheria (order Marsupialia) are found in the Americas, Australia and New Guinea, and include opossums, kangaroos, koala bears, native cats, the Tasmanian devil and the banded anteater. Marsupial young are born at a very early stage in their development and are minute, naked, blind and embryonic in appearance, but have powerful forelimbs for gripping the mother's fur. The newborn young, or embryon, makes its way unaided from the birth canal to the mother's teat. It then grips the nipple in its mouth and remains attached to it for the first part of its development. The third subclass of mammals, Eutheria, possess a well-developed allantochorionic placenta which enables its members to supply nutrients to the embryo for longer, thus allowing them to give birth to

1

young in a more advanced state of development. The newborn young of many eutherian mammals such as antelopes, cattle, horses, elephants, guinea pigs and dolphins are able, after a few minutes, to follow the herd, since their senses and power of locomotion are well developed. Eutherian mammals are highly successful both in terms of the large number of living species and the wide variety of ecological niches they have come to occupy. An outline classification of the mammals is given in Appendix Table 1, while Appendix Table 2 defines technical terms used in the text.

1.2 Social communication

Communication is difficult to define, although it invariably involves the passage of information from one individual (the signaller) to another (the recipient) and usually results in the modification of the recipient's behaviour or physiological state (see Lewis and Gower, 1980). This statement, however, does not provide an unambiguous definition of communication; if one animal is eating a meal, information passes to others and may even modify their behaviour, but eating cannot be regarded as a form of social communication. The sight of a hunting lion may change the behaviour of a herd of wildebeest, but the lion cannot be said to be communicating with them.

Probably the best way to define social communication is from an evolutionary and functional viewpoint. A social signal is behaviour which has evolved to convey information to a conspecific with the object of modifying its behaviour for the benefit of the signaller. As Dawkins and Krebs (1978) have pointed out, social signals enable one individual to manipulate the behaviour of a conspecific without the use of direct force. A signal such as a threat or a loud vocalization, which may drive a rival away without physical violence, has clear advantages over the use of direct force, because it both conserves energy and reduces the risk of injury.

There are basically two types of social signal, discrete and graded. The alarm call of a ground squirrel, a chemical signalling oestrus, or the territorial song of a gibbon are all discrete signals with a typical form. Behaviour such as aggressive vocalizations and threat displays, however, often consists of a series of graded signals, variations in which may reflect the emotional state of the sender.

Darwin noticed that an aggressive dog stands stiff-legged with raised hair, ears and tail, snarling and revealing its upper canine teeth by drawing back the lip. In complete contrast, a submissive dog crouches with head low, limbs bent, tail between the legs and ears flattened. These two postures represent the extremes of aggressiveness and submission and are completely opposite in the disposition of the various expressive parts of the anatomy. Lorenz (1966) however, realized that the two postures identified by Darwin were simply extremes on a continuum of graded signals. He extended Darwin's findings by interpreting individual canine expressions as a reflection of the conflict between two motivational factors: the inclination to attack (rage), or to flee (fear). Although he did not provide quantitative data to support this interpretation, it is one which has generally been accepted. Andrew (1963a, b) appreciated that primates also have a wide repertoire of facial expressions and he carried out a comparative survey which showed that the equivalent facial expressions occur in similar contexts in a range of primates. He also considered the possible evolutionary origins of different facial expressions (see also Redican, 1975; Van Hoof, 1962, 1967).

Huxley (1966) believed that displays have evolved from behaviour normally associated with that which is predicted, but that they have become exaggerated or carried out at a slower or more deliberate rate. For this evolutionary process he coined the term 'ritualization'. Ritualization is a process whereby an action becomes converted into an unambiguous signal. To take a simple example, when attacking a rival many mammals fix their gaze on it, make a rapid charge, open the mouth and finally bite it. These three actions which precede an attack have been ritualized into three forms of aggressive threat, namely, staring, lunging and open-mouth threat (see Chapter 4). When used as simply threats, however, these actions are exaggerated and slowed down so that they no longer simply function as precursors to fighting but convey information on the individual's internal state and hence its probable future behaviour.

It seems clear that, in most cases, an exchange of information through display is likely to be beneficial to both of the interactors, and the traditional view of ethologists has been that animal signalling has evolved for the mutual benefit of signaller and recipient (see Marler, 1966; Cullen, 1966; Smith, 1968). For example, the female's emission of scent at oestrus stimulates the male rat, rhesus monkey or dog to mate. By giving a clear indication that she has reached the fertile point in her reproductive cycle, the female is able to avoid forced attempts at mating at other times – for example, when she is already pregnant – and sperm is not wasted on infertile females.

Situations often arise, however, in which the two individual's interests are in conflict as, for example, when one is attempting to intimidate another by display. Maynard-Smith (1974) and Dawkins and Krebs (1978) took the view that an individual would not, in a conflict situation, be expected to give away truthful information to an antagonist about its next move, as this would benefit the opponent at the signaller's expense. The signaller would be expected to attempt to manipulate the opponent's behaviour to his own benefit, giving an impression of greater confidence than was actually the case; an element of bluff was therefore to be expected in conflict situations because telling the truth is not an evolutionarily stable strategy (see glossary for definitions).

However, the recipient of the signal would also be expected to resist persuasion which was against its best interests, so that an evolutionary 'arms race' is predicted. Natural selection would favour individuals who successfully manipulated others to their own ends, but it would also select for the ability to resist such manipulation. This situation is analogous to the way in which selection favours both predators who can catch their prey and prey which can effectively evade predators. The whole question of the truthfulness of displays and the extent to which they provide a means of manipulating others has been discussed by Caryl (1979, 1981, 1982) and Hinde (1981).

1.3 Altruism and inclusive fitness

The emphasis throughout this book will be on evolutionary and functional aspects of mammalian social behaviour, and the ways in which behaviour can affect the survival and success of the individual. From the standpoint of evolution, life can be regarded as a game in which each player attempts to gain the highest score in terms of its personal 'fitness'. Fitness can be defined as the genetic contribution that an individual makes to subsequent generations, and is measured by the number of its offspring which survive to breed.

Because natural selection operates in favour of the individual who leaves more offspring than others, it is to be expected that there should be competition, particularly between individuals of the same sex. This is reflected in the way of life of many primitive mammals such as shrews and opossums (*Didelphys*) which live in isolation and are hostile to adults of their own species, with the exception of fertile females. Some mammals, however, live in large groups and display little hostility to one another. They may even assist individuals other than their own offspring and defend them against predators, groom them, and in some cases even help to care for another individual's young (aunting or allomothering).

When an individual expends energy or runs risks in helping another, its behaviour is termed 'altruistic'. Altruistic behaviour lowers the 'fitness' of the altruist, while increasing that of the recipient, so that it is, at first sight, difficult to understand how such behaviour could have evolved. Three theories, namely group selection, kin selection and reciprocation, have been suggested in attempts to accommodate altruism within current evolutionary theory.

Group selection. This hypothesis proposes that groups of individuals who support and help one another may have an advantage over groups whose members are selfish. This is an appealing idea, but its major drawback is that it is not an evolutionarily stable strategy (or ESS) because a selfish individual in an altruistic group would inevitably increase his own fitness at the expense of altruistic group members. A gene for selfishness would therefore spread throughout an altruistic group (see Dawkins, 1976). It is, of course, difficult to visualize how a gene for altruism could have survived to spread throughout a selfish group in first instance. See Wilson (1975) for a discussion of this problem.

Kin selection. Perhaps the most convincing explanation for the evolution of altruistic behaviour is that proposed by Hamilton (1964). It relies for its validity on the proposition that group members may be genetically closely related. The adaptive significance of parental altruism towards offspring has never been disputed because each offspring inherits half of its genes from each parent; parental care therefore helps to ensure the persistence of parental genes into the next generation. Hamilton realized that, as the parent-offspring relationship is not the only one where genes are shared by common descent, natural selection might also favour altruism between other close relatives.

The relationship between two individuals can be expressed as a fraction (known as Wright's coefficient of relationship, r) which reflects the proportion of genes which two relatives share by common descent. For unrelated individuals r is approximately equal to zero, while for identical twins $r = 1$. The relationship between parent and offspring is $\frac{1}{2}$ and the average relatedness of non-identical siblings (brothers and sisters) is also $\frac{1}{2}$. For half-siblings, grandchildren and grandparent, and for uncle and nephew relationships, $r = \frac{1}{4}$, while for full cousins $r = \frac{1}{8}$.

As altruism, in the form of parental care (where $r = \frac{1}{2}$), is a common phenomenon, Hamilton suggests that altruism between siblings might also be expected to evolve in situations where individuals lived in association with close kin. By helping a close relative, an individual can promote the survival of shared genes.

If an individual behaves altruistically to a relative, the consequent gain in 'fitness' is dependent on two factors; firstly, the cost of the altruistic actions in terms of energy expended and risks incurred, and secondly the closeness of relationship of the recipient. Altruistic behaviour might be expected to evolve where the cost (c) to the altruist is less than the gain to the beneficiary (b), multiplied by the coefficient of relationship between the two individuals (r). This can best be illustrated by taking a hypothetical example where a brother defends his sister against a predator. Let us imagine that the sister is certain to be killed by the predator if her brother does not come to her aid. If he does so, let us assume that the risk of his being killed by the predator is one in four. By behaving altruistically, the brother increases his fitness because the risk to him (c) $= \frac{1}{4}$ while the benefit to his sister (b) $= 1$ and their coefficient of relationship (r) $= \frac{1}{2}$. Thus $c < br$ ($\frac{1}{4} < 1 \times \frac{1}{2}$). In general, for altruism to be selected, the cost:benefit ratio must be less than the coefficient of relationship, i.e. $c/b < r$.

It will be clear from this theoretical example that the likelihood of altruism between two individuals becomes more remote if the relationship between them is distant because the cost:benefit ratio must decrease proportionately. Hamilton termed selection which favours altruism between close relatives (other than offspring) 'kin selection'. Fitness or genetic contribution to the next generation is measured by the number of surviving direct offspring, but Hamilton (1964) realized that it should also include the effects of an individual's behaviour on its neighbours, weighted according to the closeness of their relationship. Thus he introduced the concept of 'inclusive fitness', which he defined as the personal fitness which an individual actually expresses in its production of adult offspring stripped of all components due to the individual's social environment. This quantity was augmented by fractions of the quantities of harm and benefit which the individual itself causes to the fitnesses of its neighbours. The fractions in question are the coefficients of relationship appropriate to the neighbours who are affected: where this fraction was negligibly small it was regarded as zero.

The concept of inclusive fitness has revolutionized sociobiology. Grafen (1982) however, has pointed out that this concept has frequently been misused and misdefined, even by the authors of major textbooks of animal behaviour.

Reciprocation. If it were possible to rely on altruistic behaviour by an individual being reciprocated by the beneficiary at a future date, no close relationship need exist between them for such behaviour to be maintained by natural selection. Such a system of reciprocal altruism, as it has been termed, could play an important role in mammalian societies if it were proof against cheating. In other words, any individual which cheated by accepting altruism but failing to reciprocate would be identified and punished by being excluded from the social group or by having future help to it withdrawn. Reciprocal altruism would be most likely to operate in highly social, long-lived mammals with high intelligence and a good memory.

There is a dearth of information on reciprocal altruism but Packer (1977) found that immigrant male baboons assisted unrelated males to acquire access to an oestrous female who was being guarded by a third male. The helper did not himself attempt to take over the female but, on a subsequent occasion, Packer observed this help to be reciprocated in a similar situation. Seyfarth and Cheney (1984) also observed reciprocal altruism in vervet monkeys, where they found that grooming between unrelated individuals increases the likelihood that they will respond to one another's solicitations for help. No such correlation between grooming and aid-giving was found in kin groups, where there was a high level of altruistic behaviour.

So far, these are the only quantified examples of reciprocal altruism but it is conceivable that the phenomenon may be more widespread than is at present realized.

1.4 Determinants of mammalian social organization

From the hypothesis of kin selection, it might appear that an individual mammal which has adopted a gregarious way of life should never leave its social group but remain there to help its closest relatives. This rarely occurs in practice because most animals have mechanisms which avoid the genetic disadvantages of excessive inbreeding (see Chapter 3). In group-living mammals, the commonest situation is for males to emigrate and breed in another group, while females remain in their natal group; social groups of mammals are therefore generally matrilineal, consisting of groups of closely-related females and their offspring. This provides the ideal environment for the evolution of altruistic behaviour through kin selection, and matrilineal groups are known from species as diverse as elephants, ground squirrels and monkeys (macaques and baboons).

As regards the extent of their sociability, it is possible to distinguish a number of different types of aggregation in mammals. There are species which live together in groups where very little co-operation exists between adults, for example, herds of giraffe or breeding herds of seals or sea lions. In these instances, the individual lives gregariously either because of the attraction of a limited resource, such as food, or a breeding area, or as a protection against predators (see Chapter 6). Where true societies are found, the colony or band has a fixed membership and there are well-defined personal relationships between individuals, who are hostile to non-group members; it is in these societies that the highest levels of co-operation are found.

One important aspect of mammalian behaviour, which has had a profound influence on the forms taken by mammalian social behaviour, is the fact that the female suckles her young. This not only demands a close relationship between mother and offspring but also eliminates the need for a father to feed his offspring. Most female mammals rear their infants unaided, so that the male's presence is supernumerary. Two aspects of mammalian sociobiology appear to be closely related to this fact: firstly, monogamy is rare in mammals (only approximately 5% of mammals are monogamous according to Kleiman, 1977) and, secondly, the matrilineal character of most mammalian societies may partially be attributed to the close mother-offspring bond initiated during lactation. This relieves the male of parental responsibility, so that he can be relatively unsociable without prejudicing his offspring's survival. Most male mammals are polygamous or promiscuous, adopting a strategy of mating with as many females as possible while having minimum contact with their offspring (see Chapter 3); the mother and her young therefore form the basic social unit of most mammalian societies.

1.5 Summary

1. All mammals show some social behaviour. Individuals may be dispersed, aggregated into a herd or colony, or members of an organized society. The majority of mammals are solitary but the social organization of some species may be complex and may include high levels of altruistic and co-operative behaviour.

2. There are three distinct living groups of mammals represented by the subclasses Prototheria, Metatheria and Eutheria. They differ in reproductive physiology and hence in the early relationship between mother and offspring.

3. Mammals have evolved a repertoire of social behaviour which can communicate information about motivational state and act as a pointer to likely future behaviour. Some displays may indicate a degree of motivational conflict.

4. Lactation by the female not only forms the basis of a social bond between mother and offspring but also reduces the need for the male to participate in

parental care. This situation predisposes mammals to form matrilineal societies where males alone emigrate from their natal group to breed.

5. The matrilineal society composed of closely related females and their offspring provides the ideal environment for the evolution of altruistic behaviour through kin selection.

6. In gregarious species, male mammals tend to be less sociable than females and they generally complete for the opportunity to mate. Most mammalian societies are therefore polygynous.

CHAPTER TWO

SENSES AND SOCIAL COMMUNICATION

Social communication has already been briefly referred to in Chapter 1. The present chapter is concerned specifically with the use of different sensory modalities for conveying messages. Mammals generally employ some, or all, of four methods of communication, i.e. chemical, acoustic, visual and tactile. Each method has unique advantages and limitations which will be considered briefly before examining signalling in more detail.

Olfaction is a pre-eminent sense in most mammals, which also possess special scent glands which secrete odours of communicative significance. Odours may be used to communicate directly with a conspecific either in close proximity or at a distance. An olfactory message has the unique advantage that it can be deposited at a site in the individual's home range and subsequently perceived in the absence of the signaller. Not only can it convey information about the individual which deposited it, but chemical changes and changes in concentration may indicate the age of the scent mark and, thus, how long ago it was deposited. Olfactory communication, including direct contact between individuals, frequently provides information about the age, sex, status and physiological state of the signaller.

Acoustic communication also has the advantage that it can be effective when the signaller is some distance away. Loud calls or songs can be used to indicate the presence of an individual or social group in an area, and the physical nature of the sounds employed often gives accurate information as to an individual's location at the time. Such signals can be used to repel strangers or attract group members. Such conspicuous advertisement may however attract predators, and loud calling is consequently restricted to species which are subject to minimal predation or, for example to arboreal species which are relatively inaccessible to predators when they signal. Vocalizations are also used in intimate situations and in highly sociable species. Acoustic communication is particularly flexible, because through modulation of frequency (pitch) or amplitude (loudness), it lends itself to the production of graded signals which may subtly reflect changes in underlying motivational states.

Visual signals can only be used where individuals are in close proximity, and so reach their highest complexity in large mammals living in open habitats or in highly sociable species. Because vision is not a primary sense in most small nocturnal mammals, which also need to remain inconspicuous, visual signalling in the majority of mammals is much less complex than that of birds. Some mammals, however, such as wolves, higher primates and plains ungulates have evolved elaborate visual displays and, in those with the most complex societies, such displays can convey information about rapidly changing motivational states.

Tactile signals may be important in maternal, sexual and amicable behaviour, particularly in highly sociable species, but they also occur in agonistic situations where a tactile signal such as a push or an inhibited bite may be substituted for a serious assault.

We shall now consider each of the four modes of communication in more detail.

2.1 Chemical communication

2.1.1 Perception and production of odours

Most mammals have a highly-developed sense of smell; the olfactory sense organs are borne on a group of scroll bones termed the endoturbinales, and sensitivity to odours relates to the number of receptors, which can be approximated from the surface area of these bones. Their area in the German Shepherd dog is $200 \, cm^2$ as compared with $4–5 \, cm^2$ in a human being; this disparity is reflected in the fact that a dog can detect acetic acid molecules at a concentration 100 million times less than the minimum which can be perceived by the human nose. Some mammals possess an independently innervated additional olfactory organ known as the vomero-nasal or Jacobson's organ, which lies anteriorly on the roof of the mouth and may connect with the nasal cavity. Lip curling or 'flehmen' is associated with the possession of this organ and is seen in many mammals during courtship (e.g. stallions on scenting the urine of an oestrous mare). It occurs in marsupials and several orders of placental mammals (see Stoddart, 1980).

Correlated with the well-developed sense of smell in most mammals is a chemical communication system which involves the possession of special odour-producing glands. The actual odours vary from species to species; in some cases the scent results from the secretion of a single chemical such as musk (from the preputial glands of the musk deer, *Moschus moschiferus*), civet (from the anal glands of the African civet, *Civettictis civetta*) and castoreum (from the preputial glands of the beaver, *Castor fiber*). In other cases the message is conveyed by a mixture of chemicals, as in the vaginal secretion of oestrous rhesus monkeys (*Macaca mulatta*), lion (*Panthera leo*) and red foxes (see Albone *et al.*, 1974), where the odour is produced by bacterial decay of secretions. This can be demonstrated by treating the vagina of the female rhesus macaque with antibiotic, which renders her sexually unattractive to males. In many species urine may contain odorous secretions which convey messages to conspecifics. This is a common method by which female mammals signal that they are in oestrus.

The odours produced by mammals may communicate to conspecifics in either of two ways. Firstly they may have a priming effect, whereby they influence the physiological state of the recipient with a delayed behavioural effect. An example of a priming odour is the Bruce effect. If a female mouse is mated and conceived but, within five days of mating, is exposed for a minimum of twelve hours to the scent of an unfamiliar male, her pregnancy terminates and she comes back into oestrus (Bruce, 1960). Secondly odours may have a direct influence on the behaviour of a conspecific, among the best known being sexual attractants secreted by the female.

The scents of mammals are normally produced by dermal glands of two kinds. Apocrine or sweat glands secrete droplets of aqueous fluid and small pieces of cell debris. They may either be widely spread over the body, as in horses and man, or concentrated to form glandular areas such as the chin glands of rabbits and the dorsal glands of peccaries (*Tayassu* sp.)

The second type of gland is the holocrine or sebaceous gland, which produces a secretion known as sebum. Holocrine glands may be generally distributed about the body, as in the rat, or concentrated as in the ventral glands of the mongolian gerbil (*Meriones unguiculatus*), the anal glands of many carnivores and the preputial glands of rodents. Artiodactyla have well-developed preorbital, tarsal, metatarsal or interdigital holocrine glands. Some glands are under hormonal control, so that the scent of the female may change throughout the oestrous cycle. Male and female mammals may differ in their sensitivity to various chemicals; this is true even in our own species where women are more sensitive to musk-like substances than are men. Le Magnen (1950) tested the sensitivity of men and women to an artificial musk, exaltolide, and found that 40–50% of men could not perceive this substance at all. The average sensitivity of those men who could detect it was 1000 times less than that of women. There is some evidence for a link with oestrogen production, for ovariectomized women's sensitivity was found to be 100–1000 times reduced, but was restored if they were treated with oestrogen. Le Magnen also found that women's sensitivity to musks varied during the oestrous cycle, being at a maximum when blood levels of oestrogen were at a peak. The significance of these findings for human beings is not clear but they show that the mammalian reproductive cycle can influence both the secretion of odours and an individual's sensitivity to them.

In discussing mammalian odours it seems best to avoid the use of the term 'pheromone' which is commonly applied to some insect odours, as few mammalian odours elicit the stereotyped responses characteristic of pheromones.

A number of techniques have been used to determine a mammal's response to, and capacity to distinguish between, odours. Examples are: direct observation of an individual exposed to an odour, comparison with a control whose sense of smell has been eliminated (anosmic control) or discrimination experiments in which, either the animal's natural choice is recorded, or one odour has come to be associated with a reward (positive reinforcement). In some instances odours have been analysed by gas chromatogram, their active principles identified and the animal's response to synthetic odours tested (see Epple, 1979).

Mammalian chemical communication occurs in a number of different behavioural contexts, which will now be considered in more detail.

2.1.2 The use of odours in social communication

Discrimination tests using an odour from an individual's own species and that of a closely related species have shown that many mammals can recognize their species by scent, for example, guinea pigs (Beauchamp, 1973), Mongolian gerbils (Dagg and Windsor, 1971) and brown lemurs (*Lemur fulvus*) (Klopfer, 1977). The ability to discriminate, and show a preference for, the odour of their own subspecies has been demonstrated experimentally in bank voles (*Clethrionomys glareolus*) (Godfrey, 1958), blacktailed and mule deer (*Odocoileus hemionus*) (Müller-Schwarze and Müller-Schwarze, 1974) and saddlebacked tamarins (*Saguinus fuscicollis*) (Epple, 1979). An extremely important piece of information which may be conveyed by scent is the sex of an individual, and male pigs (*Sus scrofa*), guinea pigs (*Cavia porcellus*), (Beräter *et al.*, 1973), Mongolian gerbils, brown rats (Archer, 1968) and house mice (Mackintosh and Grant, 1966), can distinguish between urine from males and females. Similarly, brown lemurs and saddlebacked tamarins can discriminate between the scent marks of males and females (Epple 1978a). Dixon and Mackintosh (1971) showed that an odour in the urine of male mice influences the aggressive behaviour of other males. They rubbed castrated male laboratory mice with either male or female urine and found that the former elicited more aggression from an intact male opponent. Urine from castrated males and ovariectomized females did not produce this effect. The influence of olfactory cues on sexual behaviour has been reviewed by Keverne (1978).

Some male mammals in rut produce odours which attract females. This is true of the European hedgehog (*Erinaceus europaeus*) (see Poduschka, 1977), where a secretion produced by the penis has a stimulating effect on the courtship behaviour of the female; the rutting male's urine is also attractive. The odour of the male domesticated pig has a specific behavioural effect on the female in inducing the stance which she adopts prior to copulation. Male Asiatic elephants (*Elephas maximus*) produce a copious secretion from the temporal gland when in 'musth', a state in which they become exceptionally aggressive and sexually active for short periods of time (Poole and Moss, 1981).

Certain odours communicate the state of maturity of an individual. The urine of juvenile mice has a distinctive smell which reduces the aggressiveness of older individuals towards them (Dixon and Mackintosh, 1976), and the odours produced by the scent glands of European rabbits (*Oryctolagus cuniclus*) are less intense in juveniles, so that even human beings can roughly age young rabbits on the basis of odour alone. Adult mammals frequently recognize their own young by scent; in the case of the domesticated goat (*Capra hircus*), Gubernick (1980) has convincingly demonstrated that the mother labels her newborn kid by licking it and allowing it to take milk, which imparts the mother's own smell to her offspring and allows her to recognize it subsequently. Kids which have not been licked or suckled are rejected by the mother goat. In the case of tree shrews (*Tupaia glis*) and dwarf mongooses (*Helogale parvula*) both parents mark the young with their scent glands.

Generally female mammals are only fertile for brief periods between pregnancies or, in seasonally breeding species, at a certain time of the year. The fertile period itself may last only two or three days and most females indicate their sexual receptiveness to the male by means of a vaginal secretion. Michael and Keverne (1970) and Keverne (1976) showed that in the rhesus monkey the secretion is under the control of oestrogen, while in golden hamsters (*Mesocricetus auratus*) the male's preference for the vaginal secretion of an oestrous female is removed by castration but restored by treatment with testosterone. Female sexual receptivity may also be indicated by an odour in the urine at oestrus. When urinating, the female is able to signal her sexual receptiveness to the male even when she is not physically present, an ability which must be extremely important for solitary mammals. Male dogs, rabbits, mice and horses have all been found to be attracted to the urine of oestrous females; this phenomenon is probably widespread among mammals, but remains to be investigated in other species.

Social mammals behave differently towards strangers and members of their own colony, and, in some species, colony odours are implicated. In the case of the laboratory rat, an individual which is removed from its social group for a few days is attacked as if it were a stranger when reintroduced. If, however, the isolate is kept with soiled bedding from the colony cage, it is accepted back amicably. In such cases, the colony scent appears to be acquired from the general environment and there is no evidence for a specific colony odour. In other cases, however, the dominant member of a social group scent-marks other members of the colony, sometimes by rubbing its scent glands on the other individuals as in the case of the flying phalanger (Schultze-Westrum, 1965, 1969). Some hystricomorph rodents (*Cavia, Myoprocta, Octodon, Dolichotis* and *Cuniculus*) mark other colony members by spraying urine on to them (Kleiman, 1974); this is termed 'enuration'. In desert rodents such as *Pediolagus*, sandbathing by all family members in the same spot may be a means of maintaining a group odour.

Most mammals are capable of recognizing conspecifics as individuals. This faculty enables a mammal to recall its past social interactions with a particular individual and thus to remember whether it was aggressive or friendly, dominant or subordinate. It is the ability to recognize individuals and recall their past behaviour which distinguishes the membership of a society from simply being part of an aggregation. The ability to recognize other individuals by their odour is known to have developed in a number of mammalian orders which includes Marsupialia, Rodentia, Primates and Carnivora. The individual may not only be distinguishable by its scent at close quarters but may also leave individually recognizable scent marks throughout the area in which it lives, indicative of its personal occupancy of the area (see Chapter 5). Such behaviour is found in all mammalian orders with the exception of the aquatic Sirenia and Cetacea. The form taken by scent-marking varies from species to species; the male wolf urinates on strange conspecific urine from which Fox and Cohen (1977) deduced that the animal is essentially leaving a record of its presence as an individual.

Dwarf mongooses scent-mark, and Rasa (1973), in an experimental study, found that these animals can not only identify individuals by their scent marks, but are also capable of determining whether the scent was deposited recently.

The black rhinoceros (*Diceros bicornis*) marks its territory both by spraying urine, which it disperses with rapid vibratory movements of the tail, and by leaving faeces at definite points in its territory. Faeces are also used for marking by European badgers (*Meles meles*), weasels (*Mustela nivalis*), otters (*Lutra lutra*) and giant rats (*Cricetomys gambianus*). Hippopotamuses (*Hippopotamus amphibius*) use lateral movements of the tail to spread faeces over considerable distances.

A number of mammals mark the environment directly with their scent glands. Some species (mustelids, bush dogs, and marmosets) use the anal glands, others use preorbital glands (ruminant artiodactyls), sternal glands (Mongolian gerbils) or chin glands (rabbits). Discrimination experiments have demonstrated that individual recognition is possible from scent marks in ring-tailed lemurs (*Lemur catta*) (Harrington, 1971) and dwarf mongooses (Rasa, *loc. cit.*). This does not necessarily mean that the animal uses scent marks in this way, under natural conditions, but as a general inference it seems reasonable. More field and experimental work would undoubtedly be of immense value (but see Chapter 5).

One piece of information which may be carried by an odour is the status of an individual. To take the simplest case, a dominant may scent-mark more frequently than a subordinate, and also deposit the chemical signal more frequently both on conspicuous objects in the environment and the females of his harem (Bell, 1980). Laboratory rats and mice are capable of discriminating between the body odours of high and low-ranking males, females showing an active preference for the scent of the dominant. It seems highly probable that these differences are related to hormonal states, as subordinate mice have heavier adrenal glands and lower plasma testosterone levels (Jones and Nowell, 1973).

Some mammals produce an odour when alarmed, and those of the woodchuck (*Marmota monax*) and the black-tailed deer (*Odocoileus hemionus columbianus*) cause active avoidance by conspecifics. In some mustelids such as the European polecat (*Mustela putorius*), striped skunk (*Mephitis mephitis*) and wolverine (*Gulo gulo*), the anal glands secrete a foul-smelling fluid; in the case of the skunk this is sprayed at the predator, the active ingredients in this species being trans-2-butane-1-thiol, 3-methyl-1-butanethiol and trans-2-butenyl methyl disulphide. The extent to which these scents cause alarm to conspecifics is not known but, as the species are rather solitary, this aspect is unlikely to be important. In this case glands which are normally used for social communication in mammals have become modified to produce an aversive effect on members of other species.

A number of functions have been ascribed to scent-marking in the animal's home range. Eisenberg and Kleiman (1972) suggested that scent marks help an individual to orientate in its own living area and that a second function is to advertise to conspecifics the presence of an individual or pack in a particular region. Generally, the presence of a scent mark does not, of itself, appear to act as a deterrent to trespass, although lone wolves have been shown to avoid areas recently marked by packs, and cheetahs change direction on encountering a fresh scent mark. However, Wells and Bekoff (1981) found that coyotes trespass into areas which have been scent-marked by other individuals, making it likely that the odour in this case acts only to advertise the presence, and possibly strength of numbers, of conspecifics. The individual's past experience may tell it whom to avoid or seek out, depending upon its established relationship with the scent-marker. This aspect of olfactory communication will be considered in more detail in Chapter 5.

Brown (1979) divided social chemical signals into two kinds. The first type are identifier odours which are stable for periods of time, for example individual, colony, sex-specific, age-specific, and species-typical odours. The second type are emotive odours which are released in special circumstances and are not long-lasting, for example rut, social status, maternal and alarm odours. It must also be borne in mind that the *directness* of the social effect varies; signal odours produce an immediate effect, while primer odours have longer-term physiological effects.

Clearly, most mammals which rely heavily on chemical communication are capable of receiving a wide variety of messages by this means. Eisenberg and Kleiman (1972), in their review of olfactory communication in mammals, summarize the probable role of odours by stating that

for each individual depending upon his age, sex, mood and reproductive state there is an optimum odour field which will provide the optimum level of security. This odour field is composed of a combination of olfactory stimuli emanating from the individual, the environment, the conspecifics. If a disturbance in the odour field occurs (a) through a change in physiological state which alters the sensitivity of the individual, and his perception of the optimum odour field (b) through the introduction of a foreign odour, or (c) through a change in the odour field caused by the dissipation of scent previously deposited, then the individual will attempt to restore the previous balance by the release and deposition of scent. The changed odour field may also arouse the individual, depending upon the nature of the change, and other behaviour may be initiated.

2.2 Acoustic communication

2.2.1 Sound production

Most mammals produce sounds by means of the respiratory tract, using inspired or expired air. Sounds are usually formed in the larynx by the vocal cords and then modified by changes in shape of the buccal cavity. Some species, such as the siamang (*Symphalangus syndactylus*) and orang utan (*Pongo pygmaeus*) possess special elastic-walled vocal sacs which resonate and serve to amplify the sound and reduce harmonics in the call, while South American howler monkeys (*Aloutta* sp.) have a specialized inflated hyoid bone which acts as a call amplifier; such adaptations enable the sender to be audible over distances of several kilometres. Some gazelles can produce sounds in their noses by vibrating cartilaginous structures or folds of skin, and cetaceans use the blowhole and nasal passages to vocalize. Some mammals, however, produce sounds from structures other than the respiratory tract; many rodents grind their teeth when aggressive, mountain gorillas (*Gorilla gorilla berengei*) beat their chests while chimpanzees (*Pan troglodytes*) drum with their hands on hollow trees, and black-tailed prairie dogs (*Cynomys ludovicianus*) stamp on the ground. Species whose hair is modified to form spines, such as the Bornean rattle porcupine (*Hystrix crassispinis*) and the tenrecs (*Centetes* and *Hemicentetes*) can produce sounds by rattling their quills.

There are certain physical constraints on sound production. Most mammals are capable of making high-pitched sounds, but larger mammals are also capable of producing low-pitched sounds because the length of the vibrating structure must be adequate to produce long wavelengths (compare for example a violin and double bass) and loudness is dependent upon the extent to which the vibrator can be displaced laterally (wave amplitude); thus shrews do not roar, but lions can! It follows from this that one would expect that the lowest pitch obtained might change during the animal's development, and that a young animal would be expected to produce fewer low-pitched sounds than an adult. This is shown in Figure 2.1 for a monkey, the crowned guenon (*Cercopithecus pogonias*), which has a cohesion call that functions to keep the group together. The data shown are for a male during prepuberty and puberty phases; the mean frequency for the low-pitched component and its standard deviation are given, together with the weight curve for the individual (Gautier and Gautier, 1977).

The range of sounds produced by different species is very variable and is dependent upon the extent to which the animal also relies on other forms

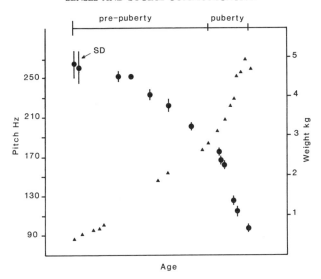

Figure 2.1 Changes in the average pitch of the low-pitched component of the cohesion call with age in the male crowned guenon (*Cercopithecus pogonias*). (After Gautier and Gautier, 1977) circles, pitch with standard deviation; triangles, weight of individual.

of communication and on its degree of sociability. For example, shrews, in which optical communication is virtually non-existent, rely heavily on acoustic messages, and the shorttail shrew (*Blarina brevicauda*) possesses a repertoire of at least five vocal signals. Highly social species of mammal may have a wider repertoire of acoustic signals. Wolves, for example, have seven and chimpanzees twenty-four classes of vocal sounds. The kinds of signal produced are also dependent upon the environment, since this places physical constraints on the effectiveness of different forms of sound. In dense woodland, for example, long-distance calls tend to have a low pitch because high-pitched sounds are easily scattered and absorbed by foliage. Other factors which reduce the effectiveness of acoustic signals are wind, high humidity, and high temperature. Marler (1970) noted that diurnal monkeys which live in dense habitats tend to have discrete calls, whereas those living in open habitats tend to intergrade.

Sound production may be different in the two sexes and in polygynous mammals such as red deer and howler monkeys the males alone produce the loud spacing call. In the great apes, Fossey (1972) showed that there is a considerable difference between the frequency of vocalizations by adult male chimpanzees and those of mountain gorillas (see Table 2.1); in the latter species, almost all of the vocalizations recorded were produced by adult males.

Table 2.1 Frequency of calling by different age/sex classes in chimpanzees and mountain gorillas (after Fossey, 1972).

% of calls made by each class member	Adult M	Adult F	Juvenile	Infant
Gorilla	92	4	0.6	3
Chimpanzee	27	25	24	24

Sample size
Number of calls: gorilla 1700, chimpanzee 2313
Number of individuals: gorilla 106, chimpanzee 44.

For its effectiveness, vocal communication depends upon the perception of the receiver, all mammals having binaural hearing which provides a mechanism for locating the source of a sound. This is dealt with in the central nervous system which estimates the differences in the time, (of arrival) differences in intensity (amplitude) and differences in phase of the waves arriving at the two ears. The distance of the caller from the recipient of the signal may be estimated from the loudness (amplitude) of the call which decreases with the square of the distance. Another mechanism which may operate depends upon the fact that the rate of attenuation, i.e. decrease in loudness, is directly related to frequency. High-pitched sounds attenuate more rapidly than those of equivalent amplitude but lower frequency. These physical principles are important for interpreting the character of different forms of acoustic communication. A social mammal faced with a predator may give a mobbing call which consists of loud, short notes covering a range of frequencies. This allows conspecifics to locate the signaller and hence the predator and, in some species, to go to the signaller's defence. Alternatively, an individual which discovers a predator may give a distress call which is usually a long call, high-pitched with a limited frequency range, providing little information as to the whereabouts of the caller. Intimate contact calls between members of a social group, by contrast, are usually intermittent, low-pitched and of relatively low amplitude, so that they can be easily located from nearby. Rhythmical variations or modulation of the frequency or amplitude of calls may also provide cues as to the whereabouts of the signaller (see Snowdon and Hodun, 1979).

2.2.2 The messages conveyed by sounds

For convenience, vocal communication can be divided into two types—firstly, distant, and secondly, intimate signalling. Alarm calls are a typical form of distance signal; they are loud and usually high-pitched, and there is often considerable similarity between the alarm calls of different species. These calls alert conspecifics to the presence of danger. Some species give different alarm calls when sighting different predators. Four such distinct vocalizations have been identified in the vervet monkey (*Cercopithecus aethiops*) in response to the following: snakes, small bird or mammal predators, large predatory birds and a major bird or mammal predator in close proximity to the caller (Seyfarth *et al.*, 1980). Belding's ground squirrels (*Spermophilus beldingi*), which are small rodents living in social groups in the Rocky Mountains, give two kinds of vocalization in response to predators, the first a chattering sound with a wide frequency range when sighting a ground predator such as a weasel, and the second a high-pitched whistle in response to an aerial predator. Clearly the chattering draws attention to the caller's, and hence the predator's, precise location in the colony, whereas the whistle simply indicates the predator's presence, its actual position being irrelevant. This example may be used to discuss the theoretical problem associated with the evolution of alarm calls.

Alarm calls present an interesting problem. An individual making an alarm call would appear to decrease its own fitness by drawing a predator's attention to itself, while at the same time increasing the fitness of other colony members. While a number of explanations have been put forward, ranging from group selection to the suggestion that the call may actually in some way deter the predator from attacking, the most plausible explanation is based on kin selection. For the alarm call to increase the individual's inclusive fitness, it must be assumed that the small extra risk incurred by the caller in drawing attention to itself will be offset by the consequent reduction of risk to a nearby related individual previously unaware of the danger. A factor which is of utmost importance in this model is the likelihood of the caller's warning a close relative; if he has no relatives in the group, he would not be expected to give an alarm call which would serve only to increase the fitness of unrelated individuals. If on the other hand the group contains a number of close relatives, the more likely an alarm call will be to save one of them and thus increase his own inclusive fitness.

Data supporting this hypothesis have been provided by Sherman (1977) for Belding's ground squirrel (*S. beldingi*). He found that predators such as weasels and coyotes were often attracted to individuals giving alarm calls, so that there could be no doubt of the decrease in fitness to the caller. In this species, males migrate to breed whereas most females remain in their natal colony. Kin selection would predict that females should give more alarm

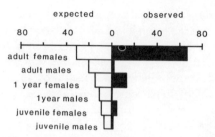

Figure 2.2 Alarm calls in Belding's ground squirrels (*Spermophilus beldingi*). Observed and expected frequencies of calling for different age/sex classes (after Sherman, 1977).

calls than males, and Sherman found this to be the case (Figure 2.2). That this was not simply a sex-linked trait was apparent from the fact that those females which had actually migrated into the colony gave fewer calls than those born into it.

Another form of long-distance calling is that associated with territory ownership and spacing (see Chapter 5). Examples are the roaring of lions, howling of wolves, calling of prairie dogs, and the loud calls of the South American howler monkey, the African black and white colobus monkey (*Colobus guereza*) and the Asian gibbons (*Hylobates*) and siamang (*Symphalangus*). Two of the best-analysed examples will be chosen for more detailed consideration: the wolf (*Canis lupus*) and the lesser apes (Hylobatidae).

The howling of wolf packs has been studied in detail by Mech and his co-workers (Mech, 1970; Harrington and Mech, 1979). Howling serves both to reassemble separated pack members and to space out different packs, i.e. it attracts familiar members and repels strangers. If, however, a howling stranger appears at close quarters, (within 200 metres), the alpha members of the pack may approach and investigate. Harrington and Mech studied radio-marked wolves from the air and also, by making simulated wolf howls, considered the effect of howling on packs and the frequency of howling in lone, as opposed to pack-living, wolves. Lone wolves howled much less than pack wolves and for a shorter period of time. Howling by the latter was particularly associated with kills, when the response of a nearby pack was to move away. As pack members howl together, it is possible that other wolves may from the howling be able to estimate pack size; in addition, each wolf has an individually identifiable howl. Generally pack howling lasts for about 40 minutes and is made up of with 85-second bouts of howling separated by 15-minute refractory periods. The wolf's howl is an extremely efficient method of territorial communication, which

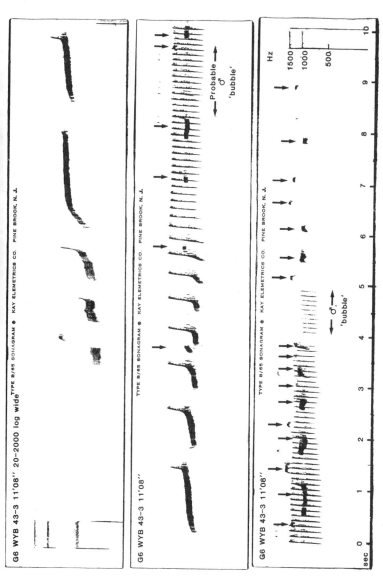

Figure 2.3 The great-call of the female pileated gibbon (*Hylobates pileatus*) showing duetting by the male partner. The positions of male calls are indicated by arrows. The male contribution usually consists of alternating high and low notes beginning during the middle of the female's great-call, and followed or interrupted by a short 'bubbling' phase about 1 s long, which here contains 10 notes given at a speed of close to 10 notes per second (bottom section of sonagram). (Sonagram W. Brockelman.)

can be detected even by the human ear at a distance of eight kilometres and is audible over an area of 200 square kilometres. It provides information on identity of callers, numbers in the pack, and location; it also enables lost members to find their social group. It is interesting that howling in the closely related coyote (*Canis latrans*), a much less sociable member of the dog family, acts only as a spacing mechanism and does not attract conspecifics.

The songs of the Hylobatidae (gibbons and siamang) are a form of long-distance territorial calling which has been studied in some detail in both field and zoo conditions. Calling normally begins just before dawn, first one group and then another becoming involved. Choruses may be all-male, all-female or male-female duets, depending upon the species. The calls are distinct as regards individual identity and sex. In species which duet, the male and female sing alternately in synchrony so that the song sounds as though made by a single individual (see Figure 2.3). It probably informs other gibbons of the mated status of the pair. Gibbons with territorial neighbours sing more than those with relatively isolated territories.

Undoubtedly the most remarkable and complex of acoustic signals produced by mammals are the songs of the humpbacked whale (*Megaptera novaeangliae*). Each song may last for as long as 30 minutes and can carry for very long distances. The song covers a great range of frequencies and each whale sings a unique song of remarkable consistency; there even appear to be dialects associated with different geographical regions. Thus the song of the hump-backed whale provides information on identity, area of origin and location; its function is, however, uncertain (see Chapter 6). Another interesting form of acoustic communication is the chimpanzee 'carnival' described by Reynolds and Reynolds (1965) where whole groups of individuals shout loudly, drum on trunks of trees with their hands, shake branches and run about, creating absolute pandemonium.

Whereas calls adapted for long-distance communication are generally stereotyped and therefore discrete, those employed in more intimate close-range situations tend to be graded and often accompanied by visual signals. Even the least sociable of mammals use vocalizations as a means of communication with conspecifics when mating. The male yellow-footed marsupial mouse (*Antechinus flavipes*), for example, makes a sound resembling 'cha-cha-cha' during the precopulatory chase and male hamsters (*Cricetus*), fennec foxes (*Fennecus zerda*) and dwarf mongooses also have mating calls. The male domesticated cat growls and the female screams when mating, and the male European polecat makes a clucking sound, while the female screams; female white-collared mangabeys (*Cercocebus torquatus*) also produce a mating call.

Aggressive behaviour is very often preceded by vocalization. A threatening Herero musk shrew (*Crocidura flavescens herero*) will emit a single sharp metallic squeak. Common shrews (*Sorex araneus*) scream at their opponents, while baboons bark or roar; male mammals as diverse as deer (*Cervus elaphus*), lions and Northern elephant seals (*Mirounga angustirostris*) roar at male rivals when defending their harem of females (Le Boeuf, 1974). Threatening growls, familiar in domesticated dogs and wolves, also occur in Olympic marmots (*Marmota olympus*) (Barash, 1973) and meerkats (*Suricata suricatta*) (Ewer, 1963). The marsupial native cats (*Dasyuridae*) make a hissing or panting sound when threatening (Eisenberg *et al.*, 1975); hissing is also common in many carnivores such as polecats (Poole, 1967) and among rodents. In some social species, individuals may attempt to steal food from one another; in the case of the meerkat, the thief is threatened with growling whilst, in common marmosets (*Callithrix jacchus jacchus*), the owner of the food produces a vocalization which has been described as 'erh-erh' (Stevenson and Poole, 1976).

The losers of aggressive encounters submit or flee but they may also vocalize, and the scream, squeak or squeal is a common sound associated with submission. This type of vocalization is characteristic of fear in mammals as diverse as rats (*R. norvegicus*), asses (*Equus hemionus*) (Klingel, 1977), polecats (Poole, 1967), and many primates, including the great apes (Goodall 1968*a*). Screaming is generally associated with fear in high-intensity agonistic interactions, usually where physical attack or fighting is involved. On the other hand, whining, whimpering or squealing which are common juvenile vocalizations, in adults are generally associated with submission to a dominant who is in proximity, or threatening but not actively attacking. These vocalizations are common in primates and canids and they may also occur in a sexual context, female primates often squeaking or whimpering when approached by a male. The general message conveyed by such vocalizations is of a lack of aggressiveness and a willingness to submit to the other individual; an example is the yelp or whine of the coyote (*Canis latrans*) which indicates subordination (Fox and Cohen, 1977).

An important type of vocalization in many gregarious species is the contact call, which enables group members to keep in close proximity when visibility is poor. Such calls are easy to locate since they are usually low-pitched (for example the grunting of pigs) or frequency-modulated (like the contact trills of marmosets). Because the call draws attention to the exact location of the signaller, contact calls in prey species are usually of low amplitude. Female mammals often have a contact call which enables them to stay close to their young. For example, mother and infant Northern elephant seals keep in contact by calling (Petrinovich, 1974). When the mother comes ashore she calls to her pup which, after 2–3 days, learns to recognize her individually by means of this vocalization. Other herd-living animals, such as artiodactyls, have mother-young contact calls. As alien young are rejected by females, the infants soon learn to recognize their own mothers so that their capacity to identify their parent is both positively reinforced by suckling and negatively reinforced by attacks from other females. In some species of mammal the infant vocalizes when separated from its mother or accidentally deposited outside the nest, as in the case of the ultrasonic 'lost calls' of rat and mouse pups. A young marmoset (*Callithrix jacchus*) separated from its family group produces a plaintive lost cry which attracts a carrier to pick it up (see Stevenson and Poole, 1976), and the 'hoo-sigh' is an equivalent juvenile lost call produced by young white-handed gibbons (*Hylobates lar*) (Chivers, 1972).

This brief description has covered only the commonest types of call found in mammals but does not include all the call types or even the contexts in which calls are made in the social Canidae and higher primates. Goodall (1968a, b), for example, lists twenty-four different types of vocalization for the chimpanzee (*Pan troglodytes*) and it is clear that other apes are similarly well endowed. Even for the meerkat Ewer (1968) listed ten vocalizations: contact sound, settling-down sound when going to sleep, satisfaction noise when feeding, fear call, fear and aggression call, alarm bark, dissatisfaction call and three distinct types of threat, namely, growl, explosive spit and harsh repetitive scolding.

As has been seen, one of the problems in using sound as a means of communication is that it may draw the attention of a predator to the caller. Snowdon and Hodun (1979) showed that the most locatable of three contact calls in pygmy marmosets (*Cebuella pygmaea*), the j-call, is used in long distance communication. This call is high-pitched (9.2–13.2 kHz) but amplitude modulated, and Snowden and Hodun took the view that, when jungle background noise is taken into account it occupies a unique acoustic channel above the highest frequency perceivable by predators. Even though high-pitched sound attenuates rapidly, the call is effective because of the restricted diameter (about 100 metres) of the pygmy marmoset's home range. Snowdon and Cleveland (1980) also showed that, in this species, individuals can be recognized from their contact calls.

2.3 Visual communication

The more primitive mammals tend to be nocturnal or live in burrows, and elaborate visual signals tend therefore to be found mainly among advanced, diurnal species. Most mammals are rather dull in colour and, unlike birds, colouring typically plays little part in their communication system, although some diurnal primates may be highly coloured (e.g. mandrill).

When Darwin (1873) drew attention to what he termed 'the principle of antithesis', which he illustrated by reference to the aggressive and submissive postures of the dog, he noted that 'when a directly opposite state of mind is induced there is a strong and involuntary tendency to the performance of movements of a directly opposite nature'. It is now clear that the principle of antithesis is only one aspect of the complex organization of the visual signalling systems of highly social mammals.

Visual signalling may involve the use of any part of the body. Mammals may raise their hair, move their ears, alter their facial expression, change the angles of head, neck or tail; their limbs may be bent or extended and their genitalia may be erected or swollen. Sometimes these actions are further emphasized by markings on the pelage, as on the face of a tabby cat or tiger. In some cases, special structures such as horns or trunks may be used to signal. Most visual signals are ephemeral, signalling the mood of the moment, but a few may convey a longer-lasting message, for example, the swollen female genital region of some old world primates and the antlers and mane of the rutting stag.

Perhaps the best way to consider visual signals is to examine the way in which the different parts of the body may be used for this purpose.

2.3.1 Head

Even primitive mammals, which possess well developed teeth, may signal aggression or defence by opening the mouth and displaying the dentition (see Figure 2.4). In some species of mammals such as wolves and baboons, the lips can be drawn back in a snarl. The extremely mobile lips of the great apes (Pongidae) enable them to show a wide variety of facial expression; they may alter the shape of the mouth without showing the teeth, or may reveal upper teeth, lower teeth, or both, each expression being indicative of a different emotional state—see van Hoof (1970). Facial expressions change when vocalizing as in the case of the scream in polecats and primates such as the common marmoset.

In some cases the tongue is used for signalling; cotton-topped tamarins (*Saguinus oedipus*) use the tongue in-and-out movement in situations inducing mild alarm. In Old World monkeys, lip-smacking has probably been derived from grooming movements and also normally occurs in a

a

b

c

Figure 2.4 Facial expressions in some mammals. (*a*) Open-mouth defensive threat in the Tasmanian devil (*Sarcophilius harrisii*); (*b*) lip retraction in the Gelada baboon (*Theropithecus gelada*); (*c*) mobile lips of the orang utan (*Pongo pygmaeus*). (Photograph (a) Zoological Society of London, (b) R. I. M. Dunbar, (c) H. M. Poole).

friendly context. Pouting is another movement made with the lips in many Old World monkeys and apes; it may have derived from suckling. Another expression, the open-mouth play face, occurs in carnivores and primates. The mouth is widely open, revealing the teeth, but there is no accompanying snarl or frown.

The eye, which may be opened or closed, is another facial feature which can be altered, even in the most primitive mammals with rather immobile faces. In many diurnal primates such as monkeys, the eyes can be half closed or slitted. The closure of eyes often occurs in an aggressive context, as it does, for example, in fighting mice where the eye nearest to the opponent is usually closed, probably for protection (Andrew, 1963*a*). Chance (1962) suggested that closure of the eyes in an aggressive context also serves to cut off the fear-inducing stimuli emanating from the opponent and coined the phrase 'cut-off' to describe this phenomenon. In addition to changing eye shape, mammals with forwardly directed eyes can lower the eyebrows to produce a frown. This is common in social carnivores and higher primates, and is indicative of anxiety or threat.

In carnivores, horses and the more primitive primates the mobile ear

Figure 2.5   Common marmoset showing contrasting ear tufts. Notice that the infant, which is being carried by the male, lacks the white tufts.

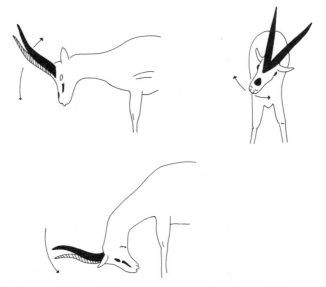

Figure 2.6   Threat: ritualized butting movements carried out by a male Thomson's gazelle. (Redrawn from Walther, 1977.)

pinnae are often used for communication. Submissive dogs and threatening horses lay back the ears. Common marmosets can flick the ears when aggressive; the movement is emphasized by a tuft of white hairs surrounding the ear which contrasts with the generally black colour of the head (see Figure 2.5). The cotton-topped tamarin raises or lowers the hairs of the crown of the head when threatened or alarmed.

Sometimes the head bears special structures in the form of horns of antlers (see Clutton-Brock, 1982) which emphasize the display, as for example Thomson's gazelle (*Gazella thomsoni*), which tosses its head to symbolize butting movements (see Figure 2.6). The head of the Thomson's gazelle is also patterned to emphasize the effect of the horns (see Ewer, 1968). Primates which have good colour vision may use colour or pattern to emphasize displays, for example, the blue eyelids of the crab-eating macaque (*Macaca fascicularis*) and the red and blue facial markings of the mandrill (*Mandrillus sphinx*). The red-bellied tamarin (*Saguinus labiatus labiatus*) has striking white lips which help to accentuate its open-mouth displays.

The facial expressions of social canids and higher primates bear marked resemblances to one another, and van Hoof (1962) has compared 14 facial expressions for wolf, coyote and dog with those of a typical primate. There do seem to be considerable resemblances and it seems probable that these are a result of parallel evolution in the two lines from simpler flight, approach and defence intention movements.

2.3.2 Body

The mammal may use its body as a means of communication in three main ways, i.e. by piloerection, by posture or by movement of the whole or parts of the body. Often two of these methods of display are used in combination, and the display usually serves to emphasize particular parts of the body. The body fur in most mammals can be raised as a whole or in patches, one effect being to make the animal appear larger and so deter an opponent from attack. The familiar arched defensive posture of the domestic cat illustrates this point. Piloerection displays have undoubtedly evolved from the natural response of the animal to a stressful situation when production of adrenalin, which prepares the body for flight or fight, also results in the erection of the hair through the contraction of the arrector pili muscles. This reaction may, as in humans, have little obvious functional value or it may serve as the basis of a display. In some cases, erection of the hair may be emphasized by body patterning as, for example, in the case of the striped flanks of some ground squirrels. The aardwolf (*Proteles cristatus*) is of special interest because it is an anteating hyaena whose teeth are reduced to small pegs. In colouring it resembles, and possibly even mimics, its relative the spotted hyaena (*Crocuta crocuta*); its defensive threat display is also similar but, unlike *Crocuta*, which, of course, has a full and impressive dentition, *Proteles* does not reveal its teeth, the normal accompaniment to piloerection displays in carnivores (see Ewer, 1968).

Bodily posture may serve as a form of social communication and Grant and Mackintosh (1963) described a whole series of postures in rodents, such as upright defensive posture and sideways posture, which appear in a number of different social contexts. In many ungulates, visual bodily signals may be extremely conspicuous. For example, the male ibex (*Capra ibex*), like many other Caprinae, stands on its hind legs when threatening (see

Figure 2.7   Ibex (*Capra ibex*) threatening a rival by standing on its hind legs. (Redrawn from Walther, 1977.)

Figure 2.7), while a subordinate Marco Polo sheep (*Ovis ammon*) kneels to the dominant. Juvenile or subordinate wolves roll over on to the back with inguinal region displayed and front paws retracted. The red-bellied tamarin sits up on its hind legs, displaying the golden-red belly.

Many species display the genitalia and, in some monkeys and the chimpanzee, the anogenital area swells up and may also become brightly coloured during the female's periovulatory period (i.e. just before and just after ovulation) (Figure 2.8). Female chimpanzees present their genital

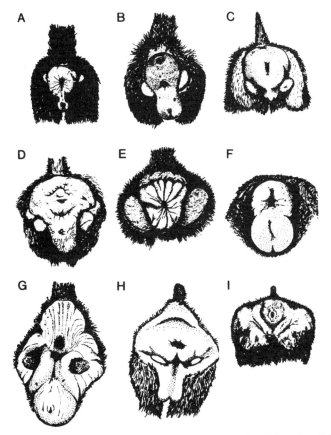

Figure 2.8 Appearance of the female sexual skin at mid-menstrual cycle in various Primates. *A, Cercocebus albigena; B, C. atys; C, Mandrillus sphinx; D, Papio ursinus; E, Colobus verus; F, Pan troglodytes; G, Miopithecus talapoin; H, Macaca nemestrina; I, M. nigra.* Reproduced with permission from Dixson, A. F., *Adv. Study of Behaviour* **13**, 63–106 (1983). Academic Press, New York, etc.

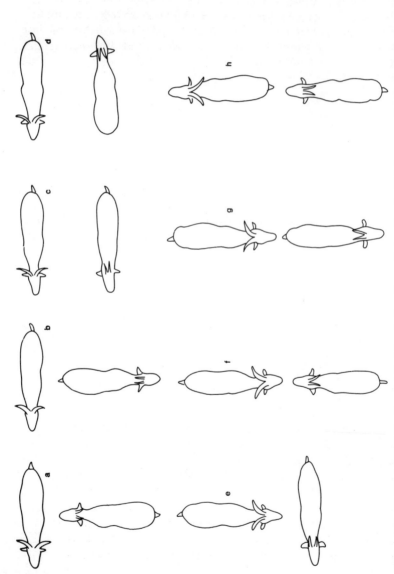

Figure 2.9 Directional signalling by a territorial male Grant's gazelle to a female of his harem, male with larger horns. Interpretations and drawings after Walther, 1977: (*a*) Stop! do not advance in this direction! (*b*) Do not turn round! (*c*) Stop or go ahead! (*d*) Do not turn round! (*e*) Continue in your direction and speed up! (*f*) Turn round and withdraw! (*g*) Go ahead! (*h*) Follow me!

areas to males, and this may also serve as submissive behaviour in many primates, especially macaques and baboons. Presenting the rear to other individuals is practised not only by females but also by males and is a submissive signal. A dominant male may mount the subordinate and thrust. Display of genitalia, however, may signify an aggressive or dominant status. In common marmosets for example, the tail is raised and the genitalia displayed by presenting the hindquarters towards rival groups. In squirrel monkeys, the male displays his erect penis and the frequency of penis display is positively correlated with the male's rank. This, like female presenting in Old World monkeys, is an intragroup display. Wickler (1967) discusses the significance of genital displays in primates in relation to human behaviour. Some male primates have coloured genitalia which emphasize the display, for example the vervet monkey which has a bright orange prepuce and blue scrotum. In the case of the gelada baboon (*Theropithecus gelada*), the pattern on the genitalia is repeated on the animal's chest so that a similar signal appears even if the animal is in the sitting position, which it commonly adopts when feeding. Sexually receptive females commonly present the genitalia to the male, for example, rats which adopt a special position known as 'lordosis' in which the hindquarters are raised, the genitalia displayed and the tail deflected to one side. Female lions also display their genitals by raising the tail and walking alongside the male with the pelvic region raised.

Walther (1977) has pointed out that ungulates may use the whole body to manipulate the behaviour of others. Grant's gazelle (*Gazella granti*) males herd their harem of females by using a series of movements which he has interpreted in the way depicted in Figure 2.9. From this diagram it can be seen that the male can exercise considerable control over the direction of movement of his females.

2.3.3 Tail

In many mammals, where this organ is well developed, the tail may be used to communicate with conspecifics. Not only can its position be varied but it can, to varying degrees, be piloerected (see Figure 2.10). In tamarins (*Saguinus*) the tail can also be coiled. Ring-tailed lemurs smear the tail with scent from the wrist glands and hold it aloft. As it is ringed with black and white bands, it is very conspicuous and so acts as both a visual and olfactory signal. Aggressive dogs and wolves also hold the tail aloft while mice thrash it from side to side ('tail rattling'). The extent to which these movements are of communicative value is not known (see Kiley, 1976).

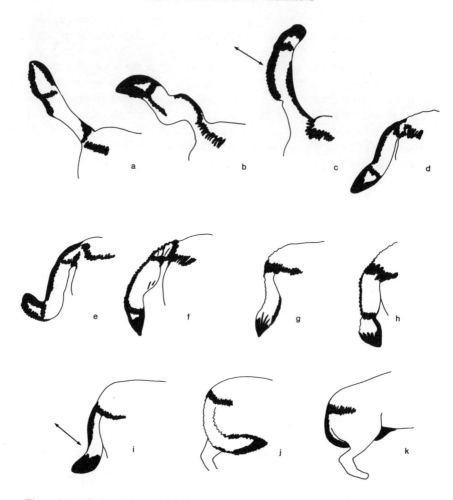

Figure 2.10 Tail positions and their contexts in the wolf (*Canis lupus*): arrows indicate lateral movement.
(*a*), (*b*) confident, in locomotion
(*c*) confident, threatening
(*d*) relaxed position
(*e*) slightly apprehensive threat
(*f*) relaxed position, usually eating or watching
(*g*) tense
(*h*) defensive threat
(*i*) submissive
(*j*), (*k*) extremely submissive
(Drawings and interpretations after Schenckel, 1948).

Clearly the division of visual signals into head, body and tail is highly artificial, as often more than one part of the body is simultaneously involved, particularly in highly social species issuing graded signals (see Figure 2.9). Movement is very often used to reinforce the bodily signal. Threats may be emphasized by charging at the opponent, as in baboons, or circling it, like the African buffalo (*Syncerus caffer*). Low-ranking animals may slink past dominants, or look away, giving a strong impression of nervousness, while high-ranking individuals appear confident and decisive in their movements which are unrestricted by the presence of others.

Some species recognize individuals visually. This is quite clearly true of human beings who are capable of picking out a familiar face in a crowd of a thousand strangers. This facility is probably shared with other higher primates, at least with the more socially complex of the Old World monkeys and the great apes (Pongidae). Chimpanzees are particularly easy for us to recognize as individuals from their facial appearance, so it is likely that they also use the same cues. This ability may not be confined to primates, but hard data are not available for other mammalian orders.

2.4 Tactile communication

Suckling is the earliest form of tactile communication to develop in a mammal. The sucking movements of the infant's lips not only induce milk let-down but also stimulate further milk production. Although the amount of information on other forms of tactile communication, with the exception of allogrooming, is restricted, it is clear that nocturnal, crepuscular and burrowing animals may rely heavily on this type of signalling.

While, the function of biting in fighting is undoubtedly to inflict injury, it may also serve as a form of social communication. Snap biting is a common form of warning signal in carnivores and primates; inhibited biting also occurs in both social play and sexual behaviour in many species of mammal. Male marsupial 'native cats' (Dasyuridae) such as the Tasmanian devil (*Sarcophilus harrisii*) and placental carnivores such as the black bear (*Ursus americanus*) grip the neck of the female preparatory to mounting, while the lesser hedgehog tenrec (*Echninops telfairi*) bites the spines on the female's back to stimulate her. The male greater hedgehog tenrec (*Setifer setosus*) actually bites the female during intromission, and she responds by trying to evade the bite, thus raising her back and improving the presentation of her genitalia to the male (Poduschka, 1977).

Body rubbing, which may also involve the transfer of body odours, often occurs in a sexual or affectional context and is common in tenrecs. Many mammals have highly developed vibrissae which may be used in social communication. Nuzzling is certainly common in sexual and affectional behaviour so that the vibrissae, in species where they are well developed, are likely to play some role in the sensation created. Licking of the genitalia often occurs prior to mating, but is also a common response to a member of the opposite sex in dogs. It has been suggested that genital licking has been derived from the genital grooming of infants, but it may also involve a chemical message. Dogs and wolves lick the muzzles of dominant individuals, behaviour which may have evolved from the infantile pattern of food soliciting. Kissing is a form of greeting in prairie dogs and great apes; for example, adult chimpanzees kiss when greeting and orang utan mothers kiss their infants. It is thought that kissing in primates may have been derived from oral allogrooming movements. Allogrooming, in addition to its cleaning function, is a very important form of tactile communication in most social mammals. Rats, however, show a rough form of allogrooming termed 'aggressive groom' which appears to be indicative of the aggressive mood of the groomer. Where a pair-bond develops between members of the opposite sex, allogrooming and other forms of tactile communication may be of great importance. The pair commonly sit in close physical contact (huddle) and the monogamous South American titi monkeys (*Callicebus moloch*) often sit with tails intertwined.

Social play involves a great deal of tactile behaviour, especially wrestling and rough-and-tumble play in primates and carnivores and the gentle butting of lambs and other horned artiodactyls. There is clearly considerable scope for further research on tactile communication, particularly in the more primitive mammalian orders and in relation to the role of the vibrissae (see Sebeok, 1977).

2.5 Summary

1. Most mammals communicate socially though the use of several senses because each modality has attributes which makes it of special value in transmitting certain types of message.

2. Chemical communication is a medium for both short-lived and persistent messages, which may be left for conspecifics when the sender is no longer present. The odour may either have an immediate effect on the recipient or it may act as a primer which affects its physiology directly and thus has a long-term effect on behaviour. Olfactory signals may be concerned with reproductive state, sex, status and mood, also with species, colony and individual recognition.

3. Acoustic communication enables some mammals to advertise their presence over long distances and provide information on age, sex, location, breeding status and individuality, or to warn others of the presence of danger. At close quarters vocalizations can be used to maintain group contact, to convey mood, to greet and to indicate status.

4. Visual signals are confined to communication at close quarters, but can be used to indicate age, sex, reproductive state, aggression, submission, affection, fear and playfulness. Extremely elaborate graded visual signals may be used in social canids and higher primates.

5. Tactile communication, apart from allogrooming, has been rather poorly investigated. Apart from biting, which generally occurs in aggressive, sexual and playful contexts, most tactile signals are associated with amicable approaches.

CHAPTER THREE

REPRODUCTIVE BEHAVIOUR

3.1 Sexual behaviour

3.1.1 Theoretical considerations

The function of sexual behaviour is to ensure the fertilization of the ovum in the female reproductive tract, and all mammals make contact with a member of the opposite sex for mating. As females are not fertile when pregnant or, in many species, during lactation, the total amount of time when the female is receptive to the male is restricted to between two and seven days in the year even in species without a restricted breeding season. Consequently, sexual behaviour does not play a large direct role in the day-to-day life of even the most sociable mammals. Nonetheless, mating systems are important determinants of the forms taken by mammalian social organization (see Chapter 5).

Optimal mating strategies tend to be different for the two sexes. A male has the capacity to fertilize, and father the offspring of, a number of females (as many as 100 in northern elephant seal harems) so his fitness increases in direct ratio to the number of exclusive matings he can achieve. To do this, however, a male must compete with other males who are employing the same strategy. A one-to-one sex ratio is normal in mammals so that, for each additional female which a male acquires, he must effectively eliminate one male rival.

Two factors influence a female's sexual strategy, firstly her heavy parental investment and secondly the fact that she needs only one male to fertilize her and father a particular litter of young. The most significant way in which a female mammal can influence the fitness of her offspring, on theoretical grounds at least, is through careful selection of the father (see Bateson, 1983). It is hard to imagine a mechanism whereby a female could *directly* measure the fitness of a prospective mate, but some attributes may be reliable indicators of male quality. The size or status of a male may reflect his competitive ability. Age is an indicator of his capacity to survive and vigour of courtship may reflect his general physical condition. The quality of a male's territory may not only be of practical value in a female's choice of mate but may also indicate his overall fitness, since the highest-quality males might be expected to hold the most desirable territories. Some male mammals bear secondary sexual characteristics such as horns, antlers or manes which may bear a direct relationship to their competitive ability and Darwin (1871) suggested that these attributes evolved and became elaborated as a result of mate choice (intersexual selection). Halliday (1978), Arnold (1983) and O'Donald (1983) have recently reconsidered this theory.

There may be a conflict of interest in the optimal mating strategies of the two sexes in some species. Downhower and Armitage (1971) found such a divergence of interest in the yellow-bellied marmot (*Marmota flaviventris*). A male leaves the maximum number of offspring when he has a harem of 2–3 females, while females have the greatest reproductive success if their mate is monogamous. This conflict of interest appears to be resolved by a compromise, since the majority of males hold a harem of only two females.

Mammals may adopt a number of mating strategies, and some attempt must be made to define them. Promiscuous mating occurs where there is no long-term exclusive relationship between members of the opposite sex. Mating is essentially opportunistic and the association between two individuals is confined to the period of the female's fertility. At the end of this association, the male moves away to seek further sexual opportunities. If the female is still fertile when the male deserts her, she may also mate with one or more other males.

Both monogamy and polygamy imply some long-term association between sexual partners which persists beyond the fertile period of the female. In the first instance, a heterosexual pair form an exclusive mating relationship, while in polygamous species a member of one sex has several mates but those of the other sex mate only with a single individual. Polygamy, where one male has several female mates, is common in mammals. No unequivocal example of polyandry where a single female mates with several males has been recorded.

Bearing in mind these theoretical considerations, sexual behaviour will be described under three main headings: mating, factors influencing mate choice, and inbreeding avoidance and dispersal.

3.1.2 Mating

Typically, female mammals living relatively solitary lives advertise their receptivity by scent or urine marking as they travel about their home range.

Males with overlapping foraging areas perceive the signal and seek out the female. If more than one male finds her, active competition may take place, which may involve fighting and the formation of a male dominance hierarchy. This has been observed in short-nosed echidnas (*Tachyglossus aculeatus*) by Griffiths (1968), cheetahs (*Acinonyx jubatus*) by Eaton (1974) and domestic cats (*Felis catus*) by Leyhausen (1965). Although tomcats form a dominance hierarchy, there is an element of female choice, for the female does not necessarily mate with the highest-ranking male.

Female mammals may also signal their receptivity by showing pro-ceptive behaviour, which advertises their receptive state to a male or males. Female shrews (*Blarina, Sorex, Crocidura*) and hamsters (*Mesocricetus auratus*) simply cease to be aggressive towards the male; in other species female mammals actively solicit the male by displaying the genitalia, for example, bottle-nosed dolphins (*Tursiops truncatus*), chimpanzees and orang utans, or by tonguing and lip-smacking, for example, common marmosets. Some female Old World simians, particularly semi-terrestrial forms which live in multimale/multifemale groups (baboons, rhesus monkeys, chimpanzees), have conspicuous swollen circumgenital areas during oestrus as well as giving chemical and behavioural signals (see Dixson (1983) and Figure 2.8).

Many male mammals guard oestrous females and ward off competitors. This behaviour is termed consortship and has the effect of increasing the chance of the guarding male's paternity. Consortship is found in a variety of mammals. Where a dominance hierarchy exists, the dominant male consorts with the female at peak oestrus, as in the case of macaques (*Macaca*), baboons (*Papio anubis*), wolves, African buffalos and elephants (*Loxodonta africana*). Some male mammals, e.g. the red deer, acquire a group of females or harem and defend it against other males; in these circumstances, young males may attempt sneak copulations when the harem owner is preoccupied with challenging an opponent, so males which attempt to acquire exclusive mating rights to females must constantly guard them during peak oestrus. The male of even the monogamous common marmoset remains close to the female and grooms her more during the period around oestrus. In laboratory mice, if a female is exposed to the scent of a second male within 48 hours of mating she aborts the original male's offspring (the Bruce effect). This would indicate that consortship may also be critical to ensure paternity in this species.

Some male mammals, for example weasels, set up territories which encompass the home ranges of one or more females; males which do not hold territories are nomadic and subordinate to territorial males (Lockie,

1966; King, 1975; Erlinge, 1974, 1979*a*). In the common tree shrew Kawamichi and Kawamichi (1979) found that most males were monogamous, with a territory completely overlapping that of a single female, but a small number of males had larger territories which included the home ranges of two or three females. Among nocturnal prosimian primates, males of Demidoff's bushbaby (*Galago demidovii*) have territories including the home ranges of several females, while males without territories are peripheral and non-breeding (beta males). In white rhinoceroses (*Ceratotherium simum*) breeding is also associated with the holding of a territory in the male (see Chapter 6). Where males are territorial and females live in mobile herds, as in many African antelopes such as the Uganda kob and the blue wildebeest (*Connochaetes taurinus*), and in some bats (e.g. *Hypsignathus monstrosus*), the male may show an elaborate precopulatory display which attracts females. To these species female choice appears to be of paramount importance and many ungulate males show extreme sexual dimorphism, frequently having horns, manes and striking patterning.

Courtship among antelopes has been described by Leuthold (1977) and usually commences with 'flehmen' by the male (see Section 2.1). The male then drives the female, he approaches, she retreats. The male bontebok (*Damaliscus dorcas dorcas*) lays his horns back and stretches his neck towards the female meanwhile showing an upwardly curled tail, a signal of submissiveness. This is followed by leg beating (*laufschlag*) in which the male lifts his foreleg stiffly under the female's rear from behind or the side. Some species, such as the greater kudu (*Tragelaphus strepsiceros*), substitute laying the head over that of the female for leg-beating. Licking the vulva and nuzzling also occurs. The visual and tactile signals described may be accompanied by soft vocalizations referred to as 'pleading'. The male may mount prior to ejaculation without showing an erection.

Some quantitative studies of mating have been carried out in the laboratory, but the results must be treated with caution because of the confined conditions and lack of mate choice. Laboratory studies have also tended to emphasize the active role of the male in copulation, while neglecting the influence of the female. A good example of recent research which illustrates these points is that of McClintock and Adler (1978) on the brown rat (*Rattus norvegicus*). From previous laboratory studies it had been concluded that the initiative lay with the male but this investigation showed that, given adequate space (more than two body lengths between the partners), the female actively solicits. Female soliciting consists of approaching the male with a stiff-legged gait from a distance of at least four body lengths, putting her head alongside the male's and grooming his neck, crawling over his head or dragging herself under his chin. If the male fails to respond to these overtures, the female presents her genital area to his head while grooming his genital area simultaneously. The male orientates to the female and grooms her; finally the female runs away from the male with the 'dart-hop' gait or a stiff-legged jerky run. She stops at intervals to wait for the male and, if he follows, then shows lordosis. Female courtship was evident in 90% of matings. McClintock and Adler further showed that the pattern of courtship and even of copulation were female-, rather than male-, determined.

The form taken by copulation varies considerably from species to species as regards the number of intromissions, presence or absence of pelvic thrusting, the number of ejaculations and the presence or absence of a post-copulatory lock or tie (see Dewsbury, 1972). Most of these data, however, are based on observations in confinement and may not be typical of the wild. Considerable differences in duration of copulation have been recorded for free-living mammals. The greater bushbaby (*Galago crassicaudatus*) may copulate for over two hours (Van Horn and Gray Eaton, 1979) and the black rhinoceros for 30–40 minutes (Goddard, 1966), whereas some gazelles copulate in a matter of seconds while walking (Leuthold, 1977). Mating has also been observed in wild lions (*Panthera leo*) by Rudnai (1973) and Bertram (1975) and is characterized by very high frequency of copulations. Rudnai found each mating sequence to last for 55 seconds with intervals between matings averaging 17 minutes (range 4–148). A low level of competition between pride-living males is characteristic of this species (see Chapter 5, Packer and Pusey, 1982), and one male was observed by Rudnai to mate twice, followed by the second male of the pride mating thirteen times, all in the same day.

Mating has been described in the rhesus monkey by Mitchell (1979). It commences with presenting by the female, who turns the hindquarters towards the male's face and raises her tail to reveal the genitalia. The female may also make quick, jerky movements of one arm, bob or duck her head, or move it laterally. The male yawns and mounts the female, holding the fur on her flanks with his hands and clasping her legs with his feet. Meanwhile the female looks back and touches the male's thigh and scrotum. Males often chew and gnash their teeth. When ejaculating the male bares his teeth and squeals, while the female looks at him and lip-smacks. She may also squeal and clutch the male. Copulation in this species consists of a series of mounts with intromission and pelvic thrusting; it is terminated by ejaculation, after which the male eats the ejaculate remaining on his genitals.

In many mammals such as polecats, the male immobilizes the female by biting her neck, which produces ataxia in the oestrus female. The male places his forepaws behind the female's shoulders. Mating takes a minimum of 15 minutes, and the male makes a series of pelvic thrusts with rests between, finally ejaculating. After a quiescent period lying together, the pair separate.

A post-copulatory tie or lock has been observed in marsupials, insectivores, rodents and primates. In the dog family (Canidae) the tie lasts up to 15 minutes after copulation. The male ceases to mount the female but his penis remains fixed in the female's vagina. The lock is caused by contraction of the vaginal muscles of the female and the swelling of the bulbous region of the male's penis. The function of the tie is unknown, but it may reduce post-copulatory competition from other males.

Aquatic mammals may copulate in the water. This is obviously unavoidable for the permanently aquatic Cetacea and Sirenia, but it has also been described in some amphibious mammals. In the sirenian manatee (*Trichecus manatus*), a number of males follow the oestrous female and embrace her. Mating is ventro-ventral (see Figure 3.1). In the monogamous spotted seal (*Phoca largha*), mating was observed in captivity by Beier and Wartzok (1979) in a tank 3.6 × 3.6 × 1.4 m containing 20 000 litres of sea water. Courtship by the male takes place over a number of weeks before intromission is achieved. Courtship sequences are highly variable, involving six male and five female vocalizations (growl, drum, chirp, bark, chirp and, in the male only, 'squeaky door'), together with nosing, gentle biting, synchronous spiralling, chasing and bubble-blowing. The male also shows

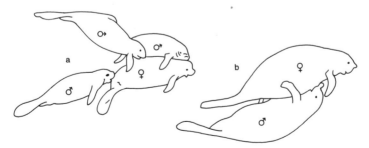

Figure 3.1 Aquatic courtship and mating in the manatee (*Trichecus manatus*). (*a*) Female followed by the 'oestrous herd' of males; (*b*) copulation embrace. (After Hartman, 1979)

'ballooning' where he draws in his head and neck and lies still, giving the impression of being puffed up. Courtship also includes jaw chopping and breathing at one another; the female frees herself from the male by solitary spiralling. During copulation the male grips his mate with foreflippers and often holds her neck or back with his teeth.

The platypus (*Ornithorhynchus anatinus*) is an example of an amphibious mammal which practises aquatic courtship and mating. In captivity the male platypus was observed to court the female for several weeks (Strahan and Thomas, 1975). He groomed her and seized her tail in his mouth, and both male and female rubbed against and crawled over one another. During mating the male seized the female by gripping her neck. A sequence of aquatic courtship and mating is illustrated in Figure 3.2.

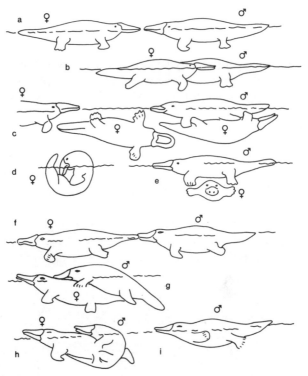

Figure 3.2 Aquatic courtship and mating in the platypus (*Ornithorhynchus anatinus*). Female proceptive behaviour, *a-e*: (*a*) head on approach (*b*) side passing (*c*) ventral passing (*d*) grooming cloacal region (*e*) underpassing. Male courtship, *f-i*: (*f*) tail holding (*g*) neck holding (*h*) sitting posture (copulation ?) (*i*) stretching. (Redrawn from Strahan and Thomas, 1975.)

In some mammals copulation has a physiological effect upon the female. For example, in the rabbit and the domestic cat (*Felis catus*) it stimulates ovulation. Such species are known as 'induced ovulators' as they only ovulate if induced to do so by copulation. If the mating is sterile it may be followed by false or pseudo-pregnancy where ovulation is followed by the luteal phase of the reproductive cycle. The brown rat ovulates spontaneously but pseudo-pregnancy follows a sterile mating. Thus copulation initiates only the luteal phase of the reproductive cycle in spontaneous ovulators. In a further group of mammalian species, ovulation and lutealization are spontaneous, e.g. guinea pig and primates; in some primates the breakdown of the uterine wall after cessation of formation of the corpus luteum results in menstrual bleeding (see Hogarth, 1978).

Most temperate mammals and even some tropical species, such as the rhesus monkey, the ring-tailed lemur and artiodactyls such as the Uganda kob (*Adenota kob thomasii*), show well-developed breeding seasons timed to coincide with favourable environmental conditions. Such species show no sexual behaviour outside the rut and males become more competitive during the period when the females are in oestrus.

A curious phenomenon, known as the 'Whitten effect', has been demonstrated in laboratory mice. If a group of females are kept together and a male then introduced, the females' oestrous cycles become synchronized. The nature or significance of this effect is poorly understood, but it has been claimed that it may occur in other species including humans. If female mice are kept together but isolated from males, they show irregular cycles and long periods of anoestrus, known as the Lee-Boot effect (see Lee and Boot, 1956).

Domesticated mammals generally differ from their wild relatives in their sexual behaviour. Laboratory rats and mice breed continuously, whereas wild males of this species are seasonal breeders. Most breeds of dogs (*Canis familiaris*) breed twice annually, whereas wolves (*C. lupus*) have only one oestrus per year. Laboratory rats are also relatively more fertile than wild rats (see McClintock and Adler, 1979). These features of the reproductive behaviour of domesticated mammals can probably be attributed to artificial selection for fecundity.

Sexual behaviour between members of the same sex has occasionally been observed in mammals. Low-ranking male monkeys present their genitalia to high-ranking males and are often mounted by the dominant. Mutual masturbation by rubbing the penis against the body of another male has been observed in manatees who were following an oestrus female (Hartman, 1979). Female homosexuality is commonly observed in domesticated cows in the absence of a bull and takes the form of mounting (see Beach, 1968).

3.1.3 Factors influencing mate choice

Although a male mammal's reproductive success can be maximized by mating with as many females as possible, a small number of species have adopted a monogamous strategy which has several advantages. Firstly, it enables the male to have guaranteed exclusive mating rights to one female because he can easily guard her against other males when she is in oestrus. Secondly, parental investment by the male may also become worthwhile, because of the high degree of certainty of paternity. As Trivers (1972) pointed out, however, it is still to the advantage of a monogamous male to take any opportunities which may arise to mate with additional females. Such behaviour has been observed in the field in the monogamous South American titi monkey (Mason 1974a, b).

Monogamy has evolved through the development of a reciprocal social bond between a male and a female which must be distinguished from the attraction which exists between male and oestrous female. In all mono-gamous species which have been investigated in detail, there exists a strong attraction between the male and female outside her fertile period. This attraction is usually referred to as the 'pair bond' and has been found in elephant shrews, carnivores, antelopes and primates. In an experimental comparative study between the monogamous titi monkey and the poly-gynous squirrel monkey (*Saimiri sciureus*), Mason (1974b) found that titi monkeys associated with members of the opposite sex, whereas squirrel monkeys associated with members of their own sex, thus suggesting that the basic types of social structure in the two species were reflected in their companion choice. In a laboratory study of the common marmoset Evans (1983) found that the male female social bond is characterized by simultaneous piloerection displays, grooming and con-tact. Sexual soliciting (tonguing and lipsmacking) was common before, but not after, the establishment of a stable pair bond.

Some monogamous mammals live in a social group consisting largely of their own offspring but sometimes also including unrelated individuals, so that there may be several adult members of a pack. In this situation the alpha male may actively prevent other males copulating with the alpha female, as observed in the dwarf mongoose by Rasa (1977); alternatively, the alpha female may interfere with other females' breeding attempts. In the African hunting dog, *Lycaon pictus*, van Lawick (1974) observed an alpha female, who had cubs, attacking and killing cubs of a second female in the pack.

In some monogamous mammals, young are expelled from the family group before they reach maturity and Chivers (1974) witnessed a subadult male siamang being driven out by his father at a time when his mother was in oestrus.

In common marmosets Abbott and Hearn (1978) found that, in a subadult group of two males and two females, only one of the females subsequently bred and the subordinate female failed to show reproductive cycles. In this species, therefore, a physiological block to breeding appears to operate.

In polygynous species there may be more than one sexual strategy available to the male to maximize his reproductive output. Male water-bucks (*Kobus ellipsiprymnus*) are territorial, with exclusive mating access to a group of females living within their territory. Some males join bachelor herds while others become satellite males (see Wirtz, 1981). A satellite male helps the breeding male to defend his territory, which benefits the territorial male by decreasing his risk of being wounded in territorial defence. The satellite male also appears to benefit as he is twelve times more likely to become a territory-holder than he would had he remained in the bachelor herd.

Male Walia ibex (Dunbar and Dunbar, 1981) associate with males of a similar age and attach themselves to the female herd. Most of the mating, however, is performed by lone old males who are visited by the females. Nonetheless, younger males may attain some matings by remaining in continuous contact with females.

Dominant male Northern elephant seals have access to a group of females and defend them against rivals. Young males may attempt either to achieve sneak copulations when the dominants are otherwise occupied, or wait in the sea for the females to return, when they attempt to mate them forcibly. Similarly, low-ranking male red deer attempt to achieve sneak copulations when the harem owner is involved in a dispute with another male.

Barash (1981) considered male sexual behaviour in the hoary marmot (*Marmota caligata*) and found that there are two alternative strategies which a male may adopt. The first is mate-guarding, to avoid cuckoldry, and the second is 'gallivanting', i.e. wandering about in search of other reproductive opportunities. Clearly the two strategies are incompatible. Barash made several predictions, all of which were fulfilled. As he expected, guarding was prominent early in the year when females were fertile, and occurred more often in breeding areas where females were easily accessible to other males with the attendant high risk of cuckoldry. Polygynous males mate-guarded more than monogamous males, since the risk of being cuckolded was greater. Frequency of gallivanting was highest among males whose females were unreproductive in a given year, and was inversely proportionate to the number of neighbouring males. Gallivanting and seeking proximity to the opposite sex were, as expected, exclusively male forms of behaviour. Thus the choice of male breeding strategy was strongly influenced by the risks and benefits likely to accrue.

Reproductive behaviour has also been studied by Tutin (1979b) in chimpanzees. She found three mating systems in operation: (1) opportunistic or promiscuous, where an oestrous female was mated by males who happened to be present—Goodall (1968a) had reported one occasion when seven males had mated in turn with an oestrous female; (2) possessive, where a male monopolized an oestrous female and prevented other males from mating with her; (3) consortship, where a male associated with a female and the pair avoided other males. The frequency of occurrence of the three mating strategies is shown in Table 3.1, together with the success rate for different methods. From the table it would appear that exclusive mating (2 and 3) which accounted for only 27% of the observed matings resulted in 64% of conceptions. Although the sample is small, it does suggest that exclusive mating is more likely to succeed than promiscuous mating. From the male's standpoint the three strategies result in different levels of success but also have different costs. Opportunistic mating has low costs and low success. Possessiveness is only likely to be effective for a high-ranking male but has a high payoff. Consortship, whilst yielding high success, also involves high risks. The consorting male may meet a party of strange males who attack and displace him, or he may meet a high-ranking member of his own group who may supplant him. Much depends upon the female with whom he consorts remaining quiet and not attracting attention.

Table 3.1 Mating strategies in chimpanzees (after Tutin, 1979b).

	Frequency (%)	Conceptions resulting (%)	Cost	Success
(1) Opportunistic	73	36	Nil	Low
(2) Possessive	25	64	Low for Alpha	High
(3) Consortship	2		Risk of	High
N =	1137	14	attack	

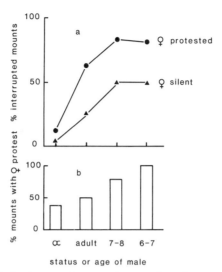

Figure 3.3 The relation between the age and status of a male attempting copulation and protests by the female in Northern elephant seals (*Mirounga angustirostris*). (After Cox and Le Boeuf, 1977)

The examples quoted above largely involve male mate choice, but data arc increasingly becoming available which indicate that female choice may also be an important factor in some species. Sometimes female selection is relatively passive, for example in common langurs (*Presbytis entellus*) and gelada baboons, but a male cannot easily take over a harem group from another male without female support. A male gelada baboon attempting to take over a harem sits on the periphery of the group threatening the alpha male and making friendly overtures to the females. In the case of the Northern elephant seal, females protest and call if a low-ranking male attempts to mate with them. This draws the attention of the dominant who immediately chases the intruding male away. With a dominant male mating her, however, the female remains silent. This is illustrated in Figure 3.3 (Cox and Le Boeuf, 1977).

Where males are territorial and females are mobile, a female may select a male by remaining in his territory although the male may also attempt to prevent a female from leaving by placing himself between her and the territorial boundary; this occurs in Steller sealions (Sandegren, 1976), and white rhinoceroses. The factors which influence female choice have not been studied, but female pronghorn (*Antilocapra americana*) appear to select males whose territories contain the best food sources (Figure 3.4). In

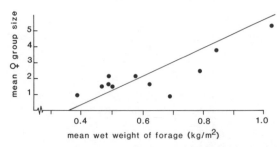

Figure 3.4 The male's reproductive success in the pronghorn (*Antilocapra americana*) appears to be dependent on the quality of his territory. The mean size of the group of females in a male's territory is positively correlated with its productivity. (After Kitchen, 1974.)

some cases, however, where food resources are not involved, territories may be small and serve simply as sites for mating. Such an arrangement is referred to as a lek (see Chapter 5). Here sexual selection must be at a maximum. Leks have been observed in antelopes such as the Uganda kob and in the hammer-headed bat (*Hypsignathus monstrosus*). In both cases, visual and vocal displays by the male attract females; the phenomenon will be discussed in more detail in Chapter 5.

Figure 3.5 Sexual dimorphism in the orang utan (*Pongo pygmaeus*). Two large adult males (far left and far right) can be seen, there is an adult female with an infant in the centre, while the other two individuals are seven-year-old juvenile males. (Photograph H. M. Poole)

One of the features related to sexual strategy is sexual dimorphism. In most mammalian species which show this phenomenon the male is larger than the female (Figure 3.5) (but see Ralls (1976) for exceptions). Several explanations have been put forward to account for this phenomenon and these are discussed by Ralls (1977). Female sexual selection for larger males is an explanation commonly put forward; another is that there has been an evolutionary arms race which gave large males the advantage over smaller ones. As larger males usually take longer than females to mature, thus reducing their lifelong reproductive capacity, there must be a compromise between the time spent in growing to a large size, the sacrifice in breeding opportunities during this period and the ultimate gain in competitiveness.

Sexual dimorphism, in which males are larger than females, is generally associated with a polygynous mating strategy, absence of paternal care (see Chapter 6, Table 6.1) and strong male/male competition. Alternative explanations exist, however. Brown and Lasiewski (1972), for example, suggested that the sexual dimorphism of weasels had the effect of reducing food competition between the sexes; Erlinge (1979) confirmed that the sizes of prey taken by the sexes differed during spring and summer, but did not believe that food was likely to be a limiting factor and attributed the larger size of males to intrasexual competition for the opportunity to mate. Powell (1979) pointed out that the most sexually dimorphic of mustelids are long thin animals which are consequently energetically inefficient. He suggested that the small size of the female reduces her basic energy requirements, which may be a critical factor during gestation and lactation when she has to be entirely self-reliant because the male makes no contribution to her feeding. Powell also pointed out that within the Mustelidae there is a positive relationship between body elongation, sexual dimorphism, extent to which the species relies on mammalian prey and intrasexual territoriality.

The degree of sexual dimorphism in some species has been related to the degree of polygyny, as indicated by the average number of females in a harem. Clutton-Brock et al. (1982) and Jouventin and Cornet (1980) showed a positive correlation between sexual dimorphism (weight of adult male divided by that of the adult female) and harem size in deer (Cervidae) and seals (Phocidae) respectively.

At first sight it seems self-evident that, for the male, polygamy must be a more efficient mating strategy than monogamy, unless paternal care makes a major contribution to offspring survival. What must also be appreciated, however, is that the number of females mated by a male in a single breeding season may be a poor reflection of his lifetime reproductive success, and it is this which determines an individual's fitness. In any mating system with an even sex ratio, average lifetime reproductive success is equal for males and females. What differs in polygynous systems is that there is a much higher variance for males as compared with females, whereas in monogamous species, variance is equal for the two sexes.

In a study of the red deer on the island of Rhum Clutton-Brock *et al.* (1983) found that there was a very considerable difference in reproductive success for males and females in this polygynous species. Hinds produced 0–13 calves in a lifetime while males fathered 0–25 offspring. They compared the reproductive success of males and females which produced at least one offspring which reached the age of one year. The lifetime average number of young for such males and females did not differ greatly (mean: females 7.38, males 7.64) but the variance was much greater in males (variance: females 6.05, males 38.73). Apart from the red deer, few data are available for long-term reproductive success in any species. There are also practical difficulties in measuring an individual's lifetime reproductive success because a male's strategy may change with age. A young male, for example, may achieve some success through sneak copulations, so that measurements of harem size and length of tenure may only be a reflection of reproductive success in fully mature individuals.

3.1.4 Inbreeding avoidance and dispersal

The problems of inbreeding were briefly mentioned, in Chapter 1, but its influence on sexual strategies will now be considered in more detail. Bateson (1983) recently reviewed inbreeding and outbreeding in animals and assessed the theoretical costs likely to be incurred. To summarize, the disadvantages of inbreeding are: the danger of recessive deleterious genes being inherited from both parents and thus becoming expressed, the reduction of heterozygous combinations and loss of heterozygous advantage, loss of genetic variability and greater competition between genetically similar offspring. The costs involved in outbreeding are the loss, or suppression, of genes for adaptation to a specific environment, break up of co-adapted gene combinations, poorer representation of parental genes in the next generation and increased danger of infection; in addition, the risks involved in attempting to travel to and gain mating opportunities in another group may be unacceptably high and skills acquired in one environment may not be useful in another. Finally, any mismatch of habits between mates can reduce parental efficiency.

There are few field data relevant to these conclusions for mammals and

Table 3.2 Olive baboon (*Papio anubis*) viability of outbred offspring compared to viability of BRM's offspring in A troop (from Packer, 1979a).

Offspring	Died in first month	Survived > 1 month
Sired by BRM	4	4
Sired by other transferred males	6	32

the only well documented instance of a disadvantage apparently attributable to inbreeding is provided by data on the reproductive output of a single male olive baboon (*Papio anubis*) (BRM) who transferred into an offshoot of his natal group. Packer (1979a) compared the reproductive performance of this male with that of outbred transferred males and found a significant difference in viability between the two. Only 50% of BRM's offspring survived beyond the age of one month, whereas 84% of other transferred males' offspring did so (see Table 3.2).

In most species there is indirect evidence for the disadvantages of inbreeding in the existence of various mechanisms which facilitate outbreeding. One example is that male chimpanzees do not mate with their mothers. In the olive baboon, high-ranking natal males, which remain in their social groups, show little sexual behaviour and will yield an oestrous female with whom they are consorting to an immigrant male (Packer, 1979a). Young female common langurs avoid mating with the reproductive male in their natal group if they were born after his arrival, since he is then likely to be their father. Instead they solicit males from outside the harem. Male olive baboons, during development, show sexual behaviour towards familiar females at first, but as they grow older and reach sexual maturity, this declines and they become attracted to females in other groups.

Many mammals show a stronger sexual attraction to unfamiliar individuals, who are unlikely to be related, than towards familiar ones. Grau (1982) has shown that white-footed deermice *Peromyscus leucopus* behave differently towards unfamiliar kin, as opposed to non-kin; males are more aggressive to non-kin males but females are more inclined to approach them. These experiments control for familiarity, so it appears that kin recognition in this species may operate on a genetic basis. Kareem and Barnard (1982) also showed that laboratory mice (*Mus musculus*) can distinguish unfamiliar half-siblings ($r = 0.25$) from unfamiliar unrelated strangers ($r < 0.125$). Thus kin recognition does occur in some species and the explanation cannot be based simply on familiarity, although this may be used by the animal as a rule of thumb.

One means by which inbreeding is avoided in natural populations is by the dispersal of a mammal from its natal group before it breeds. Dispersal is defined as the movement made by an animal from one group or site to another place or group in which it reproduces. Greenwood (1980) reviewed dispersal in birds and mammals and showed that it is generally the male mammal who disperses while females usually breed in their natal group. There are a few exceptions to this situation, e.g. monogamous mammals and some polygynous species such as yellow-bellied marmots (*Marmota flaviventris*) where both males and females disperse (Downhower and Armitage, 1981). This is also true of a number of other rodents such as house mice, some voles (*Microtus* sp., *Clethrionomys glareolus*), the Southern elephant seal (*Mirounga leonina*), the fur seal (*Arctocephalus pusillus*), the plains zebra (*Equus burchelli*), the white-handed or lar gibbon (*Hylobates lar*) and Kirk's dik-dik (*Madoqua kirki*). In a few species females emigrate, notably the chimpanzee, the mountain gorilla, the hamadryas baboon (*Papio hamadryas*), the American pika (*Ochotona princeps*), the greater white-lined bat (*Saccopteryx bilineata*) and the African hunting dog. Of sixty-eight mammalian species for which dispersal data are recorded, forty-six (71%) showed male dispersal, six (9%) female dispersal and in thirteen (20%) both sexes dispersed. According to Woolpy and Ekstrand (1979), wolves are unusual in that they appear to be highly inbred, recruitment from the pack being apparently from young born within it. Wolf packs are also extremely hostile to strangers, being essentially family groups. In a computer simulation, these authors showed that the elimination of disadvantageous homozygous genes would only take six generations. Their data drew attention to the fact that extreme inbreeding is more deleterious in naturally outbreeding species (such as coyotes) but, after a time, the offending genes would become eliminated from the group. Thus disadvantageous homozygous genes would cease to be a problem in an inbred population. There are, however, as Bateson (1983) has pointed out, a number of other possible disadvantages to inbreeding which were not considered by Woolpy and Eckstrand, although in general it can be stated that the costs of outbreeding in the wolf must be greater than the penalties incurred in inbreeding.

Something is known of the factors which promote dispersal. A prominent factor in many species is the attraction of unfamiliar females; in others, such as toque macaques (*Macaca sinica*) and African elephants (*Loxodonta africana*), adolescent males are actively expelled from the group. In Japanese macaques (*Macaca fuscata*), males appear to leave voluntarily during the breeding season, sometimes with other related members of their family (Sugiyama, 1976).

After an individual has moved to a new group, especially if he is a male who takes over a harem, there will come a time when he has sexually mature daughters in the nursery group. Some male mammals such as plains zebras allows their daughters to be kidnapped by other males, while vicuña (*Vicugna vicugna*) males drive their sexually mature daughters out of the social group. In other cases, e.g. langurs, the situation rarely arises because the average male remains in the same breeding unit for only 2–3 years. This is also true of olive baboons. An effect of repeated troop transfer by breeding males is the avoidance of incest with female offspring, but the proximal cause may simply be the presence of oestrous females in a neighbouring group. Finally, it must be emphasized that extreme outbreeding or extreme inbreeding are likely to be disadvantageous and most species adopt an intermediate strategy which Bateson (1983) terms optimal outbreeding. Optimal outbreeding is usually achieved by the dispersal of some individuals of one or both sexes.

3.2 Adult-young interactions

3.2.1 General attributes

Lactation ensures that all mammals provide some degree of maternal care after the birth of their young. The adaptive value of parental care is to raise the parent's fitness by increasing the chances of its young reaching reproductive age. Trivers (1974) pointed out, however, that this relation is not necessarily completely harmonious because it may involve a conflict of interest as to how much parental inventment is optimal. Trivers defined parental investment as 'any investment by the parent in an individual offspring that increases the offspring's chance of survival (and hence reproductive success) at the cost of the parent's ability to invest in other offspring'. Clearly the offspring will attempt to take as much as possible from its parent(s), while the parent will resist over-investment in any particular young, because this will detract from future reproductive success. For example, lionesses do not return to oestrus while they are lactating, so that a greedy cub which continued to suckle beyond normal weaning age would decrease its mother's long-term reproductive success. The Galapagos fur seal (*Arctocephalus galapagoensis*) produces a single pup which it suckles for 2–3 years. If the mother gives birth to a second pup a year later, during the next breeding season, this infant is most unlikely to survive the suckling competition from its elder sibling. With a two-year gap, however, the neonate is much more likely to survive, so that the older infant restricts maternal breeding. The older sibling is probably not operating against the mother's long-term fitness because it could not survive at one year old without an adequate milk supply which would be denied to it by a younger competitor, and the mother might ultimately fail to rear both young.

Alexander (1974) took the view that, in a conflict of interest between parent and offspring, the parent must always win because parental care must have evolved to increase the fitness of the parent rather than that of the offspring. Thus, an infant which tries to take more than is necessary for its survival may be selected against, not only because it reduces future parental reproductive output but also because, if the trait is inherited, its own young may in their turn reduce its own fitness. In addition, an offspring which deprives its siblings of resources will also ultimately lose through the resulting decline in the inclusive fitness derived from its brothers and sisters.

Polygynous mammals are often sexually dimorphic, males being larger than females. As a male offspring usually grows more rapidly, it puts a greater strain on its mother during lactation, and may also be suckled for longer. In many mammals, including man, there is a period of infertility associated with suckling (lactation anoestrus). This inhibiting effect depends upon the frequency with which the young is suckled. Clutton-Brock *et al.* (1982) showed that the male offspring of the red deer are suckled more frequently than females and that as a result, a hind with a previous male offspring comes into oestrus, on average, 11 days later than an individual with a female calf. Thus, in red deer there is a higher level of maternal investment in male as compared with female offspring. Loudon *et al.* (1983) showed that the frequency of suckling in red deer was negatively correlated with forage quality and that consequently a delay in return to breeding condition occurred when nutritional levels were low.

Another important concept relevant to maternal care is that of *r* and *K* selection. At one extreme are long-lived mammals which produce few young per litter, have long inter-birth intervals and show a maximum of parental care. These are said to be *K*-selected. They live in a relatively constant and benign environment and show strong adaptation to personal survival, being generally of a larger size and having well defined antipredator strategies and competitive abilities. Their populations show relatively small fluctuations over a large period of time. At the other extreme are *r*-selected species which are short-lived, have large litters, breed frequently, develop rapidly and show minimal parental care. Individuals of such *r*-selected species are generally small and show wide fluctuations in numbers over a period of time. A fluctuating environment with frequent catastrophes favours *r*-selection (see Horn, 1978).

Typical examples of *K*-selected mammals are higher primates, elephants, antelopes, and cetaceans, all of which give birth to single young. In contrast, shrews (*Sorex, Blarina, Crocidura*) voles, field mice and Virginian opossums (*Didelphys virginiana*) live in a variable environment, are short-lived (2 years), and produce large litters of 5–15 individuals; these are said to be *r*-selected. Although these two extremes are part of a continuum, the concepts of *r* and *K* selection are convenient for comparing the reproductive strategies of different species (see Pianka, 1970; Horn, 1978). Sometimes even members of the same genus may adopt different reproductive strategies, for example mice of the genus *Peromyscus* (see Mace and Eisenberg, 1982). It must be borne in mind that the terms *r* and *K* selection, when applied to mammals, are relative. All mammals are *K*-selected in comparison with oysters or codfish which can produce thousands or even millions of young.

The brown marsupial mouse (*Antechinus stuartii*) is an extreme case of *r*-selection in a mammal (see Diamond, 1982). Its 3–8 young are born in May, mating occurs in August and adult males are all dead by the end of the month. Young are weaned in December and most females die soon after. Thus the species is semelparous (i.e. it only breeds once in a lifetime) and males exist only *in utero* between the end of August and beginning of September (see also Lee *et al.*, 1982).

It is probable that, for most species of mammal, maternal behaviour is triggered off by the mother's post-partum hormonal state. Experimental evidence has been provided to show that prolactin is the hormone responsible in rabbits, while oestrogen operates in domestic ewes (*Ovis aries*) and brown rats. The appropriate hormonal state may not be essential, however, because virgin rats shown maternal behaviour towards rat pups. After an initial hormone trigger, normal maternal behaviour appears to be under nervous control; this marks the commencement of the non-hormonal phase of maternal behaviour, during the latter part of which the presence of the young itself acts as a stimulus to maternal behaviour. The termination of maternal behaviour may result from the birth of subsequent young (in baboons), the disappearance of the young (the Antarctic fur seal) or by active aggression from the mother (many primates, some monogamous antelopes and hoary marmots) (see Slater, 1970).

Unless there are other closely-related mothers in the social group, it is rare for mammals to suckle alien young and it is clear, especially in social mammals where young are attractive to all members of the group, that mechanisms are likely to exist to prevent it. The suckling of alien, and almost certainly unrelated, young has only been observed occasionally. It happens in some bats (*Miniopterus schreibersii* and *Tadarida brasiliensis*) (Bradbury, 1977*a*), where mothers enter the creche of infants, pick one up at random and nurse it. Bradbury does not believe that kin selection operates in these species, so that an interesting problem is raised; he even found milk in the stomachs of some adult females.

Fogden (1968) observed grey seals (*Halichoerus grypus*) feeding alien pups on disturbed beaches. Lionesses nurse cubs other than their own but this may be of benefit in two ways; firstly, all females are closely related (mean $r = 1/8$) and secondly, the success of male cubs when they grow up to take over a pride is related to the number of male companions born in the same breeding period in the same pride. Thus by feeding other cubs the lioness is increasing the chances of survival of males to collaborate with her own male offspring (see Bertram, 1975; Bygott, *et al.*, 1979; Packer and Pusey, 1982; Bertram, 1983). The majority of mammals, however, avoid suckling alien young and a strong maternal bond has evolved. Recognition of the female's own young is not necessary in mammals where the mother can associate her young with a nest site. In species in which there is a common den, or the offspring are in a creche, as in most bats, pinnipeds and hyaenas, however, mothers can usually recognize their young individually. Firm maternal attachment occurs in most cursorial mammals and in species in which there is a long period of maternal care which extends to the stage in which young are well co-ordinated and can move with the social group (e.g. kangaroos).

Maternal behaviour may, in addition to nursing, include huddling with the young to keep them warm, grooming and cleaning, bringing food, carrying and transporting, providing shelter, and defending them against both predators and conspecifics. Svare (1981) discusses the phenomenon of maternal aggression, which has been observed in a wide variety of mammals including rats, rabbits, cats, squirrels, baboons, sheep and moose, which have even been known to attack horses and bears. Maternal aggression is directed both to predators and conspecifics. The female mouse (*Mus musculus*) attacks the neck and flank of a conspecific intruder, a pattern usually only shown in males. Experimental work has shown that maternal aggression is at a peak when the young are 3–8 days old. Removal of the young for five hours eliminates aggression, but replacement of the pups for five minutes restores it. Physical contact is not essential. Female mice are attacked less than males and castrated individuals less still. There is a correlation between maternal aggressiveness, rank of mother and number of offspring born; high-ranking females generally do better (Lloyd and Christian, 1969).

3.2.2 Lactation

The period during which mammals suckle their young ranges from ten days in many small mammals to over two years in the walrus (*Odobenus rosmarus*). The two or more mammary glands secrete milk which provides a complete diet for the developing young. Milk composition changes as the young grow older and their dietary requirements alter. The female red kangaroo (*Macropus rufus*) is even capable of secreting two different kinds of milk simultaneously, one for an active joey following her on foot, and the other for a neonate attached to the nipple in the pouch. Monotremata lack nipples and the mammary glands simply open on to the surface of the skin; the young employ a munching, sucking action to the appropriate parts of the mother's body.

The patterns of suckling and amount of contact between mother and young vary greatly between species. The female common tree shrew lives in a separate nest from her 1–2 young, visiting it (or them) once every 48 hours for approximately five minutes when she provides it with up to two-thirds of its body weight in milk and removes faeces and urine (Martin, 1968). A similar situation occurs in rabbits and hares which visit the young every 24 hours and in short-nosed echidnas where the young is fed every $1\frac{1}{2}$–2 days with approximately ten per cent of its body weight in milk. At the other extreme are most higher primates which carry their young around and essentially feed on demand.

A very interesting situation exists in the Pinnipedia which come to land to breed and lactate. Female Phocidae (true seals) do not feed, but live on fat reserves when lactating, providing a rich milk for a short time, 9–10 days in the harp seal, 16–21 in the grey seal and 4–6 weeks in the harbour seal. In spite of the very short lactation period in the harp seal, the young increase in weight from 10.8 to 34.4 kg, a rate of 2.5 kg per day, 1.9 kg of which is blubber (fat). In contrast, sea lions (Otariidae) and walruses (Odobenidae) do have the long lactation periods typical of large mammals (4 months—3 years) and, after the first week, leave the young at intervals to feed at sea. The Antarctic fur seal (*Arctocephalus gazella*) alternately spends four days at sea and then two days with the pup on land, making about seventeen trips in all.

Daly (1979), in discussing why male mammals do not lactate, makes the point that male lactation would only be expected to occur where paternity was certain, as in the case of monogamous species. As the majority of mammals are promiscuous or polygynous it is not surprising that male lactation has not evolved. In considering why monogamous male mammals have not subsequently evolved the capacity to lactate, Daly makes three points: firstly, a sexually dimorphic lactational physiology had already evolved; secondly, there is no evidence that female lactational capacity is a limiting factor to breeding success; and, finally, monogamous male mammals generally contribute to their offspring's welfare through other forms of parental investment which may be more effective.

The question which remains to be answered is why mammals lactate at all, bearing in mind their wide range of reproductive strategies. The general view appears to be that lactation evolved once, in the stock which gave rise to all mammals, because of the histological similarity of all mammary glands. Milk is the ideal baby food; essentially the mother can continue her normal adult diet and convert it into food precisely adapted to meet the infant's changing needs. The ancestors of mammals appear, from the record of fossils, to have been small insectivorous or carnivorous animals whose infants would be particularly susceptible to any failure in food supply. A few days' poor hunting might prove fatal to an infant relying on its parent(s) bringing prey back to the nest. Lactation may enable the mother to utilize fat reserves built up over a period of time and thus provide the developing infant with a more predictable food supply. This is particularly critical for warm-blooded animals whose food requirements are approximately six times greater than a cold-blooded predator of similar size.

3.2.3 Maternal care and developmental needs of the young

Young of monotremes. The spiny anteater, *Tachyglossus aculeatus*, lays a single egg which the female incubates for ten days in a pouch which develops only during pregnancy. The hatched young is carried in the pouch for ten weeks, after which the female leaves it in a nest and visits it at 24–36 hours intervals (see Griffiths, 1968). The reproductive behaviour of *Ornithorhynchus anatinus* is similar but there is no pouch and the mother incubates the 1–2 eggs in a nest (see Burrell 1927; Fleay, 1944; Griffiths, 1978).

Premature young of marsupials. The young of the Virginian opossum like all marsupials, are born in a semi-embryonic state. The mother licks the embryon at birth so that, in cases where the embryonic membranes are intact, she breaks them. She also licks a trail between the birth canal and pouch. The neonate crawls unaided to the pouch, possibly using olfactory cues in the mother's saliva; certainly the young has a well-developed, fully innervated, vomero-nasal organ even at this stage. The embryon attaches itself to a teat and, provided that more than one young becomes attached, the mother lactates and the neonates suckle using pumping movements of the tongue (see Hunsaker and Shupe, 1977). Apart from cleaning the pouch, maternal care is minimal at this stage and the offspring remains attached to the teat by a mechanism that involves barbs in the buccal cavity interlocking with grooves in the nipple. Any attempt to interfere with the pouch area results in ferocious kicking and growling by the mother opossum. At 29 days, the young can re-attach themselves to the nipple if removed and they vocalize between 37–41 days. They develop the ability to leave and re-enter the pouch when ten weeks old, and the mother orientates towards crying, separated young, making a clicking sound which enables her offspring to recognize her.

The closely-related mouse opossum *Marmosa*, which lacks a pouch, will retrieve her young after a few days of suckling even though they are not able to re-attach to the nipple until ten days old; in the laboratory this species will even retrieve mouse pups. Young of both *Marmosa* and the banded anteater (*Myrmecobius fasciatus*), which also lacks a pouch, simply cling to the mother's body surface. Young *Didelphys* are weaned between 100–110 days and all leave the nest by five months. Both *Marmosa* and *Didelphys* build nests, usually out of leaves. *Didelphys* collects about 30 cubic centimetres of nest material, using its coiled tail to carry it.

The large herbivorous red kangaroo (*Macropus rufus*) gives birth to a neonate weighing 0.5 g at birth, which is 180 000 times less than the adult weight of the animal (90 kg). The young joey remains in the mother's pouch for eight months (see Figure 3.6), but, after leaving the pouch, continues to suckle and follow its mother on foot. If it is separated, the young gives a lost call which attracts its mother to it. At this stage the female can recognize her young as an individual, in marked contrast to the earlier pouch phase when it is possible to cross-foster infants, even between different species of kangaroo.

Placental mammals. The nature of maternal behaviour in placental mammals is dependent upon the stage of development of the newborn young. Three types of mammalian young are recognized. 'Altricial' neonates are born naked, blind, deaf and incapable of locomotion or of

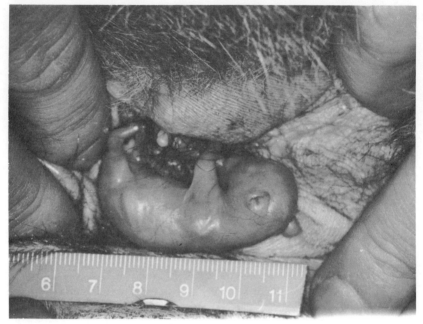

Figure 3.6 The pouch young of Bennett's wallaby aged 3 weeks. The infant remains permanently attached to the nipple at this stage. (Photograph Zoological Society of London.)

thermoregulation (e.g. the young of mice (*Mus musculus*) and rats (*Rattus* spp.). Semi-altricial young are furred, capable of some degree of thermoregulation, but blind, deaf and incapable of locomotion (e.g. cats and dogs). Finally, precocial young have fully developed senses and locomotion at birth (e.g. guinea pigs and goats). The division into three groups is artificial because intermediates exist, but it is a useful framework in which to consider the parental care of placentals.

Mammals with altricial young generally make a nest to provide protection and insulation; this is usually in a hollow tree or burrow in the ground. The female rabbit, for example, uses grass to construct a nest in her burrow. She lines it with fur from the ventral surface of her body. The loosening of the ventral fur just before parturition appears to be under hormonal control. Numerous other mammals make nests, including most small species with altricial young, such as shrews, mice, rats, and weasels.

Extensive studies of the maternal behaviour of the mouse (*M. musculus*) have yielded the following information. Before parturition the female mouse, under the influence of the hormone progesterone, builds a brood nest. It contains more material than the normal sleeping nest; after parturition, however, the presence of the young is alone sufficient to stimulate the maintenance of the brood nest. After cleaning the young and eating the placenta, the female lies on top of the pups in the lactating position and retrieves any which inadvertently stray from the nest. Retrieval is a function of the age of the mouse pup – the older it is, the less willing is the mother to retrieve it; even virgin mice will retrieve newborn pups. Female mice clean their young, licking the perineal region and removing urine and faeces, and mothers also provide special faeces called caecotrophe which are rich in bacteria; the young eat them, and this is believed to provide them with their gut flora. As previously described in Chapter 2, young rodents utter ultrasonic calls which stimulate maternal retrieval when outside the nest; the stimuli which elicit crying are lack of contact and lowered body temperature. Often the young are carried out of the nest because they remain attached to their mother's nipple. King (1963) compared the behaviour of two species of the rodent *Peromyscus* in the laboratory and found that the young of *P. bairdii* became displaced from the nest much more frequently than those of the more arboreal *P. gracilis* which normally nests in trees. Many rodents defend their young against interference both from their own species and from predators. King discovered that *P. bairdii* attacked a ten-inch pair of forceps which was used to remove young from the nest, while *P. gracilis* rarely did so.

As young house mice become more active, maternal nest building decreases; the young huddle together in small groups and show declining attachment to the nest site. Their mother then rejects them and returns to oestrus. The young of carnivorous or insectivorous mammals often go through a period during which they follow their mother on foraging excursions. Young crocidurine shrews form 'caravans' behind their mother, each holding the tail of the one in front in its mouth. Semi-altricial young are characteristic of carnivores and primates. Carnivores usually seek a quiet secluded place to give birth, often an underground den, as in hunting dogs (*Lycaon pictus*) and spotted hyaenas. Any disturbance will lead to the parents' picking up the young in the mouth and transporting them to another site.

The maternal behaviour of the domestic cat can be regarded as typical (see Schneirla *et al.*, 1963). The mother licks the newborn young, removing the birth membranes, breaking the umbilical cord and eating the placenta; after giving birth to 3–4 kittens she lies on her side with eyes closed, the nursing position. The kittens root for the nipples, each apparently finding one by touch; after two or three days some kittens develop a preference for

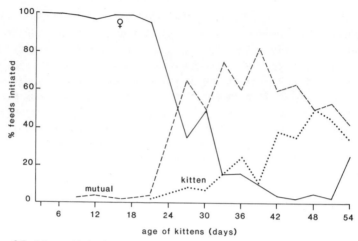

Figure 3.7 Maternal behaviour of the domesticated cat (*Felis catus*). Suckling initiations by mother and kittens for three litters of cats over a series of three-day periods. (After Schneirla *et al.*, 1963.)

a particular nipple but others suckle indiscriminately (Figure 3.7). The mother grooms and cleans her young and removes urine and excrement. Like many other mammals with altricial and semi-altricial young, she licks the perineal region to stimulate urination.

The kittens' eyes open after a week and by three weeks of age they are active and approach their mother to feed. Both mother and kitten may vocalize. When the young are over a month old, the initiative for suckling shifts to the kitten. At this stage wild or feral cats bring prey home to their kittens so that they come to rely less and less on milk. The mother avoids the kittens for much of the time by sleeping in a place which is inaccessible to them but after the 45th day the young are able to follow.

The young of many species of cat remain with their mother until fully grown. Tiger cubs (*Panthera tigris*) stay with their mother until 17–18 months old, sharing her kills and assisting in the hunting and killing of large prey (Schaller, 1967). Cheetahs show similar behaviour, so that most cats, although solitary as adults, spend a considerable time as a member of a family group (see also Fenton, 1974). The more social Serengeti lions, which live in prides, not only learn to hunt by observing adults of the group, but the females of the pride, who do most of the hunting, may take the cubs on practice hunts after food supplies have been assured. The practice hunts give the lion cubs a chance to learn how to capture prey themselves (Schaller, 1972).

Hyaenas and dogs are cursorial pack-hunting carnivores, often travelling over very considerable distances. Their prey is generally large and cannot be brought back to their cubs in one piece. As the young are semi-altricial, they must be left in a den until they reach an age when they can keep up with the pack. Hyaenas and wild dogs have found different solutions to this problem. In an African hunting dog pack, a single female breeds, producing a large litter of 9–16 puppies. She remains to guard the young, sometimes with the help of babysitters. Other pack members feed on the kill and regurgitate to the mother and pups when they return. This system of confining breeding to a single female with a high productivity enables the maximum number of hunters to go foraging, and also provides the maximum number of stomachs for regurgitation. This 'communal stomach' system of rearing young involves kin altruism, for all members of the pack are closely related. When the young are old enough to follow the pack, their mother punishes them if they attempt to suck by growling, snapping or snarling at them. Domesticated dogs shake the pup or hold it down with a paw. Similar behaviour has been observed in hyaenas.

Spotted hyaenas adopt a totally different method of breeding. Each female produces one or two young. Numerous females in the pack breed and cubs are left behind in a communal den. Each female lactates for twelve months, but, because she has few offspring to feed, she can hunt with the pack. Hyaena cubs do not rely to any great extent on food brought back to them by the pack; instead each female gorges herself and turns the prey into milk.

The semi-altricial young of some mammals cling to their mother; such young are characteristic of sloths, flying lemurs or colugos, pangolins, bats and primates. Of these the best-studied are primates, and Altmann (1980) describes the maternal care of the yellow baboon (*Papio cynocephalus*) under natural conditions. Infants are normally born at night. Initially the infant is cradled by the mother while it cries and gives rooting responses in an attempt to reach the nipple. Experienced mothers lift the infant to a position where it can suckle. By the end of the second week, the infant can move around on its mother and make its first attempt to leave her; mothers tend to restrain their infant's movements at this time. At three months, however, mothers often leave their infant and train it to follow by moving a short distance away and waiting for the infant to catch up. During the third and fourth months infants begin to play with peers and develop social relationships within the group.

Mothers rarely attack or punish their offspring but, after four months, they begin to resume their pre-partum way of life. They may ignore or move away from the infant, or shake it off when it tries to climb on. This often results in the infant having tantrums in which it throws itself on to its back, screeching and cackling while waving its tail about. This generally lasts five to ten minutes and is ignored by the mother. By five to six months, infants are supplementing their mothers' milk with solid food, and at six to eight months the young will stray more than 20 metres from their mothers. At six months the infant spends only 32% of its time in contact with its mother, declining to 10% by the tenth month. Dominance becomes apparent in infant dyads from 9–12 months and by one year the average infant is capable of surviving even if its mother dies. Mothers return to oestrus after 8–12 months, but infants sleep with their mothers and occasionally take a nipple in their mouths up to the age of eighteen months when the next infant is born.

Altmann divided the baboon's development into dependent (0–4 months) and semi-dependent (4–18 months) stages. During the dependent stage the mother clutches and supports her infant and even dead infants are treated in this way. Low-ranking mothers are more protective to their young and they become independent later than those of high-ranking mothers. The young of low-ranking mothers generally show a higher survival rate but, in the event of their mothers' death, are less likely to survive because of their high dependency. Another interesting fact, described by Altmann, was that low-ranking females produce pre-dominantly male offspring, while the reverse is true for the high-ranking females. As the ranks of mother and offspring are correlated and males emigrate to breed, it may be that this is the optimum strategy; high-ranking females can produce high-ranking female group members, while low-ranking females produce males whose rank, when they emigrate, is more likely to be independent of their status in the natal group. Female mortality was found to be greater when an infant was present, showing that maternal investment is costly for a female. Trivers and Willard (1973) predicted for sexually dimorphic polygynous vertebrates, in which males are larger than females, that high-ranking females should bias the sex-ratio of their offspring in favour of males. This supposition was based on the view that high ranking females are those most capable of affording the extra parental investment necessary to produce larger, more competitive male offspring.

While this hypothesis did not hold for baboons, for the reasons already outlined, red deer, however, do behave according to this prediction. Not only do high-ranking females produce relatively more male young, but there is a positive correlation between maternal rank and male offspring's breeding success, but no corresponding correlation for female young (Clutton-Brock *et al.*, 1984).

The experimental work of Harlow and Harlow (1966) showed that infant rhesus monkeys reared in social isolation proved to be severely abnormal in sexual and maternal behaviour when they became adults. Hinde and Spencer Booth (1969) found that one or six-day separations of semi-dependent infants in this species had long-term effects which, surprisingly, were still apparent $1-2\frac{1}{2}$ years later; infants who had been separated in this way were less exploratory and less willing to play with strange objects, although their behaviour was otherwise normal. However, even the drastic separation technique of Harlow and Harlow, while affecting the isolate's response to its first infant, had diminishing effects on the rearing of subsequent young; thus, self-correcting mechanisms appear to operate on maladaptive behaviour resulting from abnormal early experiences. Harlow and Harlow also found that rearing infants without mothers, but in company with peers, reduced abnormality. These results show that the infant's behaviour cannot be regarded as an extension of that of its mother, but must be viewed as an integral part of the social milieu in which it develops.

Some slow-developing primates retain a close social relationship with the mother even after the birth of the next sibling, for example, chimpanzees (Goodall, 1968*a*) and Japanese macaques (Sugiyama, 1960). Precocial young are fully-furred and capable of sensori-motor co-ordination shortly after birth. They are typical of cursorial, placental mammals and are found in hystricomorph rodents such as guinea pigs and acouchis (*Myoprocta pratti*), some lagomorphs (hares), all hoofed animals, elephant shrews and aquatic mammals such as whales, sea cows and pinnipeds. Precocial infants show one of two types of behaviour immediately after birth, being either 'hiders' or 'followers'. In both instances the young are capable of loco-motion soon after birth, but 'hiders' remain apart from their mother after birth, usually concealed among vegetation where the mother visits them at intervals to feed them. By comparison, 'followers' are immediately capable of joining the herd and accompaying their mother wherever she goes.

The precocial young of the pig family, Suidae, are unusual among un-gulates in that they are born in a nest constructed by their mother. Piglets establish a teat order, the most dominant individuals occupying the most productive nipples. The sow utters soft grunting sounds to call the young to feed and they can recognize her voice. Warthogs (*Phacochoerus ae-thiopicus*) actually nest in burrows, frequently those dug by aardvarks. The temperature of the burrow is maintained at about 30° C with a relative humidity of 90% and there are normally three young. After a period of two–three weeks, the mother rejoins a group and the young follow her.

Altmann (1963) described the behaviour of the elk (*Cervus canadensis*), a 'hider' species. The mother seeks cover to give birth to her fawn, which, for the first 18–20 days, remains separate from the herd. The mother leaves her young during the daytime to rejoin the herd, visiting the fawn only at intervals for nursing. Sometimes several hinds place their young in the same area and a distress call from one fawn attracts all the hinds with young in the area. Mother and young can, however, recognize one another. The strategy of maternal defence depends on the size of the predator. If the threat is from a wolf the mother makes a noisy retreat from the area, but elk

Figure 3.8   Red deer (*Cervus elaphus*) hind suckling calf. (Zoological Society of London.)

attack smaller predators such as coyotes. At three weeks of age the fawn begins to follow its mother into the herd, and the relationship between mother and calf remains close until the birth of the next offspring. In antelopes it has been shown that the choice of hiding place is determined by the young, not the mother (see Leuthold, 1977).

The maternal behaviour of the common hare (*Lepus europaeus*), another 'hider' species, has been studied by Brockhuizen and Maaskamp (1980). The hare gives birth to 2–4 precocial young which are born above ground in a shallow nest in the vegetation. They remain there for a day or two and their mother visits them at intervals. After this, however, the leverets separate but assemble at the old nest site between 1900 and 2000 each evening to be fed. The female only feeds young which turn up and does not search for an individual which fails to appear.

The young of pigs, red deer, elk and hare, although capable of locomotion, (Figure 3.8) are all relatively inactive after birth. This is also true of the young grey seal studied by Fogden (1971). The cow seal bears her young on a beach, where she defends a small territory against all other females. After giving birth to a single pup, she spends most of her time in the sea but returns at intervals to nurse. She responds to the pup's call which she can recognize individually. On approach, she presents her venter to the pup which searches for one of the two erected nipples. She helps the pup into an appropriate position (Figure 3.9).

Precocial mammals of the 'follower' type occur in hystricomorph rodents of which the guinea pig can be taken as an example. Neonate guinea pigs are extremely well developed, with all sensory systems functioning. They can even eat solid food from the day of birth but are also well provided with stored fat accumulated *in utero*. Under laboratory conditions, they have been reared from birth without milk but, even under optimal feeding conditions, there is a high mortality (40%) during this period and guinea pigs normally suckle for three weeks. Neonates can groom themselves and eliminate from the day of birth. There is a loose social bond between mother and offspring, but the mother appears to do little apart from suckling and familiarizing the young with its home range by leading it (see Fullerton *et al.*, 1974). The closely related green acouchi (*Myoprocta pratti*) uses a purring vocalization to maintain contact with her offspring. It is possible to hypothesize that some hystricomorph rodents could be an evolutionary pointer towards the ultimate elimination of the need for lactation. It is not known, however, how typical the guinea pig is of cursorial hystricomorph rodents as a whole, particularly as it is a purely domesticated species.

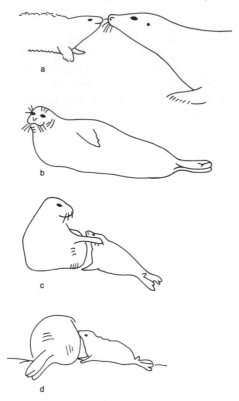

Figure 3.9 Behaviour associated with suckling in the grey seal (*Halichoerus grypus*) after the female has hauled out: (*a*) mutual nuzzling, (*b*) mother displays nipples to pup, (*c*) mother guides pup with flipper, (*d*) suckling. (After Fogden, 1971.)

'Follower' young are also typical of elephants, zebra and rhinoceroses and, although most cattle and antelopes (Bovidae) have 'hider' young, 'follower' types are found in wildebeest and African buffalo. The maternal care of the blue wildebeest (*Connochaetes taurinus*) has been described by Estes and Estes (1979).

In 'follower' species the onus for maintaining contact is generally on the mother. The female caribou (*Rangifer arcticus*), for example, grunts and bobs her head as a means of communicating with her calf. In many species, however, a process similar to imprinting operates, and the calf follows the individual with whom it is in contact at birth; it is therefore possible for human beings to 'adopt' lambs, Uganda kob and lesser kudu (see Leuthold, 1977). After attachment to a parent or foster-parent, the offspring learns to recognize the object of its attachment as an individual (see also Chapter 2).

Many aquatic mammals have 'follower' precocial young. These include all Cetacea, Sirenia and some Pinnipedia such as the common seal (*Phoca vitulina*) which suckles its young in shallow water on the sea shore. The female bottle-nosed dolphin maintains contact with its offspring by vocalization. Reviews of maternal behaviour in mammals are provided by Shillito-Walser (1977) and Gubernick and Klopfer (1981).

3.2.4 Paternal care

Theoretically, male care for infants is likely only to occur in situations of where paternity is certain, which restricts it to monogamous and harem-forming species. In the latter, paternal behaviour would be expected to be confined to offspring born after the male took over the harem, and in fact the most extensive paternal care is recorded in monogamous species.

Evidence for male infant care comes from two sources, firstly from captive animals and secondly from field studies. Caution must be used in interpreting laboratory studies, if there is no evidence that the behaviour occurs under natural conditions. If a male rodent, for example, is confined with an infant in a restricted space it may groom it or huddle with it, but this should not be regarded as paternal behaviour as the animal may behave similarly towards any conspecific, even another adult male.

Before continuing further to consider specific examples, the nature and form of paternal care must be considered. Apart from lactation, a male mammal is potentially capable of all other behaviour patterns shown by a mother, which may be any of the following: (1) cleaning or grooming, (2) transporting, (3) retrieving, (4) bringing food, (5) defending the young, and (6) babysitting. Males may also indirectly contribute to the welfare of young by huddling, playing and socializing with them, as well as by acquiring suitable resources and maintaining and defending them. These last behaviours, however, should not be regarded as paternal care because they may benefit the male himself and may also be directed towards individuals other than his offspring. Male exploitation of infants will be discussed later in this chapter.

Species in which males are known (from field studies) to show behaviours 1–6 are listed in Table 3.3. In addition to these, there is evidence that most male Canidae provide food for their young and are monogamous (see Kleimann and Malcolm, 1981). Most of the species in the table are monogamous and the two polygynous species, zebra and Indian langur,

Table 3.3   Mammals in which paternal care has been observed under field conditions (from Kleiman, 1982)

Species	Mating Systems	(1) Groom	(2) Transport	(3) Retrieve	(4) Feed	(5) Defend	(6) Babysit
Elephant shrew	M	+	–	–	–	+	–
Beaver	M	–	+	–	+	–	–
Deer mouse	M	+	–	+	–	–	±
False vampire bat	M	–	–	–	–	–	–
Wolf/jackal/coyote	M	–	+	–	+	–	+
African hunting dog	M	+	+	+	+	+	+
Dwarf mongoose	M	+	+	+	+	+	+
Titi monkey	M	+	+	+	+	+	+
Siamang	M	?	+	+	?	+	+
Phillip's dikdik	H	+	–	+	–	+	–
Indian langur	H	–	–	–	–	+	–
Zebra	H	–	–	–	–	+	–

only defend or retrieve young threatened by danger. More field data are urgently needed, particularly for small mammals such as rodents where laboratory studies have indicated that many species may be monogamous and show paternal care, for example the prairie vole (*Microtus ochrogaster*) (see Thomas and Birney, 1979) and the Mongolian gerbil (see Elwood, 1975). Elwood showed that the male gerbil not only demonstrates all the behaviour, (apart from lactation) shown by the female, but the pair also behave in a complementary manner, so that if one is away from the nest the other is present.

Field studies of the monogamous South American titi monkeys have shown that the mother only takes the infant when nursing; the rest of the time, infant care is entirely the prerogative of the male. The male siamang takes care of the infant after an initial period during which the mother cares for it exclusively (Chivers, 1974).

In their review of paternal care, Kleimann and Malcolm (1981) list paternal behaviour (Table 3.3, patterns listed 1–6) in Marsupialia*, Insectivora*, Macroscelidea, Chiroptera, Primates, Lagomorpha*, Rodentia, Cetacea, Perissodactyla, Artiodactyla and Carnivora. Data for the orders with an asterisk are derived solely from captive studies.

It is clear from this brief account that extensive or costly male/infant care is characteristic of monogamous species so that, consequently, it is rather uncommon in mammals.

3.2.5 Alloparental behaviour

In many species of social mammal, members of the group other than an infant's parents may care for it (see Spencer-Booth, 1970; Hrdy, 1976). Such behaviour is referred to as 'aunting' or alloparental behaviour. There are two main theories as to how this behaviour came to have evolved. The first possibility is though kin selection; individuals, particularly those who are not breeding themselves, may increase their inclusive fitness by caring for infants of close relatives. Thus alloparenting is most likely to occur in monogamous species with extended families or matrilineal polygynous species with well-defined kinship groups. A further possibility is that alloparental behaviour provides the caring individual with experience which may prove valuable when it gives birth to its own young; the two hypotheses are not incompatible.

Alloparental behaviour has been recorded from rodents, bats, dolphins, carnivores and primates: it resembles parental behaviour and consists mainly of one or more of the following: grooming, transport, retrieval, feeding, defence and babysitting (see Table 3.3). The phenomenon has been best investigated in the field in carnivores and primates.

In many species it has been shown that infants are attractive to all conspecific adults, not only to their mother, and it has long been established that virgin rats and mice will care for infants. Lorenz (1943) drew attention to the fact that infant birds and mammals have different facial proportions, a short muzzle, rounded cranium and relatively large eyes, which he believed to be a source of their attractiveness, particularly to human beings. Sternglanz et al. (1977) provided quantitative data from human subjects which confirmed, for this species, that the optimum combination of features supported Lorenz's contention. Hrdy (1976) drew attention to the fact that some primate infants possess coats which contrast markedly with those of adults of the same species, and which she referred to as 'flamboyant natal coats'. Infants of the silvered leaf monkey, *Presbytis cristatus*, for example, have white skin and orange fur while adults are grey. Flamboyant coats are also common in other arboreal colobine monkeys but the differences between adult and infant pelage are much less noticeable in terrestrial and semi-terrestrial monkeys. The function of distinct infantile colouring is not known for sure, but it seems likely to be a contributory factor to the attractiveness of infants.

For some mammals, alloparental behaviour is an essential part of their way of life and this is true of some Carnivora. Pack-hunting wolves and African hunting dogs assist in feeding the young of a single breeding female by regurgitating food at the den site in response to begging from pups and babysitters. The success of the litter is entirely dependent upon paternal and alloparental care by both sexes (see Malcolm and Marten, 1982). Owens and Owens (1984) have shown that the extent of helping behaviour in brown hyaenas is greater in females, who show alloparental behaviour to relatives as distant as second cousins. By contrast males will only provision half sibs. This finding lends further support to the hypothesis that altruism is most frequent between close kin, because male brown hyaenas emigrate more frequently from their natal group than do females. A most remarkable example of alloparental care has recently been discovered in the South African naked mole rat (*Heterocephalus glaber*) which is the only mammal known to show the phenomenon of eusociality. A eusocial animal is one which has evolved a sterile caste (the workers) whose members assist the reproductive caste by caring for young and foraging. Jarvis (1981) reported the results of field and laboratory studies on *H. glaber* which live in large colonies underground. She found that each burrow system contains a single breeding female together with three other castes: these she termed 'frequent workers' which forage, dig and nest-build; infrequent workers', which are larger and work at less than half the rate of frequent workers; and finally, 'non-workers' which are the largest individuals in the colony and assist in the care of young and form the nucleus of sleeping huddles. All females in the three castes have sexually inactive gonads while males are fertile, and it is thought that non-worker males fertilize the breeding female. The breeding female or 'queen' resembles a non-worker in appearance but has prominent teats and a perforate vagina. Both sexes carry and care for young and weaned juveniles join the frequent worker caste. Their growth rate determines their final caste. Rapidly-growing individuals become non-workers or replace breeding females, while slower-growing individuals remain permanently in the worker castes. Jarvis suggested that faster-growing individuals show age polyethism, which is a progressive change of roles as they grow larger. Removal of the breeding female results in her replacement by a fast-growing infrequent worker. It appears that female non-workers have lost the ability to become repro-ductive, and that recruitment to the female reproductive class must come from a growing individual which is still in the infrequent worker class. Jarvis attributed the suppression of reproduction in females to 'phero-monal' influences and direct body contact. Reproductive females are highly aggressive to other similar females from another colony and, if two colonies are mixed in the laboratory, one reproductive female kills the other. This social system appears to provide very considerable protection for the reproductive female who is highly fertile, producing up to twelve in a litter, four times per year. Food is brought to her and care of young is provided by other colony members. The kinship of the different individuals has not yet been established but, as juveniles appear to be recruited to the worker and non-worker castes, it seems likely that the colony is basically a family.

Alloparental behaviour in some primates appears to be an essential part of their way of life while, in others, it may seem to be optional. The South American Callitrichidae (marmosets and tamarins) live in social groups in which a single female breeds, producing in the genus *Callithrix* twin young every five months. The infants are carried, groomed, defended and retrieved and food is shared with them by all members of the group over ten months old (Stevenson and Rylands, in press). Circumstantial evidence from the field, the presence of a single breeding female, and a wealth of laboratory studies support the view that this genus is monogamous and that the social group is an extended family. The evolution of alloparenting may well have made feasible the successful rearing of twin young, which is typical of the family Callitrichidae, but is unusual in other monkeys. The advantage to the alloparents may derive from their close relationship to the infants, full siblings in a monogamous family group. In a related species, the cotton-topped tamarin (*Saguinus oedipus*), however, this explanation seems unlikely because juveniles commonly transfer between breeding units (see Neyman, 1978) but still show alloparental behaviour in their new group. In an allied species, the saddle-backed tamarin (*Saguinus fusicollis*), Epple (1978) found in a laboratory study that prior experience of infant care significantly improved the reproductive success of primiparous females, so it is conceivable that care for alien young also provides valuable experience for juvenile *S. oedipus*.

The extent of allomothering in Old World primates is very variable and is dependent upon the permissiveness of the mother in allowing other group members to interact with her infant. Macaques (*M. fuscata, M. radiata* and *M. nemestrina*) are very protective and tend to remain in close contact with their offspring until it begins to depart of its own accord. In marked contrast, colobine monkeys (*Presbytis entellus, P. obscurus, P. cristatus, P. johnii* and *Colobus guereza*) are very permissive, mothers allowing other group members to handle their infant within a few hours of birth. There is, however, some within-species variation, socially confident mothers being more permissive than others.

Most (93%) of the grooming of the offspring in the Nilgiri langur (*P. johnii*) is done by allomothers. In Old World monkeys, alloparental behaviour appears to be commonest among leaf-eating monkeys (Colobinae); McKenna (1979) has put forward the hypothesis that females of these species are less competitive, so that there is a less well-defined female hierarchy and consequently less risk to infants. Certainly instances are known of high-ranking female cercopithecine monkeys taking infants from low-ranking mothers and not returning them, so that the infants died.

Clearly there are advantages and risks in allomothering to all three parties involved, namely the infant, mother and alloparent. From the mother's point of view the ideal alloparent is one of slightly lower rank, preferably not too young, so that it has experience with other infants; from the infant's viewpoint the alloparent should be as high-ranking as possible so as to provide protection and access to food. From the standpoint of the alloparent, experience of mothering, if it is a female, is best acquired when it is nulliparous, i.e. has not yet had any young of its own, and in fact Hrdy (1971) found that allomothering in langurs is commonest among nulliparous females. Allomothering often leads to a friendly relationship between mother and caretaker so that it is beneficial to the latter if the mother is high-ranking. From all points of view, it is advantageous if mother and alloparent are close relatives and, in chimpanzees, for example, allomothering is the prerogative of an elder daughter.

Hamilton *et al.* (1982) observed that 4–5 year old male and female chacma baboons (*Papio ursinus*) adopt orphaned infants who are likely to be close relatives.

Infant 'exploitation' by male monkeys. In a number of species of macaques and baboons, a male interacting aggressively with another male has sometimes been observed to be carrying an infant. During the interaction the infant adopts a passive role. Deag and Crook (1971) first drew attention to this phenomenon and took the view that carrying an infant reduced the male's likelihood of being attacked, so they termed the phenomenon 'agonistic buffering'. The hypothesis was that the male was exploiting the infant to gain access to an oestrous female or food (see Deag, 1980). Packer (1980) found that in olive baboons there was a positive correlation between carrying an infant, when in conflict with another male, and caretaking of the same infant. He also found that infants who were treated in this way, by natal males in the troop, were close relatives and that immigrant males only carried and looked after infants born after their entry into the troop. Packer took the view that the dangers of 'exploitation' (i.e. carrying against another male) were outweighed by the benefits of caretaking.

Smith and Pfeffer-Smith (1982) failed to find any relation between infant-carrying by males and agonistic behaviour in Barbary apes (*Macaca sylvanas*) and rejected the theory of 'agonistic buffering'. Busse and Hamilton (1982) argued that infant-carrying by males, in polygamous primate groups, is a form of paternal care whose object is to protect offspring from infanticidal immigrant males. Busse and Hamilton found that olive baboon males carry infants who are likely to be their offspring, and protect them against immigrant males. Nine out of ten infants who were carried were conceived when the carrier was a member of the troop, and nine out of ten protecting males were higher-ranking at the time of the infant's conception that at the time of carrying. In most cases, the infant was protected against a higher-ranking immigrant male, and the carrier had lost status since the infant's conception. Most of the carried infants were unweaned and their mothers were antagonistic to the high-ranking immigrant male but not to the carrier.

Fundamentally the data presented by Packer (1980), Smith and Pfeffer-Smith (1980) and Busse and Hamilton (1982) are in agreement and suggest that carrying by males in polygamous primates is a form of parental protection and that the hypothesis of 'agonistic buffering' should be rejected.

3.3 Summary

1. Male and female sexual strategies differ. Males can mate with a number of females to increase their reproductive output whereas females can only give birth to their own offspring, so polygyny is common in mammals.

2. Female mammals may exert some mate choice.

3. Precopulatory behaviour consists of a male identifying an oestrous female and attempting to compete for her and court her. Courtship has been identified in both male and female mammals.

4. Patterns of copulation vary considerably among mammals. Some species have a post-ejaculatory lock or tie. Both terrestrial and aquatic mating is described for a number of mammals.

5. Monogamous mammals usually form a strong bond between sexual partners, irrespective of the female's oestrous condition. The dominant pair usually suppress breeding in other group members.

6. In polygynous species, dominant males acquire mating rights to a group of females but subordinate males may also adopt strategies to optimize their reproductive success.

7. A breeding male in a social group may adopt more than one strategy to father as many offspring as possible.

8. The importance of sexual selection by females has hitherto been neglected, but examples are given of species in which female choice of mate is known to play a significant role.

9. Inbreeding can be genetically deleterious and various methods of inbreeding avoidance have been identified.

10. Dispersal involves leaving one group to breed in another; generally male mammals disperse, while females breed in their natal group.

11. The duration of lactation is very variable, ranging from 10 days to nearly three years. Feeding may be on demand or at infrequent intervals of up to 48 hours in some species.

12. Both the egg-laying monotremes and the marsupials with their premature young have a long period of maternal dependence. Maternal behaviour includes cleaning, grooming, nest building and consuming urine and faeces.

13. Eutherian young may be relatively helpless or altricial, and be cared for by their mother in a den or nest. Many eutherians, however, produce offspring which are fully-furred with open eyes and which are capable of a degree of independent locomotion from birth. Some precocial young may even be capable of following the adult group very soon after birth. Between these two extremes are the semi-altricial young of carnivores and the clinging young of primates.

14. Maternal care usually goes through three phases; initially suckling is initiated by the mother, then the young seek her out and, finally, at weaning she avoids or rejects attempts to suckle.

15. Weaned young of insectivorous or carnivorous mammals often accompany their mother on foraging expeditions before becoming fully independent.

16. In addition to caring for the young, most female mammals defend them against predators and sometimes from the attentions of conspecifics.

17. The status and behaviour of young in some primates relate to that of the mother. Low-ranking mothers may be more restrictive than high-ranking mothers.

18. In some mammals, individuals other than the mother may help to care for the infant. This may take the form of grooming, transporting, retrieving, bringing food, defence and babysitting.

19. Paternal care has been identified in monogamous mammals. In some polygynous species, however, the male has been observed to come to the defence of his offspring.

20. Alloparental care by females other than the mother is common in some species. There is usually a close kin relationship between mother and allomother. The main advantage to the mother appears to be temporary relief from the infant's demands and, for the allomother, experience in mothering and a gain in inclusive fitness.

21. Some pack-hunting carnivores are dependent on alloparental care, particularly feeding and babysitting, for the survival of their young.

22. Adult male macaques and basoons in multimale/multifemale groups may care for and carry infants. There is evidence that these males may be protecting their offspring against high-ranking immigrant males.

23. The only known eusocial mammal is the naked mole rat, which has reproductive and non-reproductive castes.

CHAPTER FOUR

COMPETITIVE AND AFFILIATIVE BEHAVIOUR

4.1 Agonistic behaviour

Agonistic behaviour is that which is associated with attack and defence. Because an individual's reproductive potential is greater than the carrying capacity of a stable environment, intraspecific competition for the limited resources available is inevitable. Some of this competition takes the form of defending assets which can be monopolized, and this is the commonest situation in which agonistic behaviour is shown. To acquire and defend a resource, an individual must be capable both of obtaining it in the face of rivals and then of defending it in the event of a challenge. The assets which are most commonly defended are a mate, a food supply, living space, a resting site safe from predators, or the superior status which gives priority of access to such resources.

In a situation of conflict an individual can either challenge its rival, or retreat. The advantage of challenging lies in the chance of winning the resource, which will be referred to as the payoff. The cost of challenging can be assessed in terms of the energy utilized in the conflict and the risk of serious injury. For the stronger opponent, challenging is the best strategy; for the weaker, retreat alone will provide the maximum benefit. In unequal contests it is clearly beneficial to have some method of assessing relative strengths which will allow the weaker individual to withdraw without physical injury. Such an assessment will benefit both individuals if physical conflict can be avoided, and commonly occurs where a clear discrepancy in fighting potential exists between two individuals. The stronger individual displays and the weaker withdraws.

Even in situations in which two individuals are equally matched it would obviously be advantageous if a conflict could be resolved, without resort to physical violence, simply by display. Non-injurious contests of this type have been termed ritualized fighting and, until the early 1970s, many ethologists believed that ritualized fighting had evolved because it benefited both partners and hence ultimately the species. However Maynard-Smith, Price and Parker carried out a theoretical analysis of aggression using game theory which cast serious doubts on such an interpretation, and their views have been summarized by Dawkins and Krebs (1978) to which readers are referred for a more detailed account. In essence their argument is as follows: if all individuals in a population (henceforth referred to as 'mice') settled disputes by ritualized fighting and an individual appeared who employed escalated injurious fighting (a 'hawk'), the 'hawk' would win every time. Thus, the strategy 'mouse' is not an evolutionarily stable strategy (or ESS) for it can always be defeated by a 'hawk'. (It will be recalled that an evolutionarily stable strategy is defined as a strategy which, if adopted by most members of a population, confers greater reproductive fitness than any alternative strategy.) To continue, as a 'hawk' would always succeed in a conflict with a 'mouse', the genes for 'hawk' would spread throughout the population. The time would come, however, when the probability of a hawk meeting another hawk in a conflict would increase to such a point that serious injury among hawks would be common; mice would then come to be at an advantage. Thus 'hawk' is not an ESS either and in this example, assuming that the cost of injury was greater than the benefit of winning, the final ESS would be an equilibrium point with a particular proportion of mice and hawks. The exact percentages of hawk and mouse can be calculated by game theory for various values of costs and payoff for the two strategies.

Maynard-Smith (1976c) appreciated that this scenario is simplified and that, for example, an individual might display conventionally against a mouse but escalate when confronted with a hawk. He termed this strategy 'retaliator' and showed that it can be an ESS in situations where the cost of injury exceeds the benefit of winning.

This type of analysis is helpful to our understanding of aggression by providing realistic models which can easily be quantified. The examples so far considered have made the assumption that the two individuals are evenly matched in the sense that each rival has a 50:50 chance of winning. In nature, however, conflicts are often asymmetrical; this may be because one individual is stronger (has greater resource-holding potential, or RHP), or one has greater need of the disputed resource, or because one individual is already holding the resource while its rival is a challenger attempting to take over.

In such asymmetrical contests, information regarding the resource-holding potential of the combatants may be available. Geist (1966) found that, in mountain sheep (*Ovis dalli*), a strange ram's position in the dominance hierarchy is partially determined by relative size, especially horn-size, and he observed only fights between rams of approximately equal size. Thus, it must be assumed that a ram is capable of assessing, on the basis of body and horn-size, the RHP of its rival in comparison to its own.

Where individuals are unable to detect differences in RHP, they might be expected to behave as if they were evenly matched. This would lead either to an impasse or to damaging fighting. Maynard-Smith and Parker (1976), however, have shown that an arbitrary rule could be used to settle such disputes amicably. The rule which they suggested was that where two individuals appear to be equally matched the resource-holder wins, and it is apparent that such a convention would save time in display and avoid injury. What is surprising however, is that they found that the application of this arbitrary rule is an ESS having a higher payoff than either 'mouse' or 'hawk' strategies (see Dawkins and Krebs, 1978).

The rule 'resource-holder wins' is common to most territorial mammals but may also occur in competition for females. In a lion pride, for example, a male who is already consorting with a female is seldom challenged (see Chapter 3) and Kummer (1974), in an experimental study of the formation of sexual bonds in hamadryas baboons found that a male will not challenge a pair which he has observed forming only fifteen minutes earlier. Prior ownership of a female confers the right to retain her, but it applies only where the resource-holding potential of the two males is similar. If the first male is obviously smaller than the second, the latter may challenge the owner and acquire the female. Kummer also found that conflict developed when a male was removed from the troop and his females taken over by other males. On returning to the troop, the original male challenged the new owner and attempted to regain his females by force.

Whether or not escalated fighting occurs is also dependent upon the scarcity of the resource, conflict being more likely if a resource is highly restricted, when the payoff will be high. Escalated fighting is also more likely to occur in species in which the risk of serious injury is low and these two factors must be taken into account in any investigation of fighting.

4.1.1 Weapons and fighting techniques

The majority of mammals possess weapons which may be used in attacking other individuals. The primitive mammal has a battery of at least 44 sharp

a

b

Figure 4.1 Fighting techniques: (*a*) the male golden hamster (*Mesocricetus auratus*) aims to bite the opponent's flank; (*b*) the male polecat (*Mustela putorius*) on the left of the photograph retains a bite on his opponent's neck.

teeth adapted for piercing the carapaces of insect prey or killing small vertebrates; these make effective weapons against conspecifics. Biting is the most primitive form of aggression and is employed by most mammals (see Figure 4.1).

Where biting is the major offensive strategy, the mammal must both succeed in biting its opponent and itself avoid being bitten. Mice (*Mus musculus*) attack parts of the opponent's anatomy remote from its jaws such as the back and flank, followed by very rapid withdrawal, thus employing a series of sharp nips. In contrast, male Northern elephant seals make brief slashing bites at the opponent's head, neck and pendant nose; though deep wounds may be inflicted, these heal rapidly (Le Boeuf, 1971). Most terrestrial carnivores also use their teeth in fighting, in many cases biting the neck of the opponent as, for example, polecats. Cats also use their claws (see Leyhausen, 1979) and primates may hit the opponent with the hand. Ungulates may use their hooves but some have, in addition, evolved special weapons such as the horns and antlers of ruminants. Geist (1966) regarded these appendages as having evolved for intraspecific aggression, as opposed to defence against predators, and Leuthold (1977) gives four reasons for this view:

(1) The weapons are rarely used against predators.
(2) For attacks on predators straight pointed horns would be the most effective; most species have branched antlers or curved horns.
(3) The horns or antlers of females are usually either absent or less well developed than those of males.
(4) Cervidae (deer) usually only develop antlers for the rut.

When fighting, horned artiodactyls generally lock their antlers together and push one another, making the fight more equivalent to a wrestling match than a sword fight. Nonetheless, it is possible for one individual to make a broadside attack and inflict a severe injury, if it can get past its opponent's guard. In species of ungulate where both sexes are horned all the year round, such as many antelopes, Kiley-Worthington (1978) takes the view that their horns prove very effective weapons against predators. She does not, however, dispute that they are of importance in intraspecific aggression and cites the example of the eland (*Taurotragus oryx*) in which the female has long thin horns suitable for delivering quick stabs, while the male has more robust weapons suitable for horn-wrestling with other males (see Figure 4.2).

Elephants fight by pushing one another, using the tusks to prevent the opponent's head slipping sideways; rhinoceroses club their adversary's head with their nasal horns. Zebras (*Equus burchelli*) bite and also kick with

Figure 4.2 Eland (*Taurotragus oryx*) using their horns in fighting. (Photograph Zoological Society of London.)

their hooves, rising up on their hind legs. Amongst the most bizarre forms of fighting is that of the giraffe (*Giraffa camelopardalis*), which is termed 'necking'; the animal swings its whole neck and head towards the opponent, aiming for the shoulder. One of the most remarkable weapons possessed by any mammal is the male narwhal's (*Monodon monoceros*) single long tusk which is also believed to be used in intraspecific fighting. Many mammals which fight have thickened skin in regions where they are likely to be attacked, e.g. rhinoceroses, elephant seals and polecats.

Fighting, apart from that of pinnipeds, is difficult to observe in the field because it rarely occurs, and many agonistic encounters which are observed may be between individuals who have met previously and already established their status in relation to one another. In many species fighting is of short duration and thus difficult to analyse, but escalated fighting in male polecats, which may last for as long as nine minutes, has been subjected to a detailed cine analysis in the laboratory (Poole, 1974*b*). The

Table 4.1 Orientation and duration of bites in polecat's fighting for 917 bites with a total duration of 41.96 seconds (60 418 frames of cine film at 25 fps).

	Bites	
	No.	Mean duration (seconds)
Face	14	2.0
Neck	832	3.0
Chest	1	2.7
Shoulder	50	1.8
Back	49	0.8
Flank	31	1.5
Belly	1	0.8
Anal region	22	1.0

fighting technique in this species consists essentially of biting the opponent and holding on for as long as possible. Biting occupies approximately 40% of the time, and the individual which can sustain its bites longest wins.

Over 80% of the polecat's bites are directed to the neck of its opponent, a region well protected by skin and subcutaneous fat. It might appear that polecats bite their opponent in an area where they can do least damage, in line with Lorenz's (1966) suggestion that natural selection favours non-injurious fighting which promotes species survival. Further examination of the data, however, shows that bites to the neck are retained far longer than those on other parts of the body (see Table 4.1). As winning is associated with the duration of biting it is clearly to the individual's advantage to bite the neck in preference to other regions. The fact that the neck is well protected is therefore hardly surprising. These data also support Maynard Smith and Parker's (1976) view that escalated fighting is only likely to occur where minimal injury is likely to be inflicted.

4.1.2 The role of aggressive displays

One of the few species of mammal for which a detailed analysis of aggression is available under field conditions is the red deer which has been extensively studied by Clutton-Brock *et al.* (1979, 1982). In the rut, each stag attempts to acquire access to a group of hinds (a harem) which he then defends against rivals. In situations in which a stag is likely to be challenged he shows threatening behaviour in the form of roaring and walking parallel to his opponent. Should the other male continue to challenge, however, the antlers are used and a fight develops.

Fighting stags lower the head and ram the opponent with the antlers. As the rival faces his attacker, their antlers lock together and a pushing match ensues. Each stag attempts to get uphill from his opponent and to push him backwards. The loser finally withdraws and takes to flight. Pursuit is rare because attacking involves lowering the head which reduces the male's speed. If, however, the loser slips or falls, the winner will take the opportunity to jab the flank of its fallen rival, often wounding it severely. Fighting success is positively correlated with reproductive success and, in turn, with antler size. Success in fighting can therefore lead to a considerable gain in a male's fitness, but it also involves risks, as there is a $1:17$ chance of its being seriously wounded. As a seriously-wounded stag has little chance of survival, it is apparent that the optimum strategy is to avoid contests with superior rivals or those in which there is a high risk of injury.

Clutton-Brock *et al.* (1979) investigated the displays which occurred prior to fighting to determine their significance and likely function. They found that stags roar most in conditions in which they are likely to be challenged and that the pitch of roaring is related to the size of the animal, larger stags having lower-pitched roars. Roaring provokes other stags to reply, and the frequency of the replies is positively correlated with the frequency of the roars heard. Generally stags roar alternately, each facing its opponent. If one contestant withdraws at this stage, the winner is the individual which has the maximum number of roars per bout. Human observers can predict the outcome of a contest by comparing the two stags' roaring rates. Clutton-Brock *et al.* concluded that roaring appears to function for the two stags as a means of assessment. If the protagonist remains after the roaring contest, the contestants generally commence parallel walking. This occurs most commonly when opponents are well matched. The fact that there is a strong correlation between the duration of parallel walking and that of subsequent fighting again indicates a trial of strength; very long parallel walks, however, are less likely to be followed by a fight.

These data support the view that roaring and parallel walks provide a means whereby rival stags can assess one another's fighting potential. Stags seldom challenge older, larger individuals, so that roaring contests rarely occur if there is an obvious visible discrepancy in size; very powerful stags of approximately equal strength, however, generally do not fight after long parallel walks, thus avoiding serious injury. Clutton-Brock *et al.* discuss how roaring and parallel walks might be related to fighting ability; they regard parallel walking as a test of stamina and they put forward the view that roaring and fighting both involve the same thoracic musculature.

These results can be interpreted using Maynard-Smith and Parker's analytical approach. Contests are usually asymmetrical; one individual holds a harem while its challenger does not. The rivals confront one another and assess each other's fighting ability, without actual combat, either by size discrepancy or vigour of display. This method of assessment is probably relatively immune to cheating. If the two individuals come to regard one another as equals they then adopt the convention 'resource holder wins'.

The above discussion has considered only cases where individuals simply advertise their strength; in other situations individuals may avoid showing their weaknesses. Young male stags roar less than older ones when in possession of a harem, thus avoiding the attention of older, larger stags. Packer (1979a) has shown that, in male olive baboons, fighting ability is related to canine wear, and open-mouth yawns are used to display the canines to opponents. Males with long, sharp canines yawn more frequently than those with worn or damaged ones. There have been few other quantitative investigations of the effects of different displays on the opponent, or the degree to which future behaviour can be predicted. Chalmers (1968), however, provided some information on three displays in sooty mangabeys (*Cerococebus albigena*) (see Table 4.2). It is apparent that yawning and staring convey an aggressive intent, while lipsmacking appears to be friendly. Chalmers also found that the orientation of the yawn influenced the behaviour of its opponent. Yawning directed towards an individual more often resulted in its flight than did yawning away from it.

From the above discussion it is apparent that, in some species, display may function to settle a dispute without physical conflict which could prove

Table 4.2 Subsequent behaviour of signaller and recipient after three facial displays. Data from a field study of mangabeys (*Cercocebus albigena*) by Chalmers (1968).

Behaviour	Next behaviour			
	Individual	Attack	Remain	Flee
Stare	Signaller	6	12	0
	Recipient	0	2	12
Yawn	Signaller	9	16	19
	Recipient	1	7	6
Lipsmacking	Signaller	0	21	9
	Recipient	0	14	0

Figure 4.3 Aggressive confrontation between two male gelada baboons (*Theropithecus gelada*) showing staring and stiff-legged posture by the dominant male (third from left). The follower (second from left) does not threaten. (Photograph R. I. M. Dunbar)

injurious (see Figure 4.3). By advertising its fighting potential, the individual conveys information to its rival and at the same time may receive information about its opponent's strength.

4.1.3 Submissive and defensive displays

In situations in which there is a difference in resource-holding potential (RHP) between two individuals, the weaker may display to indicate his non-combatant status. The two main types of display concerned are termed *submissive* or *defensive*.

Submission indicates that the individual will not retaliate, even if attacked, and a common form of this behaviour is rolling over on to the back or crouching. Brown rats (*R. norvegicus*) also utter an ultrasonic cry which inhibits the dominant from attacking (Lehman and Adams, 1977). Submissive canids lie on the back and expose the inguinal region, sometimes also showing a submissive grin. Submissive displays are commonly shown by the young towards older group members, by females towards males and by very low-ranking adults towards high-ranking dominants.

Defensive displays, often referred to as 'defensive threat' signify that the animal will not spontaneously attack its opponent but may retaliate if attacked. It is commonly used where two closely-ranking individuals are in proximity, or where a lower-ranking individual is holding a disputed resource. In many species defensive threat involves displaying the teeth as, for example, in some marsupials, primates and carnivores (see Figure 2.4, 4.4). Defensive threat and submission occur in situations where the signaller wishes to avoid conflict or the resumption of a previous fight, the difference in RHP between the interactors being greater in the case of submission. In species which live in social groups, memory of the outcome of previous conflicts with a particular individual must be the important factor in determining the nature of the display and it is in the more sociable mammals that the most elaborate forms of agonistic displays have evolved.

4.1.4 Agonistic displays and their underlying motivation

Aggressive, defensive and submissive displays have been defined and discussed independently. In highly sociable species, however, forms of display intermediate in form between these categories have been identified. They have generally been interpreted in terms of a conflict between the motivation of aggression (urge to attack) and fear (urge to flee) (see Lorenz, 1966; Leyhausen, 1979), but few quantitative data are available to support this view as regards mammals. Maynard-Smith (1974), Dawkins and Krebs (1978) and Caryl (1979, 1981, 1982) have, as already stated, questioned its validity by pointing out that, in an agonistic contest, an opponent would be at a disadvantage if he provided accurate information about his next move, and that game theory would appear to favour a bluffing strategy giving the impression of greater confidence than might be the case. Hinde (1981) argued that a display may result from conflicting motivations but convey only very generalized messages such as 'I shall attack or stay' or 'If you do do x I am more likely to attack than escape'. In the absence of relevant quantitative data for mammals, it is not currently possible to resolve the conflicting views regarding the motivation of these displays, the ways in which are interpreted by a rival, or their reliability as predictors of subsequent behaviour.

Hutson (1982) carried out a quantitative study of threat in the Australian carnivorous marsupial, the kowari (*Dasyuroides byrnei*). He took into account both the sequences of behaviour shown by the signaller and the response of the opponent. Two types of threat display were shown by this species towards conspecifics. One was the pant-hiss which was associated with a high probability of attack and significantly elicited flight from the opponent. The other was shown by a defensive individual and was associated with flight or retaliation, but not with spontaneous attack. In view of the considerable variation in intensity of the calls, Hutson took the view that the data were compatible with the conflict hypothesis of threat

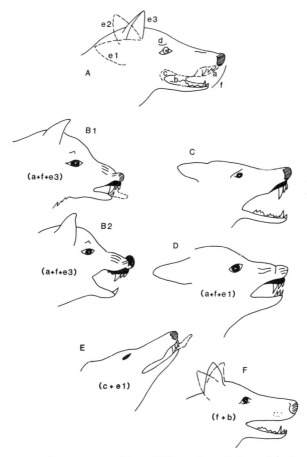

Figure 4.4 Some facial expressions of the wolf (drawn from photographs). *A*: parts of the face utilized in expressive movements, (*a*) upper lip, (*b*), (*c*) lower lip positions, (*d*) eyebrow (frown), (*e*) ears, (*f*) opening of the mouth.
B: differing intensities of confident threat
C: defensive threat
D: threat by beta male to dominant
E: friendly submission
F: open-mouth play face. (See text for explanations)

display, but did not provide data to show what effect intermediate displays might have on the opponent. He found that distance from the opponent was important, as was the context in which the display occurred – for example, whether the animal was approaching or fleeing from its rival.

A species whose aggressive displays have generally been taken to indicate conflicting tendencies to attack or flee is the wolf, together with other related canids such as the dog, coyote, fox, and jackal. We shall briefly consider some of these displays in terms of the information which they are believed, by a number of experienced observers to convey to a rival. Figure 4.4 shows some facial expressions of the wolf taken from photographs published by Fox (1975). A shows the normal relaxed face with the areas which can be moved in an agonistic display indicated by letters $a - g$. Display B indicates readiness to attack, B_1 and B_2 representing low and high levels of this display. An individual showing this behaviour is issuing a challenge: 'If you remain (or approach) I shall attack'. D is a defensive threat which is not a challenge but indicates 'If you attack me, I shall retaliate'. Behaviour E conveys the message 'I am friendly and will not attack'. The threat C is intermediate between B and D and was shown by a high-ranking beta wolf who was approaching the alpha; its precise message is unclear. On traditional grounds it would be interpreted as indicating both submissiveness (the flattened ears) and a tendency to attack if challenged. It is this type of display which needs much more clarification.

So far as the structures used in signalling are concerned, the display of the upper incisors and canine teeth appears to be indicative of the individual's capacity to bite, either in attack or retaliation, thus conveying the information 'These are my weapons, beware'. The pulling back of the lip (b) indicates a low tendency to offensive behaviour; the play face (f) is of special interest because it combines the non-display of weapons (upper incisors and canines) with the full retraction of the lower lip so that the lower teeth only are displayed.

Until more quantitative data are available no conclusions can be drawn as to the precise meaning of intermediate displays such as that illustrated in C. In this discussion no account has been taken of the vocalizations accompanying the facial displays. These are clearly of significance, growling being characteristic of B, while screaming may accompany D. The facial expressions may be directly related to the way in which accompanying sounds can be produced.

From the data currently available it is not possible to decide how precise a prediction of future behaviour an intermediate display may be. The view that it reflects underlying motivation however seems reasonable on face value. What needs to be shown is how these displays may benefit the signaller, which otherwise appears to be giving away important information about the future moves to the opponent.

An aspect of mammalian agonistic displays which is often ignored is the fact that most graded displays in species living in social groups are directed towards familiar individuals. This being the case, the contestants already know one another and are aware of any previous asymmetries in their resource-holding potential. Any display which reflects this asymmetry gives nothing away and may simply emphasize the persistence of a stable situation, thereby avoiding further challenges for the dominant. If the signaller were to bluff in this situation, it might well end up with an unwanted challenge. An important social aspect is whether a resource is involved. If the resource is valuable to the signaller but less so to its rival, the weaker individual by adopting a form of defensive threat is effectively saying that it will retaliate only if the dominant individual attempts to take over the resource. In this situation the dominant may withdraw because the cost of acquiring the resource may be greater than its value.

4.1.5 Dominance hierarchy

The concept of dominance hierarchy relates to a situation in which individuals can be ranked so that a higher-ranking individual may attack or show aggressive threat, while the subordinate avoids conflict by moving away or showing submission or defensive threat (see reviews by Bernstein, 1981; Dewsbury, 1982). In a social group the situation may exist where individual A is dominant over B, which is in turn dominant over C and so on; this is a linear hierarchy but sometimes loops may exist so that A is dominant over B who is dominant over C who dominates A. Considering only dyadic relationships, therefore, the dominant individual can threaten or displace the subordinate with impunity.

A dominance hierarchy is commonly established in one of two ways, either through fighting, in which the dominant wins, or through differences in age (age-graded rank). Packer's (1977a) work on olive baboons provides an excellent example of both arrangements in a multi-male society. Individuals born into the group have a status based on their age, older individuals being dominant over younger ones. Immigrant males, however, have rank which is not age-dependent but results from conflicts with other males. Japanese macaque females are unusual in that the status of sisters is inversely related to their age. In most social species males are dominant over females and Dittus (1977) found that, for each age group, male toque macaques dominated females.

Some authors have questioned the validity of the concept of a dominance hierarchy on a number of grounds, for example, the fact that all measures of dominance (reproductive success, access to mates etc.) may not be correlated; the possibility exists that dominance hierarchies are a product of confinement and are of much less relevance in the field, and that subordination is the critical aspect of a dominance hierarchy (for review, see Dewsbury, 1982). If the concept is confined to situations where there is a consistent asymmetry in agonistic relations, then the term would seem to be valid because dominance hierarchies have been observed in the field in many primates, ungulates and wallabies. Mech (1970) examined the value of the concept of a dominance hierarchy in a wolf pack (*Canis lupus*). He correlated a series of parameters with dominance and obtained high correlations which gave reliable ranking, and concluded that a wolf pack can be regarded as a ranked society. Dominance hierarchies have been identified in the field in marsupials, rodents, lagomorphs, carnivores, artiodactyls, perissodactyls, elephants and primates.

The degree of stability of dominance hierarchies may vary; in some species it only becomes apparent in the rut, e.g. Northern elephant seals, while in others it is a year-round phenomenon, although changes may occur during the breeding season. Jolly (1966) found that the male hierarchy of ring-tailed lemurs outside the breeding season differs from that which appears when females come into oestrus. In wild yellow baboons, Hausfater (1975) found that the female dominance hierarchy is much more stable than that of males. Changes resulting from demographic factors such as death, emigration and immigration occurred every 13 days for the male, every 57 for females, while those due to agonistic interactions took place on average every 21 days.

Two important questions which require further consideration are what benefits are associated with dominance and, if dominants do have an advantage, why subordinates remain in a social group.

The general view among ethologists is that dominance confers greater reproductive success and Dewsbury (1982) has examined the data which purport to support this hypothesis. The usual means of measuring reproductive success are numbers of copulations by dominant, as opposed to subordinate group members, and number and duration of consortships between males and females in relation to rank. One factor which should be taken into account is the stage of oestrus of the female when consortship takes place. High-ranking male olive baboons, for example, consort with a female only at peak oestrus, so that subordinate males are less likely to father offspring, irrespective of the duration of their consortship in relation to that of the dominant. Drickamer (1974) questioned the value of taking absolute measures of mating frequency in the wild; his data showed that dominant male rhesus macaques mated more frequently than subordinates but that the latter were less frequently seen and, when the data were corrected for time observed, the apparent difference disappeared. Order of mating may also be a significant factor in some species. Levine (1967) found that a female laboratory mouse which had received an equal number of ejaculations from two males bore more offspring from the first male; by contrast, female golden hamsters and prairie voles produced more offspring from the male who mated last (see Dewsbury and Baumgartner, 1981). Other factors which may influence mating success are sperm exhaustion in a dominant male which mates very frequently, as compared with a subordinate who rarely does so.

Dewsbury (1982) concluded that there is good evidence for a correlation between dominance and reproductive success in carnivores, ungulates and rabbits, while the situation appears to be much more variable from species to species in rodents and primates.

For females there is often a correlation between rank and reproductive success, measured by number of offspring produced. This has been demonstrated in captivity in deermice (*Peromyscus maniculatus*), house mice and red deer, and, in the field, in rabbits, in Japanese macaques by Takahata (1982), and gelada baboons by Dunbar and Dunbar (1975).

Dittus (1979) found that subordinate toque macaques had less access to food, fewer refuges from predators and fewer mates and sleeping sites. This raises the question of how subordinate behaviour has evolved and what advantages it might confer on the individual. By submitting to a stronger individual, the subordinate avoids an unequal contest and the danger of injury. It also saves the energy involved in a fight or flight which it can more profitably use to seek food elsewhere. If the dominant is also a relative, the subordinate gains some inclusive fitness by not committing its relative to a time- and energy-wasting conflict. Behaving in a subordinate manner allows an individual to maintain close proximity to high-ranking males of the group and to remain a member of the social group, thus gaining the benefits of group vigilance, group foraging and other advantages of social life. If a subordinate individual is younger than a dominant it may itself, in time, become dominant if it remains in the social group, or alternatively it may accept subordinate status in its natal group but, when another group is contacted, the individual may change groups and acquire a high status in the new group. Vehrencamp (1983) has put forward a quantitative model comparing egalitarian societies with those showing despotic dominance (i.e. a single dominant which manipulates resources to its own advantage). She concludes that the extent to which benefits may be restricted to a few (dominant) members of a society is dependent upon the cost to subordinates leaving the group balanced against the benefits derived from group living and the degree to which they are genetically related.

Agonistic behaviour is known to be an important factor in the regulation of numbers in *r*-selected rodents such as deer mice (see Healey, 1967), and lemmings (*Dicrostonyx, Lemmus*), but recently Dittus (1979) has shown that it is also of paramount importance in a *K*-selected species, the toque macaque in Sri Lanka. Dittus found, in a three-and-a-half-year study, during which there was no significant population growth, that agonistic behaviour was the major factor in population regulation. Females usually remain in their natal groups, while males emigrate to another one on reaching maturity. The sex ratio at birth is equal but that of individuals over five years old is biased towards females (1.56 F:1 M). Of all individuals born, 85 of females and 90% of males died before adulthood. Dittus concluded that predation was negligible and that success in aggressive competition for food was the major factor which determined survival. Subordinates were supplanted from food in 36% of all threat interactions and survival was closely related to status. Males of any age group were dominant to females, so that the most vulnerable groups were young juvenile and infant females. There was, however, a high mortality in sub-adult males which were driven by the adult males to the periphery of their natal group and subsequently suffered the hazards of emigration to another group. Dittus' data show that intraspecific aggression effectively results, under stable population conditions, in a pre-breeding mortality rate of between 85%–90% of all individuals born (see Table 4.3).

From these examples it is apparent that status can have an important

Table 4.3 Percentage mortality per annum for different age, sex, classes for the toque macaque (*Macaca sinica*). (After Dittus, 1979.)

Stage	Years	Percentage mortality per annum M	F
Infant	0–1	39.50	52.60
Juvenile (1)	1–2	7.9	15.8
Juvenile (2), (3)	2–5	7.4	5.4
Subadult male	5–7	9.95	–
Adult male	7–30	0.45	–
Adult female	5–30	–	0.61

effect on reproductive success and, as already mentioned in Chapter 3, a mother's rank can even affect the sex ratio of her offspring.

4.1.6 Infanticide

There are, in most social mammals, strong inhibitions against the killing of infants which are clearly the most vulnerable members of society. In some species, however, infanticide has been commonly observed, the best-documented cases being those of langurs (see Hrdy, 1977; Chapman and Hausfater, 1979; Hausfater and Vogel, 1982) and lions (see Bertram, 1975b). Infanticide generally occurs after a harem has been taken over by a new male.

The male increases his fitness by eliminating young which he has not fathered, thus reducing competition for his own offspring and bringing their mothers into oestrus earlier than would otherwise have been the case. In both common langurs and lions males only hold a harem for a brief period of up to two to three years, so that there must be considerable selection pressure favouring males which father infants very soon after taking over the harem. The theoretical advantages of infanticide in langurs have been discussed by Chapman and Hausfater (1979) who pointed out the importance of the relationship between mean length of tenure of a harem and the evolution of infanticide. They compared a theoretical model with the values obtained from field studies and found good agreement.

Infanticide is by no means universal in species with harems and, in fact, appears to be limited to a few species with a relatively short harem tenure. Females might be expected to oppose it concertedly, or to oppose group takeover by an infanticidal male. To take the female langur as an example, the loss of her young reduces her overall reproductive effort considerably, for she produces only seven or eight offspring in a lifetime and, through infanticide, loses a 6–15 month period of reproductive output if her 1–12-month-old infant is killed. In both lions and langurs, however, males are considerably larger than females so that individual female opposition is unlikely to be effective. Packer and Pusey (1983), however, saw a group of three lactating female lions successfully defending their cubs against a group of alien males, although all three females were wounded. Lionesses also show an indirect strategy for reducing infanticide immediately after the pride males have been driven out by rivals; females show increased sexual activity but low fertility for the next few months. This results in competition for the pride by male coalitions and takeover by the largest coalition. This, in turn, ensures a long period of tenure and hence a reduction in the frequency of post-takeover infanticide (see Packer and Pusey, 1983). Hrdy (1977) argued that females may favour aggressive males in a harem takeover, and that a more aggressive male is more likely to succeed in infanticide but is also likely to be a more effective protector than a more amicable one. Until more is known of the relation between infanticide and aggressiveness in males, this view can only be regarded as speculation.

A further factor which may be relevant is the proportion of females in a harem who are in oestrus and make takeover attractive to a male. Females may actively solicit an outside male, especially if they are daughters of the current harem-owner who are actively attempting to avoid mating with their father. Thus it may be that the takeover is influenced by a majority of females who are not vulnerable to infanticide and therefore have less to lose and probably much to gain from takeover by another male. For these females an infanticidal male may increase their fitness in two ways, firstly by removing infants who would compete with their own offspring and secondly, indirectly, through their production of infanticidal sons.

4.2 Social play

Of all the forms of social behaviour which have been observed in mammals, play is the most enigmatic. The majority of social play takes the form of playful fighting, but this is unlike true agonistic behaviour because it is non-competitive and no winner or loser emerges. Play fighting is amicable and individuals actively seek opportunities to carry it out, so that it is in marked contrast to true agonistic behaviour. I shall first attempt some definition of social play, then describe the main forms which it takes and, finally, discuss its possible function. The logic for discussing it in this chapter is that it is amicable behaviour closely resembling aggression. Solitary play will not be considered because it is outside the terms of reference of this book.

4.2.1 A definition of play

Play is characteristic of young mammals and, while difficult to define it precisely, there is good agreement between observers as to what can be regarded as social play. Smith (1982) has defined play as 'behaviour with no obvious cause or function conferring no obvious benefits on the organism'. Social play simulates fighting, chasing, fleeing and, in some species, predation. In playfights attacker and defender exchange roles; the individual which takes to flight soon itself becomes the chaser while, in predatory play, the victim of stalking and pouncing is unharmed. Playful interactions rarely include behaviours which can inflict injury or are symptomatic of fear or pain, so that they are incomplete in the sense that they fail to achieve the goal of similar but serious behaviour; thus play is essentially make-believe (Poole, 1966).

There are a number of facts which show that play is not merely a developmental stage of the equivalent serious action. The adults of some species play; coyote pups fight and establish a rank order before they develop playfighting, while common marmoset twins show uninhibited fighting at 5–6 months of age but, after a few days, return to their previous playful relationship (Stevenson and Poole, 1976, 1982).

Playfighting and serious fighting are quite different in mood, one being relaxed and gentle, the other tense and uninhibited; it is clearly implicit that the players should know from the outset that the interaction is not serious. Certain behaviour patterns characterize play and are never seen in real fighting. These are exaggerated or jerky movements of playful locomotion termed 'locomotor rotatory movements' by Wilson and Kleiman (1974) and, in primates and carnivores, the relaxed open mouth or 'playface'. These signals were constantly repeated and occupied approximately half of the time in the play of polecats (Poole, 1978). Bekoff (1977) found that play sequences in canids were preceded by specific behavioural signals. Bateson (1955) coined the term 'metacommunication' for signals of this type, which inform the reactor of the nature of the subsequent interactions.

Many authors have commented that play is pleasurable to the participants and Humphreys and Einon (1981) found that the opportunity to participate in social play acts as a positive reinforcer, i.e. is rewarding, in rats (*Rattus norvegicus*). If play is to be pleasurable, it is essential that neither player gets hurt and it has been found, where there is an obvious inequality in playmates, that the larger and stronger individual plays less roughly than he would do with an equal combatant. This self-handicapping principle has been observed in polecats, meerkats, lion cubs, dogs, and olive baboons (Owens, 1975), hamadryas baboons and chimpanzees. If play is too rough for one of the combatants it may squeal, cry or squeak, until it is released by its opponent and the interaction then reverts to a more inhibited level.

4.2.2 Forms taken by social play

Playful behaviour patterns described by various authors for a range of terrestrial mammals are listed in Table 4.4. Patterns 1–14 resemble adult fighting and pattern 15 ('mount') occurs in both sexual and aggressive

Table 4.4 Distribution of playful behaviour patterns among terrestrial mammals whose play has been the subject of detailed study—see text.
(Ro = Rodents, Ar = Artiodactyla, Pe = Perissodactyla, Ca = Carnivora, Pr = Primates).

Orders		Ro		Ar		Pe	Ca				Pr	
Behaviour patterns *Playfighting*		*Rattus*	*Spermophilus*	*Odocoileus*	*Capra*	*Equus*	*Mustela*	*Canis*	*Ursus*	*Felis*	*Callithrix*	*Macaca mulatta*
1. Aim bite	*	+	+			+	+	+	+	+	+	+
2. Bite (inhibited)	*	+	+			+	+	+	+	+	+	+
3. Nip, nibble		+	+			+	+		+		+	
4. Butt				+	+			+	+			
5. Cuff; paw, hand		+	+			+	+	+	+	+	+	+
6. Box, spar, grapple		+	+			+			+		+	+
7. Kick		+	+	+			+	?	+		+	+
8. Roll over		+	+				+	+	+	+	+	+
9. Wrestle		+	+				+	+	+	+	+	+
10. Lunge							+	+	+			
11. Arch back		+	+				+			+		
12. Push		+	+	+	+			+			+	+
13. Rear up		+	+		+			+	+	+	+	+
14. Stand over		+	?				+	+	+	+		+
15. Mount			+	+	+	+	+		+		+	+
Locomotor play												
16. Chase, follow	*	+	+	+	+	+	+	+	+	+	+	+
17. Flee		+	+	+	+	+	+	+	+	+	+	+
18. Jump away				+	+			+			+	+
19. Pounce, jump on	*	+	+				+	+		+	+	+
20. Stalk	*						+	+		+	+	
Play signals												
21. Open mouth			?				+	+	+	+	+	+
22. Mouthing		+	+				+	+			+	+
23. Head toss, neck twist				+	+		+	+			+	
24. Dancing approach				?	?	?	+	+	+		+	+
25. Play bow								+				+
No of them in species repertoire		16	16	8	8	8	19	20	17	13	20	19

contexts in many species. Locomotory play (16–20) is associated with attempts to make physical contact or to induce following. In polecats (Poole, 1978) and dogs (Bekoff, 1974) the fleer often looks back to check that he is being followed and may simultaneously show the playface. Five behaviour patterns, 'aim bite', 'bite', 'chase', 'pounce', and 'stalk', also resemble those of predation; it is of interest to appreciate that, while 'pounce' occurs in mammals such as rodents and marmosets which catch some live prey, usually insects, 'stalk' appears to be confined to carnivores which use this technique as adults to catch vertebrate prey. Behaviour patterns 21–25 are largely play initiation movements which are peculiar to playful interactions (see Bekoff, 1974).

It can be seen from this table that ungulates have rather simple play while carnivores and primates have a much wider repertoire; the playful behaviour patterns exhibited by a species reflect the way of life of the adult. Primate play is more complex than the table suggests because it includes a range of patterns, such as tickling, which are unique to play in these species and have no obvious equivalent in other species; these are therefore omitted. If, however, serious equivalent behaviour only is considered, it is apparent that for all species the majority of social play patterns simulate fighting (see Aldis, 1975; Symons, 1978). Predatory play occurs in predators, but frequently fighting and predatory patterns are not dissimilar in adults. Sexual play is uncommon and has been reported from very few species (e.g. including pelvic thrusting in black bear by Henry and Herrero (1974)), where it appears to occupy a very minor role.

Some behaviour patterns appear to be used to solicit play and Bekoff (1974) lists seven for Canidae, namely, bow, exaggerated approach, approach/withdraw, general movements, face pawing, leap-leap and barking. Bekoff assessed the efficiency of the different patterns in eliciting play and found that, for beagles, any of the actions were successful 56% of the time, but in wolves and coyotes general movements (head-tossing, eye-rolling, rapid extension and flexion of the forelimbs) and bowing (crouching with forelegs flexed and hindlegs extended) were most successful. In brown rats, charging, pouncing, inhibited biting and playful grooming are common initiating behaviours (Poole and Fish, 1975) and individual play often leads into social play. If the prospective playmate is unresponsive, its adversary may tease it until it is drawn into play. Teasing in the Columbian ground squirrel (*Spermophilus columbianus*) consists of striking with the forepaws, biting, pushing aside with the hindquarters, pulling the tail with the teeth, jumping or pouncing on the opponent (see Steiner, 1971). Polecats tease by mounting and biting the opponent's neck, dancing up to

Figure 4.5 Social play in Columbian ground squirrels (*Spermophilus columbianus*): (*a*), (*b*) rearing, (*c*), (*d*) pouncing, (*e*) wrestling, (*f*) open mouth with pouncing, (*g*) wrestling. (Redrawn from Steiner, 1971.)

1

13

3

17

7

20

10

a

23

1-17 defence

20-23 offence

Figure 4.6 Polecats playfighting. Drawings from cine film with frame numbers indicated. Each frame occupies 1/24 second. (*a*) The open mouth playface in a defensive context (1–17) and an offensive one (20–23); (*b*) (over) mutual open mouth in play.

it, jumping on or chasing it while nipping the pelvic region (Poole, 1966). Chimpanzees tease by leaping on to, biting, pulling the hair, dangling above or kicking unresponsive opponents (Goodall, 1968*a*).

Ongoing play generally consists of alternating bouts of chasing and fighting; in many species upright and horizontal wrestling are common. A number of forms of playfighting are illustrated in line diagrams derived from cine films (see Figures 4.5–4.7). During playfighting the combatants adopt the typical strategies of adult aggression, e.g. biting in carnivores,

Figure 4.7 Social play in meercats (*Suricata suricatta*): (*a*) grapple, (*b*) grapple and cheek bite, (*c*) wrestle, (*d*) clasp. Notice the open-mouth playface. (After Wemmer and Fleming, 1974.)

butting in sheep and goats and boxing and wrestling in red kangaroos.

There have been a few direct comparisons between playfighting and serious aggression. Henry and Herrero (1974) found that the frequency with which agonistic behaviour patterns were repeated in American black bears was greater in play than in serious fighting. In polecats the mean durations of behavioural elements were similar in play and serious fighting, but in serious fighting the duration of biting was significantly longer (fighting, median 4 seconds, range 0.17–308.17, playfighting, median 2.25 seconds, range 0.33–17.21) (Poole, 1978). The elements of playful behaviour have been shown to be sequentially patterned in canids (Bekoff and Byers, 1981), brown rats (Poole and Fish, 1975, 1976) and hamadryas baboons (Leresche, 1976) although sequences are generally more labile than in serious aggression. The probable reason for this is that spontaneous role reversal is common in play, so that sequences switching from offensive to defensive tactics might be expected to occur more frequently. The sequential organization of play in rats is shown in Figure 4.8.

Locomotory social play is usually very active, and its complexity relates to the way of life of the species. Thus the arboreal common marmoset plays both on the ground and in trees (Stevenson and Poole, 1982) while the

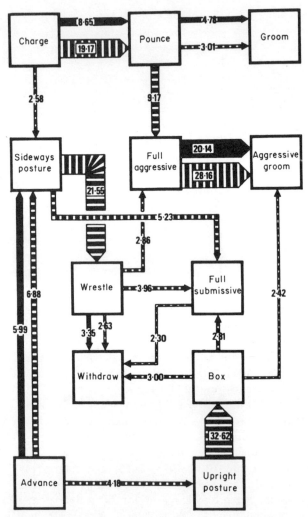

Figure 4.8 Flow diagram to show that social play in laboratory rats is sequentially organized. The figures are values of the normal deviate derived from the binomial test, all are significant at the $p = 0.05$ level. Dotted lines indicate individuals with unresponsive partners (see Poole and Fish, 1976)

amphibious American mink (*Mustela vison*) plays both on land and under water (Poole, 1978) and ibex (*Capra ibex*) play on rocky outcrops (Byers, 1977).

A number of mammals have been observed to play socially in water. Tigers, leopard cats (*Felis bengalensis*) and fishing cats (*F. viverrinus*) have all been observed playfighting in water, as have both hippopotamus and pygmy hippopotamus (*Choeropsis liberiensis*). Some amphibious mammals (mink, otters and polar bears) indulge in subaquatic social play but unfortunately there are few quantitative data for these species. The mink, whose playful behaviour on land closely resembles that of the allied polecat, differs in carrying out some of its social play both under water and on the surface. Aquatic play in this species include chasing, fleeing, neck bite, chase tail, roll and wrestle. Figure 4.9, taken from a cine film, shows role reversal between 'chase' and 'flee'.

Marine mammals which breed on land and fight for possession of females, such as Northern elephant seals, Steller sea lions (*Eumetopias jubata*) and grey seals, all show terrestrial playfighting (see Gentry, 1974) and chasing. Adult females and non-breeding adult and subadult males playfight in shallow rock pools and carry out rapid, active social locomotory play both under and on the surface of the water. Wilson (1974) found that both common and grey seals played under water, the play taking the form of chasing, fleeing, rolling, splashing and hauling out. The grey seal laid its head over its opponent's back as a play invitation. Play was accompanied by jerky locomotor rotatory movements. *P. vitulina* did not playfight on land. In some species, strong sexual differences, particularly in agonistic behaviour, may be reflected in their play. Rasa (1971) found this to be the case in elephant seals, while Gentry (1974) showed that male Steller sea lions displayed a larger number of different elements of social play and indulged in longer bouts than females; biting was also commoner in male play. Male rats (*Rattus norvegicus*) are more playful than females (Poole and Fish, 1976) and this is also true of olive and hamadryas baboons (Owens, 1975; Lereshe, 1976). Symons (1978) found that male rhesus monkeys played more roughly than females.

Fagen (1981) reviews the occurrence of play in the different mammalian orders. It was described by Bennett (1835) in the young monotreme, (*Ornithorhynchus anatinus*) which showed playfighting – biting, rolling, wrestling and gambolling – both on land and in shallow water. No-one has since reported play in this species, and obviously a modern account is desirable. Social play has been described in marsupials, and appears to be more complex in carnivorous marsupials than in pure herbivores, as is the

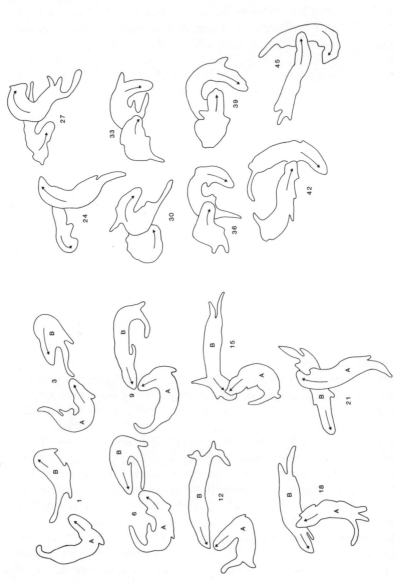

Figure 4.9 Underwater play in the American mink (*Mustela vison*) taken from a cine film shot at 24 frames per second, showing role reversal. Frames 1–21 A chases B, 24–45B chases A.

case in eutherians. Kangaroos show sparring only with their mothers and not with peers, while the tiger quoll (*Dasyurus maculatus*) a weasel-like stalking predator, shows open-mouth playface, chasing, wrestling, biting, stalking and head-shaking, with littermates.

Social play has been recorded from most orders of placentals with the exception of Lagomorpha (see Fagen, 1981). Some well-studied species such as the laboratory mouse also appear to show no social play (Poole and Fish, 1975).

Social play is not confined to the young; in wolves and hunting dogs play may precede a hunting excursion; playfighting has also been recorded between adult Steller sea lions of the same sex (Farentinos, 1971). Rolling over and playful, inhibited biting are common responses by female polecats to the sexual advances of a male when the female is not in oestrus (Poole, 1967).

The development of social play has been studied by several authors. Barrett and Bateson (1978) found, in domestic kittens, that wrestle and stalk increase in frequency with age while arch, biting and pawing decrease. In polecats the amount of chasing play increases as the young grow older (Poole, 1966). The temporal patterning of play changes with age in laboratory rats; younger pups (3–5 weeks old) tend to withdraw at an earlier stage than those over five weeks old (Poole and Fish, 1976). The character of play in polecats appears to relate to the state of physical development rather than to absolute age, for young which had been reared in small litters of one and two individuals were larger and better co-ordinated and showed more locomotory play than members of large litters of 6–8.

Partner preferences have been identified in some species. Common marmosets, for example, show a preference for their twin (Stevenson and Poole, 1982) as opposed to other sibs, while Owens (1975) found that olive baboons show a definite preference for individuals close to their own age; they also played significantly more with older siblings than with non-siblings of the same age. Laboratory rats spent more time playing with playful individuals but showed no preference for them in selecting a partner (Poole and Fish, 1976). Rats also showed marked individual differences in social play. Three out of 39 showed significantly more defensive play than offensive, while in two other cases the situation was reversed. The remaining 34 did not differ from a one-to-one expectancy.

Social play occurs in a relaxed environmental setting, where no demands are being made on the animal, so that the frequency of social play in the wild may be low if the animals are aware of the observer's presence. Fagan

(1981) estimated, from field studies in carnivores and primates, that play (most of which is social play) occurs naturally for about 3% of the time. Ungulates, however, play considerably less often. Baldwin and Baldwin (1974) found that the frequency of social play in squirrel monkeys differed in different habitats. In Barqueta, Panama, 261 hours of observation did not include any social play. Social groups were small (approximately 20 individuals), food was scattered and the monkeys spent most of their time foraging. In the Amazonian forest, where food was more plentiful and troop sizes larger (up to 300 individuals), social play was estimated to occupy one to two hours per individual per day. In an experimental study, Baldwin and Baldwin (1976) confirmed the influence of food-searching time in reducing the frequency of social play.

It can be concluded from the evidence presented, that play is an active time-consuming behaviour which may expose the player to risk of injury or attack by a predator; in a situation of food scarcity, it is effectively eliminated. It is clear that, while an individual can survive without social play, in order to justify the risks and costs incurred, this behaviour must, in some way increase its overall fitness; it is also apparent that the goal of play must be different from that of equivalent non-playful behaviour.

4.2.3 The function of social play

Over thirty hypotheses have been put forward to explain the function of social play, but these can be reduced to four main theories. The four hypotheses are not mutually exclusive but the evidence for each will be considered in turn.

Physical training and co-ordination. Byers (1977) found that Siberian ibex kids in a zoo showed significantly more locomotor play on sloped as opposed to flat areas, whereas social play occurred on both. The risk of injury was greater in locomotor play in sloped areas, but the opportunity for practising co-ordination was clearly better. It is not clear, however, why most birds and other vertebrates do not play, nor is there any evidence available to suggest that social play may have this function.

Development of competitive skills. Symons (1978) put forward the view that playfighting is practice fighting which prepares the individual for contests of a more serious nature. This view is supported by the sexual differences in play which have been identified in rats, sea lions and macaques. He suggests that rhesus monkeys learn to bite without being bitten and that they choose partners of equal development in order to ensure an even contest. On this assumption, the main function of social play which consists largely of playfighting must be to prepare for adult fighting. What is not so easily explained, however, is why the interactions should be playful, because mammals are capable of non-injurious fighting which resembles serious fighting in mood (termed 'companion fighting') (Poole, 1973). My own observations have identified such behaviour in polecats and mice (*Mus musculus*). It may be that the playful character of most non-competitive fighting is what makes it pleasurable (positively reinforcing) to the players. The movements of playfighting may also be of value in practising predation, as also are those of chasing play; the chased player makes evasive actions which may simulate both those of a fleeing opponent and prey.

The main argument against this hypothesis for the function of social play is that play movements are generally believed to be clumsy and ill co-ordinated; this is however a subjective impression for which no hard data are available.

Development of cognitive skills. Einon *et al.* (1978) found that rats (*Rattus norvegicus*) reared in social isolation were slow to reverse previously learned discriminations. Some of the isolates were exposed to non-playing chlorpromazine-dosed conspecifics, while others were placed with normal partners for one hour a day. It was found that the opportunity to play restored the speed of learning reversal to normal levels. As the experiment controls for other forms of social behaviour (chlorpromazine only reduced play), the authors concluded that social play may have a role in cognitive development.

More data are needed but the reason for the apparent relationship is not obvious.

Socialization. Some authors, particularly primatologists such as Poirier and Smith (1974) and Suomi and Harlow (1972), but also Bekoff (1978*a*) from his study of Canidae, have expressed the view that play is an important factor in socialization. It has been suggested that individuals learn their role in society, develop their social relations and communication system and form lasting social bonds through play. Play has also been said to provide information about the rank and strength of other group members, and to enable an individual to develop its social skills. There is, however, a good deal of evidence which is in direct conflict with this view. Social bonds may be forged by allogrooming, which appears to be much more useful and less energy-consuming than play. Information about status is usually provided by threat or submissive behaviour and playfighting is unlikely, because of the self-handicapping principle, to provide accurate information about an opponent's real strength. So far as the communication system is concerned, play has its own unique signals so that the player can only learn about play signals during playful interactions, and these are markedly lacking in subtlety.

Harlow and Harlow's (1966) maternal deprivation experiments are commonly regarded as evidence for the socialization hypothesis, but these authors did not control for other forms of social interaction such as allogrooming, agonistic or sexual behaviour, all of which were also eliminated.

In addition to the logical arguments against the socialization hypothesis, there are several instances of evidence which run totally counter to it which will be briefly discussed here. If the socialization theory were correct, there ought to be a correlation between the occurrence of play and the sociability of the species. This is clearly not so. Solitary species such as American black bears (*Ursus americanus*) (Henry and Herrero, 1974; Burghardt and Burghardt, 1972), polecats and mink (Poole 1966, 1978a), and the tiger quoll, a carnivorous marsupial, are all solitary species with complex social play, while the social house mouse (*Mus musculus*) does not play. Orang utans (*Pongo pygmacus*) are relatively solitary apes, but juveniles play socially together when they meet (Rijksen, 1978) and play vigorously in captivity (Maple *et al.*, 1978; Maple, 1980). In those mammals where sexual differences occur in play, it is generally the less sociable males which are more playful. In marsupials, social play is more complex in the solitary quoll than in the social macropodids.

Some mammals have been observed in the wild to play with members of another species; for example, baboons (*Papio ursinus*) have been observed to play with chimpanzees, jackals and bushbuck (*Tragelaphus scriptus*) and bat-eared foxes (*Otocyon megalotis*) with Thomson's gazelles. The existence of interspecific play, needless to say, is incompatible with the socialization theory.

While no firm conclusions can be drawn regarding the functional significance of social play, the current consensus of opinion favours the view that it is concerned with the practice of locomotor patterns. It seems doubtful, on current evidence, whether this can be extended to include the learning of social relationships.

4.3 Affectional behaviour

In many species of mammal which live in social groups such as wolves, dolphins, monkeys, apes and prairie dogs, adult individuals may develop strong personal attachments to other adults in the group. Such an attachment is referred to as a bond or social bond, and is objectively identifiable because the individuals concerned display certain characteristic behaviours. They spend more time in close contact than would normally be expected. They often groom one another, and various species demonstrate

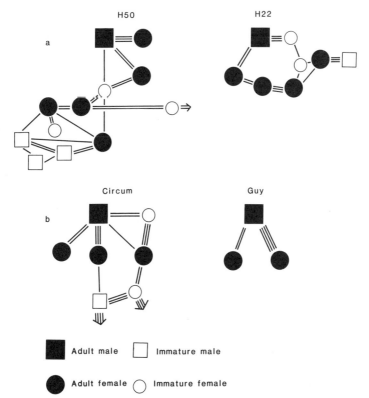

Figure 4.10 Sociograms for one male groups in (*a*) gelada baboons and (*b*) hamadryas baboons. Connecting lines indicate percentage of samples with social interactions: single line (*a*) 5–10% (*b*) 4–10%, double line 11–20%, triple line 21–30%, quadruple line 31–40%. Arrows indicate social interactions with non-group members. Notice the numerous female-female interactions in *T. gelada*, whereas *P. hamadryas* females mostly interact with their male group leader. (Modified after (*a*) Dunbar and Dunbar 1975, (*b*) Kummer, 1968). Group identifications are those of the original authors.

kissing, embracing, body rubbing, nuzzling and licking or touching the genitalia. They may also form an alliance against a third party in either an offensive or defensive context and may share food or care for each others' infants (see Chapter 3). Frequently these behavioural interactions can be expressed as sociograms which enable the observer to assess the extent of social bonding between any two individuals (see Figure 4.10).

A number of behavioural signals have evolved which are also indicative of a friendly relation between two individuals. Some higher primates (such as chimpanzees) show a friendly grin; tonguing or lipsmacking are also common patterns in primates and the open-mouth playface may be used to indicate friendliness. Both lions and domestic cats rub against one another, while male and female white-handed gibbons sing duets. In many cases the relationship is an unequal one, in the sense that one of the individuals is higher-ranking than the other, so that affectional behaviour may include an element of submissiveness on the part of the subordinate – rolling on to the back in wolves, for example.

Affectional behaviour may be used to establish social contact after an agonistic encounter in chimpanzees, where former combatants may subsequently come into non-violent bodily contact such as kissing, embracing, holding out the hand, touching and submissive vocalizing. De Waal and Roosmalen (1979) termed this behaviour between former opponents 'reconciliation'. They also observed that a third individual might come up to the victim of aggression and embrace it; this they termed 'consolation'. Although such terms may sound anthropomorphic, their use was established only after careful quantitative investigation. While affectional bonds may exist between peers in play groups, there is no doubt that the most significant social bonds, in terms of the evolution of mammalian societies, are those between adults.

In even the most primitive mammals, two types of social contact have a brief existence. There is the sexual attraction between male and oestrous female and the mother/infant bond. While these relationships do not persist beyond the period during which they are of physiological importance, they may form the basis for more lasting social ties. In mammals which show higher social organization, the development of particular non-sexual social bonds appear to determine the structural organization of the society in which they occur. It is important to appreciate that, while sexual strategy may be a factor which determines the structure of society, sexual attractiveness associated with oestrous condition is unlikely to function as a mechanism of social cohesion because of its relative inconstancy of occurrence.

Table 4.5   Long-lasting non-sexual affectional bonds in mammalian societies

Type	Coefficient of relationship (r)	Benefit	Examples
Parent/offspring	1/2	Kin selection	Wolf, beaver
Sib/sib	1/4–1/2	,, ,,	Wolf, lion
Female/female	1/8–1/2	,, ,,	Lion, *Loxodonta, Macaca, Spermophilus*
Male/male	1/8–1/2	,, ,,	Lion, chimpanzee, Gorilla, *Lycaon*
Male/female	0–1/8 max.	Exclusive mating	Gibbon, beaver, hamadryas baboon, vicuña, *Equus grevyi*

The five types of affectional bond are listed in Table 4.5, and it is apparent that in four out of the five cases the collaborative and altruistic relationships can be attributed to kin selection because of the genetic relationships of the individuals concerned. In the fifth case, the male/female bond, the relationship is based on exclusive sexual access and mating rights. It seems likely that this bond evolved initially from extended consortship or guarding (see Nagel, 1971) which assured the male of paternity and therefore made it to his advantage to remain to guard his mate. Paternal behaviour has evolved in some monogamous species, but it must be regarded as secondary to the male/female bond.

Little is known of the way in which the heterosexual bond is reinforced in mammals, partly because of its relative rarity. Once the bond is formed it is stable and most monogamous mammals pair for life (e.g. gibbons). In the few species examined, it appears that the male is primarily responsible for the maintenance of the heterosexual bond. Male hamadryas baboons, for example, punish harem females who stray by biting their necks, as a result of which errant females return to the proximity of the male. Male common marmosets follow the female and show more affectional behaviour than their mate, although means for the two sexes are correlated (see Poole, 1978b). Once a pair relationship is established, even in a harem-forming species, it is relatively stable. Assuming that two males were relatively close in status, Kummer et al. (1974) found that in an experimental situation, in captivity, the first of two males to pair with a female had an undisputed right to her, even though the second male was present in the cage.

There is no doubt that non-sexual bonds are the fundamental cohesive force which determines the form taken by society in mammals and this will be considered in more detail in the next chapter. More than one type of bond may exist within the same society and differences in their relative strengths can produce different forms of society.

4.4 Summary

Agonistic behaviour

1. Most mammals use teeth and claws, but some species have evolved special weapons such as horns and antlers for intraspecific fighting.

2. The weaker opponent usually retaliates if attacked; it is therefore advantageous to both combatants for conflict to take place without resort to physical assault.

3. Mammals may advertise their strength and future behaviour by threat displays when it is to the advantage of both contestants.

4. Three main signals are of importance in fighting. They convey the information (1) 'I am about to attack' (aggressive threat) which allows the opponent to retreat; (2) 'I shall only retaliate if attacked' (defensive threat) which tells the aggressor that his opponent is not challenging but will defend himself or his resource; (3) finally the opponent may submit which indicates 'I shall not attack or defend myself', which gives the aggressor the victory without combat.

5. The existence is known of signals intermediate between the three described. What is not known, however, is whether or not they arise from a state of motivational conflict and what message the opponent reads from them. There are good theoretical reasons for believing that the signaller will not convey his intentions if this is to his disadvantage.

6. Sex, isolation, familiarity, possession of a resource, previous experience and genetic factors have all been shown to influence mammalian aggression.

7. Dominance hierarchies arise either from direct combat, age-related status or a combination of the two. Dominance confers greater reproductive success in ungulates, carnivores and rabbits, while the situation is more variable among rodents and primates.

8. Intraspecific aggression may play a significant role in limiting group numbers even in K-selected species.

9. Where infanticide occurs it is usually practised by a dominant male on the offspring of females over whom he has just acquired exclusive sexual access.

Social play

1. Social play is a complex interaction which has no obvious goal.

2. Special signals have evolved which are indicative of the playful nature of the interaction, particularly locomotor rotatory movements and, in some species, the open-mouth play face.

3. Most social play simulates adult aggressive and defensive behaviour.

4. The complexity of social play relates to the adult ecology; predators show predatory play, arboreal species play in trees while aquatic mammals play in and under water.

5. Play cannot be regarded as a developmental stage of equivalent adult behaviour.

6. In species where males are markedly more aggressive than females, this difference is also reflected in the frequency and vigour of playfighting.

7. Play partners of a similar strength or developmental stage are preferred.

8. Four major views have been put forward to explain the function of social play: (a) that it is a form of physical training; (b) that it develops competitive skills in fighting and predation; (c) that it promotes the development of cognitive skills; and (d) that it is an important factor in the development of socialization. These theories are not incompatible but there is considerable evidence against the socialization hypothesis.

Affectional behaviour

1 Affectional behaviour between individuals can be objectively described in terms of proximity, allogrooming, mutual help and special gestures such as kissing or nuzzling.

2. Five types of affectional bond have evolved in mammals; these are not dictated by physiological necessity and are powerful determinants of the structure of mammalian society. The bonds in question are parent/offspring (persistent), sib/sib, female/female, male/male, male/female.

3. In social species, affectional bonds may be of a personal nature so that an individual may form a strong personal tie with another member of a social group.

CHAPTER FIVE

SOCIOECOLOGY

5.1 Social determinants

Most of the factors which determine the patterns of mammalian social organization have already been identified and discussed in Chapters 3 and 4, and are listed in Table 5.1

The earliest known fossil mammals from the Jurassic and Cretaceous periods provide clues as to the primitive way of life of the class. They were small and their dentition indicates that they preyed on insects or small vertebrates, like the modern insectivores and the Dasyuroid marsupials of Australia. If similar modern species are taken as typical, then for primitive mammals the nine major factors listed in Table 5.1 can be deduced to have been as follows: (1) promiscuous mating with some male competition for females; (2) no permanent grouping, just mother and immature offspring briefly foraging together; (3) intolerance of same-sex conspecifics, so spaced out and solitary; (4) no non-sexual affectional bonds between adults, with the mother-infant relationship terminated soon after weaning, (5) a simple communication system—no co-operation, chemical signals providing information on identity, sex, reproductive condition and status, vocal signals in aggression and courtship, open-mouth threat; (g) emigration from natal area mainly by males; (7) group mobility restricted to a brief period when young forage with their mother; (8) litters of 1–3 young annually or biannually, the average lifespan of a breeding individual being 5–10 years. From this simple way of life the evolution of all other forms of mammalian social organizations can be visualized. The ninth factor, ecology, will be considered in more detail later, but it is apparent that small generalized insectivore/carnivores could find an ecological niche in a variety of environments, provided that there were ample opportunities for concealment.

By far the majority of mammals are solitary, meeting members of their own species only rarely, but some are sociable, living either in aggregates or integrated social groups. An aggregate can be defined as a

Table 5.1 Determinants of mammalian social organization

(1) Mating strategy	(a)	Opportunistic, monogamous polygamous
	(b)	Degree of male or female choice
(2) Gregariousness	(a)	Solitary
	(b)	Aggregated for feeding, protection mating or nesting
	(c)	Group permanence and identity
	(d)	Personal relationships within the group
(3) Intolerance	(a)	To members of same or opposite sex
	(b)	Degree of competitiveness (e.g. defence of an exclusive area or presence of a rank order)
(4) Affectional bonds	(a)	Duration of mother-offspring bond
	(b)	Non-sexual bonds between members of the same or opposite sex and their relative strength
(5) Complexity of communication	(a)	Variety and nature of information exchanged, especially in cooperative behaviour
	(b)	Individual recognition and personal relations
(6) Inbreeding avoidance	(a)	Does one sex disperse or both?
	(b)	Differential sexual dispersal influences kinship relations in a social group
(7) Group mobility	(a)	Mobility of young
	(b)	Need for refuge (den or burrow), permanent or temporary
(8) Fecundity and longevity	(a)	Number of young produced per female per unit time
	(b)	Lifespan—long-lived mammals have the greatest potential for complex social organization
(9) Ecological factors	(a)	Food
	(b)	Space
	(c)	Climate

group of individuals which live in close proximity but where adults show no strong affectional bonds with one another. Aggregates do not usually have a fixed composition but vary from time to time. The migratory herds of ungulates or whales, the breeding rookeries of many pinnipeds, and roosting flocks of bats are all examples of mammalian aggregations. In some cases a number of adults of a species seek refuge in a confined area, but each individual forages independently; these aggregates are termed colonies and are typical of most of the more sociable burrowing rodents. Colonies may be simple aggregates or may have a more complex social structure. The most highly developed form of sociability in mammals is what Eisenberg (1966) termed the integrated social group (or society) which contains more than one breeding adult and where individuals show distinct personal relationships. An integrated social group was defined by Eisenberg as showing a complex system of communication, a division of labour based on specialization, cohesion, permanence of individual composition and a tendency of the group to be closed to extra-group

Table 5.2 A classification of mammalian social organization on the basis of sociability, sexual strategy and territoriality (for explanation see text).

Social Types	Examples
1. Solitary	
(a) Intersexual territoriality	*Blarina* (short-tailed shrew)
(b) Intrasexual territoriality	*Mustela* (weasel, stoat)
(c) Non-territorial	*Didelphys* (opossum)
2. Monogamous	
(a) Grade I	*Oreotragus* (klipspringer)
(b) Grade II	*Castor* (beaver)
(c) Grade III (Status-determined)	*Lycaon* (African hunting dog)
3. Harem-forming	
(a) Dispersed or colonial harem	*Galago* (bushbaby), *Procavia* (hyrax)
(b) Rookery	*Eumetopias* (Steller sealion)
(c) Temporary mobile harem	*Cervus* (red deer)
(d) Permanent mobile harem	
(i) Non-female bonded	*Gorilla*
(ii) Female bonded	*Presbytis* (langur monkey)
4. Territorial males, females more sociable	
(a) Male territory with absolute hierarchy	*Ceratotherium* (white rhinoceros)
(b) Male territory with nursery herd	*Litocranius* (gerenuk)
(c) Lek	*Hypsignathus* (hammer-headed bat)
5. Males spaced, females sociable	*Elephas* (elephant), *Sus* (pig)
6. Multimale/multifemale groups	
(a) Multimale/multifemale colony	*Oryctolagus* (rabbit)
(b) Multimale/multimale herd	*Macropus parryi* (whiptailed wallaby)
(c) Society	
(i) Female bonded	*Macaca* (macaque)
(ii) Non-female bonded	*Pan* (chimpanzee)
(d) Pride (some)	*Panthera leo* (lion)
(e) Multimale/multifemale group, nomadic breeding males	*Hyaena brunnea* (brown hyaena)
7. Eusocial	*Heterocephalus* (naked mole rate)
8. Ephemeral aggregate	*Giraffa* (giraffe)

conspecifics, while Wilson (1975) emphasized the co-operative nature of a society which extends beyond mere social proximity.

Mammalian social organization will be classified on the criteria listed in Table 5.1 and the different forms are listed in Table 5.2. A cautionary note must be sounded, however, for few biological classifications are completely watertight and the scheme must be regarded simply as a convenient way of considering the range of mammalian social organization. Intermediates can and do exist and some species may differ in their social organization under different environmental conditions.

5.2 Types of mammalian social organization

A classification of the forms taken by mammalian social organization is given in Table 5.2. The criteria which have been used to define the different classes will be described in the text

(1) *Both sexes solitary*

In these species individuals of both sexes are spaced out throughout their environment and mutually avoid one another. Mating is opportunistic, a female advertises her oestrous condition and any resident males in the vicinity are attracted and may compete to mate with her. Spacing may be achieved by the use of chemical markers (see Chapter 2) or, in some cases, by vocal display.

Some solitary mammals are territorial, i.e. they defend their home range against intruders, and in many instances successful breeding can occur only when an individual holds a territory. Individuals which fail to acquire a territory, or have not yet done so, are usually nomadic. The short-tailed shrew is a well-documented example of a solitary species in which individuals defend territories against intruders of either sex. Females are only tolerant of males when sexually receptive (see Platt, 1976). This social arrangement can be termed 1(*a*), *intersexual* or *exclusive* territoriality (see Chapter 6).

A situation which is also well known is that of 1 (*b*), *intrasexual* territoriality, where individuals of each sex defend their home range against intruders of the same but not the opposite sex. Usually males hold larger territories than females, so that a male's territory may include those of several females. This arrangement will increase the male's opportunity of forming sexual relationships with any females within his territory, because the territorial male will detect their oestrous condition and, by excluding other males, decrease the probability of their mating with other males. Females may also show a preference for a territorial, as opposed to a vagrant, male, so there may also be some element of female selection. Intrasexual territoriality is common in mustelids such as weasels, stoats, mink and otters (see Erlinge, 1968, 1974, 1977a; Gerell, 1970; King, 1975). The effect of male/male competition for territories which include more than one female is to produce a surplus of nomadic males which avoid male territories, unless challenging the owner, and search for vacant territories which offer an opportunity to breed.

Many solitary mammals do not defend their home range. They are, however, spaced out and may show a degree of hostility on meeting same sex conspecifics. In *solitary non-territorial* species (1c) males usually have larger home ranges than females, particularly in the breeding season. Females attract males by indicating that they are in oestrus, and several males may congregate and compete for a female. This arrangement is characteristic of many small rodents, for example the field mouse *Apodemus*, and members of the cat family. It is probably the commonest social system in primitive mammals, which do not have readily defendable resources within their home range, but, surprisingly, is also shown by one of the great apes, the orang utan (see Chapter 6).

(2) *Monogamy*

Monogamy occurs where one male and one female form an exclusive sexual relationship, but it is important, to distinguish at the outset between monogamy as a sexual strategy and monogamy as a social arrangement. Wickler and Seibt (1983) have pointed out that these two aspects are often confused, so that the concept of monogamy may be an ambiguous one.

In discussing monogamy in mammals the social relationship will be regarded as more important than the number of mates which an individual may have. For example, in populations of mammals which are typically polygynous, there will be males who have managed to monopolize only one female. Such males have adopted a monogamous mating strategy, but only because they lack the competitive ability or opportunity to acquire exclusive mating rights to more than one female. A monogamous social organization is typically one in which a breeding unit consists of one male and one female who share a unique social relationship from which third parties are excluded.

Kleiman (1977) divided monogamy into two forms; (a) facultative, where individuals are so spaced out that only a single member of the opposite sex is available for mating, and (b) obligate monogamy, where a female cannot rear her young successfully, without direct assistance from conspecifics. Fox (1975) divided monogamous canids into three types based on their group structure (see Chapter 6, p. 170). Both classifications have some merits so that a modified scheme based on both of them will be employed here (*a*) *Grade 1* monogamous mammals are those in which a male and female defend a common territory but offspring do not remain with their parent(s) after weaning. Adults may be paired permanently or only during a restricted breeding season. The amount of contact between them also varies from one species to another. Elephant shrews, for example, spend very little time in contact, although they share the same territory, defending it against same sex conspecifics. Common tree shrews have a similar social organization to elephant shrews, but a minority of males have territories large enough to include those of more than one female, so that they are sometimes polygynous. Another good example of a Grade 1 monogamous species, in which male and female keep in close contact, is the klipspringer (*Oreotragus oreotragus*) studied by Dunbar and Dunbar (1980). Both sexes defend the territory but, during the female's pregnancy and lactation, she spends more time feeding than the male, who generally spends more time being vigilant and thus allows his mate to feed in security. This division of labour enables the female to acquire the extra resources needed by the developing offspring.

(*b*) *Grade II* species are permanently paired but delay driving out their young, so that adults are accompanied by more than one generation of offspring. Many species show direct paternal care (see Chapter 3), and juveniles and subadults may assist in the caring for offspring. Colonial Grade II monogamy is found in the beaver (*Castor fiber*), where offspring remain in the family group until two years old, assisting the parents by cleaning the nest, collecting food for storage and caring for infants. Grade II monogamous mammals, which form mobile groups, include some members of the dog family (see later), the South American titi monkeys (*Callicebus moloch*) and the lesser apes (Hylobatidae). (*c*) *Grade III* species have multimale/multifemale groups where only a single male and female breed. Breeding is determined by an individual's position in a dominance hierarchy so that only the alpha male and female breed. Grade III monogamy can be regarded as status-determined monogamy; the social group is a multimale/multifemale one in which only the alpha pair breed. While non-breeding members of the group assist in the care of infants and co-operate in group hunting.

Status-determined monogamy, which corresponds to the social organization of Fox's (1975) type III canids, is found in wolves (*Canis lupus*) and hunting dogs (*Lycaon pictus*). In view of the fact that canids are generally monogamous it seems most likely that this form of organization is derived from Grade II monogamy. The pack, however, in *Lycaon*, is not simply a family, the alpha male is not necessarily the oldest male in the group, and dispersal is by emigration of the females out of their natal pack (see Malcolm and Marten, 1982). Dominance relationships within the pack, unlike those of typical monogamous species, change from time to time. The wolf pack more closely resembles a family group, although there are both male and female dominance hierarchies. In view of the close social ties between members of a wolf pack and their hostility to unfamiliar conspecifics, they appear to form inbreeding groups with negligible gene flow between packs (Woolpy and Eckstrand, 1979). Common marmosets also appear to show status-determined monogamy, as they live in multimale/multifemale groups with a dominant pair where only the alpha female breeds.

(3) *Polygyny*

A polygynous social organization is one in which a male has exclusive sexual access to several females. This arrangement depends upon females being sufficiently tolerant of one another to enable them to live in close enough proximity to allow a single male to monopolize them. If female/female hostility is high they become so spaced out that the male is forced to adopt a monogamous or promiscuous sexual strategy.

There are basically two types of polygyny. The first occurs where a male's attractiveness to individual females enables him to assemble, or take over from another male, a group of females, each of whom is socially bonded to the male but not to other females of the harem. The second type of polygyny occurs where the females in the harem are strongly bonded to each another and the female group exists as a persistent social structure in its own right. Females are usually closely related and from time to time the group is monopolized by different males, each of whom supplants his predecessor. The second type of polygyny is associated with male dispersal from the natal group.

The majority of gregarious mammals are polygynous for reasons already explained in Chapter 3. This class contains a large number of different forms of social organization which can be divided into four main types, harems, territorial males, spaced males and multimale/multifemale groups.

Harems occur where one male, sometimes accompanied by an associated satellite male, has exclusive mating rights to a group of females. Four main types of harem have been described.

(*a*) A *dispersed harem* (referred to by Martin, 1981, as 'dispersed polygyny') occurs where a male holds a territory which encloses the home ranges of several females with whom he has exclusive mating rights. The females aggregate at a sleeping site or burrow but forage independently. In the case of the nocturnal bushbabies (e.g. *Galago demidovii*) females sleep together during the day in matriarchal groups, while non-territorial males are peripheral or subordinate in the alpha male's territory. Male bushbabies emigrate to breed, while strong mother-daughter affectional bonds exist which persist into adult life. Many colonial burrowing mammals show dispersed harems where females occupy burrows in a restricted area and a male includes the home ranges of a number of females within his territory; females forage independently, and mother-daughter home ranges show complete overlap (e.g. *Procavia johnsoni* and *Marmota olympus*). Males emigrate to breed and non-breeding males are peripheral. Subadult young are tolerated in yellow-bellied marmots (*Marmota flaviventris*).

(*b*) *Rookeries*, or *breeding assemblies*, are found in highly mobile mammals which return to a restricted area to breed. Males compete to acquire a harem of females, although they also mate opportunistically with any female which strays into their harem. There is no social cohesion, females are attracted to an area where they give birth and nurse their pups, while males defend a group of females which have a post-partum oestrus. This arrangement occurs in Pinnipedia, such as Northern elephant seals and Steller sea lions and in some bats (e.g. *Pteronotus parnelli, Mormoops megalophylla*).

(*c*) *Temporary mobile harems*, where a male associates with a group of females, are typical of many cursorial mammals such as wild goats (*Capra hircus*) mountain sheep (*Ovis canadensis*) and red deer.

(*d*) *Permanent harems* are found in other species. For example the male vicuña is territorial and defends a group of 4–18 adult females, while other males live in bachelor herds which are non-territorial. Both six-month-old sons and yearling daughters are driven out of the harem, with the result that its size remains relatively constant (Koford, 1957). Permanent mobile harems take one of two forms; either the male collects a group of unrelated females (non female-bonded harems) or he takes over a group of related females (female-bonded harems). The cohesion of the group depends upon the existence of a non-sexual male-female bond. This system occurs in some bats, such as *Saccopteryx bilineata* and *Phyllostomus discolor*, where the female composition of harems varies from time to time. The best known

instances of non-female bonded harems are in primates, namely the
hamadryas baboon and the gorilla. In both species females leave their natal
breeding unit and are attracted to a male who may or may not already have
a harem. Bachelor groups do not occur in either of these species. In the
hamadryas, the breeding unit is part of a larger band which includes some
non-breeding adult males, while male gorillas tend to remain in their natal
group or become solitary and attempt to attract females from another
harem (see Chapter 6). Female-bonded harems are the type found most
frequently in mammals. The permanent group consists of a number of
related females with strong affectional bonds between them. A male simply
takes over the sexual access to the group from a previous male, defending
the harem against other males. In most cases, males outside the breeding
units live in bachelor groups, usually with a rank order. This system has
been studied in common langurs by Hrdy (1977) and gelada baboons by
Dunbar and Dunbar (1975) (see Chapter 5). It is also known to occur in
mountains zebras (*Equus zebra*) (see Klingel, 1974). Breeding units are part
of a larger troop or herd in gelada baboons and feral stallions (*Equus
caballus*), the latter being ranked independently of the size of the harem
which they hold.

(4) Territorial males, females more sociable

In some mammals breeding males are territorial, but females are more
sociable and have home ranges which overlap one or more male territories.

(*a*) A system termed by Leuthold (1977) 'territory and absolute hierarchy
combined' was found in the white rhinoceros by Owen-Smith (1975). In
this species non-breeding males lived as subordinates in a dominant
male's territory. Female home ranges overlapped those of males and
groups of one or more adult females, with their juvenile and infant
offspring, moved around together (see Chapter 5).

(*b*) In some species, non-territorial males may form separate bachelor
herds, often with a dominance hierarchy, while females form herds which
live in home ranges overlapping several male territories. This arrangement
of male territoriality with female herds is found in some African ungulates
(see p. 137). Males display to females in the rut so that there is a degree
of sexual selection by females. Males of some species such as reedbuck
(*Redunca arundinum*) and gerenuk (*Litocranius walleri*) defend their whole
home range, while others such as blue wildebeest defend only a part of it,
which may be referred to as a breeding territory.

Female herds are often matriarchal, as in the case of mountain goats.

This arrangement is found in wildebeest, Uganda kob, asses (*Equus hemonius, E. africanus*) and Grevy's zebra (*E. grevyi*).

(*c*) The most extreme form of male display and territoriality is that of the lek. During the rut males display to females on a traditional breeding ground, where each male occupies a small area which it defends against other males. Some of these territories confer greater reproductive success on a male than others, while non-breeding males live in bachelor groups. Such a system has been observed in the hammer-headed bat (*Hypsignathus monstrosus*) and the Uganda kob. The kob has a lek system with territories of 15–30 m in diameter in some areas, whereas in others it has much larger territories of 100–150 m diameter (see above). In some places both systems are found. Leks are uncommon in mammals but are known in other classes of animals including birds and insects (see p. 151).

(5) Spaced males, sociable females

Males of some mammals are not territorial, but lead a relatively solitary existence, while females are more sociable. This situation is found in the coatimundi (*Nasua narica*) (see Kaufmann, 1962), pigs such as warthog (Leuthold, 1977) and elephants (Douglas-Hamilton and Douglas-Hamilton, 1973). Female elephants form matriarchal herds led by an old female. If a female is in oestrus, males are attracted to the female herd and compete for mating. Male African elephants, however, are more sociable than their Asiatic counterparts (see Chapter 6) and 50% of African males live in loosely organized 'bull groups'.

(6) Multimale/multifemale groups

Multimale/multifemale groups are formed when adults of both sexes live together, permanently in a herd or troop. Although such groups are usually termed 'multimale' by primatologists, to avoid confusion they will be referred to here as 'multimale/multifemale' or 'bisexual'. There is usually a male dominance hierarchy which may confer priority of access to oestrous females on high-ranking individuals. Females may also have a dominance hierarchy.

(*a*) Burrowing mammals may live in multimale/multifemale colonies as, for example, the black-tailed prairie dog studied by King (1955) and the European rabbit (Southern, 1948; Bell, 1980, 1983). The rabbit lives in groups of 1–3 males and 1–5 females, often with both male and female dominance hierarchies. Breeding success for both sexes is related to status, so that the dominant buck and doe consort. The colony defends the area around its home warren; dispersal is largely by males, 70% of whom leave their natal warren while 70% of females remain; female rabbits in a colony are therefore more closely related than males.

(b) The multimale/multifemale herd is a mobile group in which there appear to be no personal relations apart from a male dominance hierarchy and the mother-offspring bond. This form of society was found by Kaufmann (1974a) in the whiptailed wallaby (*Macropus parryi*), which appears to represent the peak of marsupial social organization. It is also characteristic of the African buffalo, which also forms all-male (bachelor) herds.

(c) Female-bonded societies are the characteristic form taken by most higher primate bisexual groups. Males emigrate, while the females, which remain in their natal group, co-operate and show strong kin-related social ties with other females, often with a well marked kin-determined rank order. Males are hierarchically organized and may change troops several times in a lifetime. The best studied species are macaques (*Macaca fuscata, M. sinica, M. mulatta*).

Two species of mammal are known which form non-female bonded societies. These are the chimpanzee and the closely-related bonobo, or pygmy chimpanzee (*Pan paniscus*). The main social bond in these species is between males, and females leave their natal group to breed. Published data (see Chapter 6) indicates that there is also a strong male-female bond in *P. paniscus*. These societies have a male hierarchy and *P. troglodytes* males tend to travel in bands, defending their group territory against other males.

(d) Multimale/multifemale groups, known as prides, are characteristics of lions in some parts of their range. The social organization of the lion pride has been investigated by Bertram (1975a, b, 1976, 1978, 1983), Packer and Pusey (1982, 1983) and Schaller (1972). In some ways it can be regarded as intermediate in form between a harem and a multimale/multifemale grouping. In this species, females form the stable social group; they are closely related (mean $r = 1/8$) and relatively uncompetitive, even suckling one anothers' cubs. Dispersal is by males which are driven out during adolescence. These males which are closely related ($r = \frac{1}{4}$) remain together and, on reaching adulthood, attempt to take over another pride from the resident males. Success in takeover is related to the number of males in the group, as is success in retaining it (see Table 5.3). Pairs of males or singletons have both a low rate of success in pride takeover and short tenure, so that they frequently join unrelated males to form a coalition of two or three individuals.

Table 5.3 The frequency of occurrence of male lion groups of different sizes and the probability that they will have tenure of a pride of lionesses. (After Bygott *et al.*, 1979.)

No of males in group	No of male groups		Percentage with tenure	Significant differences
	Total	No. with tenure		
1	23	4	17	
				$p < 0.01$
2	39	23	59	
				$p < 0.01$
3	12	11	92	
4–7	9	9	100	

Packer and Pusey (1982) estimated that approximately 72% of a male's partners were relatives. Between males of the same age or size there was no dominance hierarchy and, once a male consorted with an oestrous female, other males did not challenge him and ownership therefore conveyed temporary dominance. Fights occurred mainly when ownership of an oestrous female was uncertain. The degree of competition between males was strongly influenced by the number of females in the pride. As all females tended to come into oestrous simultaneously, in a large pride every male was likely to find a consort simultaneously so that competition was minimal. Related males were no less competitive for oestrous females than unrelated ones. Female co-operation in rearing cubs is beneficial because the breeding success of males is dependent upon the presence of same age companions.

(*e*) Brown hyaenas (*Hyaena brunnea*) also form multimale/multifemale groups with a rather unusual social system. Mills (1982) found that females only mate with nomadic males and not with male members of the pack or clan. Thus the male has a choice of reproductive strategy, either to remain in his natal group as a helper or to become nomadic. Females are dominant to males and numerous females in the pack breed.

(7) Eusocial

One of the most remarkable mammals from the viewpoint of its social organization is the naked mole rat (*Heterocephalus glaber*) which is eusocial with reproductive and non-reproductive castes, female workers being sterile (see Chapter 3). The details of its social structure have been reported by Jarvis (1981).

(8) Ephemeral aggregates

Some mammals are sociable, spending much of their time in groups which represent ephemeral aggregations with no constancy of group membership. Herds of between one and 15 giraffes and eland are of this form. Solitary individuals are usually males; temporary groups may be of one or both sexes. Males are promiscuous, seeking out oestrous females for which they compete. Eland may also form nomadic female herds, while males tend to be more solitary, living in a small undefended home range; peer groups also form (see Dagg and Foster, 1976; Leuthold, 1977).

Other reviews of mammalian social organization have been provided by Eisenberg (1966, 1981); Crook and Gartlan (1966); Crook *et al.* (1976); and, for African ungulates, Leuthold (1977).

5.3 The ecology of social organization

Before considering specific examples which show a clear relationship between social structure and environmental factors, the general question of why some mammals live in groups can be considered from a theoretical standpoint. The advantages and disadvantages of group living will be considered purely from the viewpoint of individual fitness. If an individual ceases to benefit from living in a group, it will leave the group and adopt a solitary mode of life, as normally happens to members of litters of solitary mammals such as shrews, cats and weasels.

Group living has obvious drawbacks in the form of increased competition, greater conspicuousness to predators, the need to travel further to find adequate amounts of food and greater risk of transfer of parasites between group members.

The advantages of group living have been discussed by Hamilton (1964, 1971) Alexander (1974), Bertram (1978) and Gosling and Petrie (1981). There are a number of reasons why mammals may be gregarious, several of which may apply to any one species.

Some mammals aggregate because of a dearth of suitable resting sites. The roosts of bats, sleeping cliffs of hamadryas baboons and restricted breeding areas for some pinnipeds all bring individuals together. In some cases energy conservation may also be involved, as in cold climates where members of a social group may huddle together. If food is clumped in rich patches, a strategy of group searching and sharing may be the most efficient method of detecting it.

Prey species may group together for protection, for example, many species of ungulate live in herds. The protection afforded arises because group vigilance may be more effective than that of a single individual and living in a large herd also decreases an individual's chance of becoming the victim (see Hamilton, 1971). Wildebeest with calves have been seen to use the herd for cover by moving to its far side when they detect a predator. A predator may also be confused by a large herd in flight and, as a result, fail to single out an individual victim. Some mammals actually co-operate in group defence. When threatened by a wolf or coyote, musk oxen (*Ovibos moschatus*) form a circle around females with calves with their heads facing outwards, ready to attack the predator should it attempt to penetrate the herd.

Predatory mammals may also live in groups to enable them to hunt as a pack and to kill larger prey than a single individual could do. Living in groups may also be advantageous when defending a kill, or, may even permit a predator to rob a lone individual or small group of its prey. A pack of wild dogs (*Lycaon pictus*) can drive a single lion or hyaena from its kill.

Where mammals live in permanent socially-organized groups, members may be closely related so that co-operative behaviour brings benefits through kin selection, but unrelated individuals may also benefit through reciprocal altruism. Group living also makes it easier to find a mate. In some higher primates cultural traditions may spread through imitation.

A number of authors have attempted to relate the form taken by the social organization of a mammal to its ecology and three factors have been examined, namely, food, climate and terrain.

5.3.1 Diet and food distribution

Where food is distributed in a scattered fashion, but each item is relatively rich in nutrients, mammals tend to be solitary. This way of life is characteristic of small primitive mammals living on invertebrates, small vertebrates, seeds, fruit and carrion; most marsupial and placental carnivores; and small omnivorous or grazing rodents.

A good example of a mammal adopting this way of life is the Virginian opossum (*Didelphys virginiana*), which feeds on carrion, insects, birds, crayfish and snails. It is an opportunistic feeder, since its food consumption is closely related to seasonal food availability. Wiseman and Hendrickson (1950) found that *D. virginiana* travels 1.6 – 2.4km each evening, when foraging. It has a home range of 10–120 hectares, spending about half its time in one-tenth of the area. Individuals are spaced and aggressive to same-sex individuals, and the female consorts with a male only when in oestrus. This mammal is *r*-selected, being short-lived (mean 1.33 years) and prolific, producing an average of 7.5 weaned young per female per annum. The young disperse on weaning at $3-3\frac{1}{2}$ months and at once adopt the unsociable mode of life of the adults, becoming sexually mature at nine months.

When food is distributed in a clumped fashion with rich pockets scattered unpredictably in space and time, it may be of advantage to the individual to forage in a group. The African banded mongoose (*Mungos mungo*) lives in packs of up to 35 individuals and its foraging behaviour has been described by Neal (1970). This species is diurnal and, after spending the night in a den, the pack searches for millipedes and beetles; it covers a considerable area searching for elephant and buffalo dung which provide a rich source of these arthropods. The foraging technique used involves fanning out over an area, while remaining in visual or vocal contact. If one individual finds a patch of dung, its calls attract the rest of the pack. Foraging in a social group is much more efficient than doing so independently, because the pack can cover a much greater area and food patches are large enough for the finder to share with others without depriving itself. During breeding periods unweaned infants remain at the den, to which the pack returns at night.

Feeding strategies and social organization sometimes vary between closely-related species. A good example of this phenomenon is found in the African Canidae (see Bekoff, 1974). This is a family of mammals which is characteristically monogamous, so that social organization is based on the pair and their family. The side-striped jackal (*Canis adustus*) hunts singly or in pairs for small mammals, eggs, birds, lizards, insects, carrion and vegetable matter. The black-backed jackal (*C. mesomelas*) is sometimes found hunting in packs of between five and seven members, which enables it to draw on not only the same type of food supply as the striped jackal but also to overpower small antelopes and lambs. The golden jackal (*C. aureus*) may forage singly, in pairs, or in packs which include female yearlings, which often remain with their parents and assist in rearing further young. When hunting singly, *C. aureus* scavenge and take small mammals. In packs, however, they can overpower and kill adult Thomson's gazelle by disembowelling them. Kruuk (1972) found that a pair of golden jackals are more efficient than a single individual in killing a gazelle fawn because together they can overcome its mother's defence. While only 17% of lone hunters succeeded in capturing a fawn, 67% of pairs were able to do so.

The most specialized African pack-forming canid is the hunting dog (*Lycaon pictus*) which hunts in groups of 2–30, the mean lying somewhere between 8.9–9.8 according to different studies (Schaller, 1972; Frame *et al.*, 1979). Each dog weighs only 22–26 kg but, by hunting co-operatively, they are able to overpower and kill prey as large as buffalo, zebra and wildebeest. Generally, however, they take smaller antelope such as impala, reedbuck and Thomson's gazelle. The *Lycaon* pack functions as a highly organized group and, during the breeding season, the alpha female produces a large litter of up to 16 pups. She remains with the pups and nurses them for five to six weeks while the rest of the pack hunts and regurgitates food on its return. After six weeks, the breeding female rejoins the pack and guarding is undertaken by other pack members. Pups and babysitters solicit food by licking the muzzle of the returning hunter. *Lycaon* hunts by sight, prey are chased not stalked, and the pack may split, one group driving prey towards other pack members who can cut it off.

The strategy of pack hunting to run down larger prey has also evolved in the Asiatic wild dog or dhole (*Cuon alpinus*), the wolf and the spotted hyaena (see Kruuk, 1972). Whereas most cats, which hunt their prey by stalking, are solitary, lions in areas where there are large game herds form prides (see pp. 130–1). The lionesses do the hunting, using an ambush technique, and Schaller (1972) has shown that co-operative ambushing yields twice as many prey per capita as hunting alone. It also allows lions to overpower such large prey as buffalo and giraffe. While the associated male lions do not generally hunt, they perform a useful function in protecting the pride, and particularly the vulnerable cubs, from predators.

Toothed whales (Odontoceti) also show a relation between group size and hunting strategy. Inshore species which feed on small isolated prey hunt alone or in small groups, whereas open-water species such as the common porpoise (*Phocoena phocoena*) form large schools; this enables them to detect and surround fish shoals (a clumped resource) or to overpower large prey such as the large whalebone whales (Mysteceti) (see Chapter 6).

Killer whales (*Orcinus orca*) hunt co-operatively by surrounding schools of seals or porpoises and take turns to dart in to feed. When hunting large whalebone whales, some of the *Orcinus* pack immobilize the prey by holding its flippers while others attack, biting the lower jaw or tongue (see Martinez and Klinghammer, 1978).

The relation between diet and social organization has been examined in two groups of herbivores, the kangaroo family (Macropodidae) and the African antelopes (Bovidae). Kaufmann (1974*b*) reviewed what is known of the social organization and ecology of the Macropodidae, a family which includes 45 species, and tried to relate the two. The smallest and most solitary forms such as the muskrat kangaroo *Hypsiprimnodon moschatus* are insectivorous to omnivorous, while at the other extreme the larger and more sociable species such as the whiptailed wallaby (*Macropus parryi*) are grazers. Kaufmann postulated an evolutionary history for the family, commencing with small, solitary, nocturnal omnivores. As these animals developed grazing habits they tended to become more tolerant of one another, often congregating together in temporary aggregates at rich food sources, as does the present day quokka (*Setonix brachyurus*) which forms gregarious subunits with overlapping home ranges and, in competitive situations, a male dominance hierarchy. Possible intermediates between the quokka and *M. parryi* may be the banded hare wallaby (*Lagostrophus fasciatus*) and the tamar wallaby (*M. eugenii*) which live in thickets and are believed to be gregarious.

M. parryi forms permanent social groups (multimale/multifemale herds), referred to as 'mobs', which are of fixed composition and may therefore have evolved non-sexual bonds. Males are hierarchically organized, the dominants having access to oestrous females. Although there are some macropodids which are gregarious and live in thickets where visibility is poor, there is a general tendency for the more social species to live in open habitats and to be more diurnal (see Table 5.4). These data support the view that species which rely on rich but widely scattered food resources tend to be solitary, while grazers which are surrounded by food for which they need not compete can adopt a more sociable lifestyle.

The kangaroo family represents the peak of marsupial social organization and adaptation to a cursorial grazing mode of life. This ecological niche is also occupied by the placental ruminant *Artiodactyla*, and the

Table 5.4 · Sociability and other parameters for five Macropodidae. (Based on Kaufmann, 1974*b*.)

| | Group size | | | Openness | |
	Range	Mean	Food	of habitat	Diurnality
Macropus parryi	1–42	6.0	G	4	6
M. giganteus	1–15	3.7	G	4	4
M. robustus	1–9	2.1	G	4	3
M. rufogriseus	1–8	1.5	B	3	3
Wallabia bicolor	1–3	1.1	B	2	2

Key: Grazer = G
Browser = B
Openness of habitat: 4, maximum
Diurnality: 6, most diurnal

ecology and social organization of African species has been reviewed by Jarman (1974) and Leuthold (1977).

Jarman classified African antelopes into five groups according to their feeding habitats; most species are either browsers, feeding mainly on leaves and buds, or grazers feeding on grass. While grass is more generally accessible than browse and tends to grow in large stands, as grassland or savannah, it is subject to greater seasonal differences in availability. Some grazers such as wildebeest feed selectively on the new growth of grass (which contains 15% protein as compared with 7% for mature leaves and 4% for old leaves). Others, such as buffalo, are unselective. Jarman's classification is as follows.

Class A are selective browsers which may even take some animal protein. Food is distributed in small rich pockets, so that the social groups are small. These species are typically territorial and some, such as the klipspringer, are monogamous. Other species in this group are the dikdik (*Madoqua sp.*), duikers (*Cephalotus sp.*) grysbok and steinbok (*Raphicerus sp.*).

Class B are slightly less selective feeders but feed on specific parts of plants; they may be browsers or selective grazers. Their diet varies with the seasonal abundance of different foods. Males are usually solitary and territorial but females live in small groups which lack social structure and permanence; male herding may play a role in determining the existence of female groups. Example are the Bohor reedbuck (*Redunca sp.*), oribi (*Ourebia ourebi*), gerenuk (*Litocranius walleri*) and lesser kudu (*Tragelaphus imberbis*).

Class C feed on a range of grasses and also browse, but their diet is restricted to certain species and changes in accordance with the seasonal availability of different items. Breeding males may be territorial in the rut, while non-breeding males form bachelor herds. Females live in a home range in herds of 20–250 individuals. Such species as the greater kudu (*Tragelephas strepsiceros*), waterbuck (*Kobus ellipsiprymnus*), impala (*Aepyceros melampus*), Grant's gazelle (*Gazella granti*) and Thomson's gazelle (*G. thomsoni*) are in this group.

Class D are selective grazers feeding on the fresh growth. They move from area to area following the rains. Male and nursery herds are separate but, in the rut, some males acquire breeding territories which may be abandoned if conditions become unfavourable. Females are attracted to, and mate only with, territorial males. This group contains blue wildebeest, (*Connochaetes taurinus*), Uganda kob (*Adenota kob*) topi (*Damaliscus korrigum*) and Coke's hartebeest (*Alcephalus buselaphus cokei*).

Class E are large unselective grazers, or grazers and browsers. They live

Table 5.5 Antelope ecology and social organization. (Data from Jarman, 1974, and Lenthold, 1977.)

Class	Typical examples	Group size (range)	Group composition	Territory	Weight (kg)
A	klipspringer, dikdik	1–2	1M, 1–2F	M + F	5–70
B	reedbuck, gerenuk	3–6	FF	M	15–150
C	waterbuck, greater kudu	6–60	MM, FF	(M)	20–250
D	blue wildebeest, Uganda kob	6–300	MM, FF	(M)	80–210
E	buffalo	15–1000	MM, MM + FF	–	180–700

Key: MM, FF: separate male/female herds
 MM + FF: herds with both sexes
 (M): mating territory in the rut

in large herds of anything from several hundred to over a thousand individuals. The buffalo is typical of this group. Adults of both sexes coexist in breeding herds, but bachelor herds may also exist. Herds are mobile and move around the home range. Male access to females is determined by a dominance hierarchy, and females have a long-lasting relationship of 2–3 years with their calves. The Beisa oryx (*Oryx beisa*) may be territorial but other members of this class – eland (*Taurotragus sp.*) and gemsbok (*Oryx gazella*) – appear not to be.

Jarman's classification provides a useful framework for relating the social structure and feeding habits of cursorial herbivores, and Table 5.15 compares the different classes of antelopes for a number of parameters. As in Macropodidae, group size is smallest in selective feeders living in an exclusive territory on scattered supplies of rich food, while it is largest in unselective grazers which are surrounded by poorer food for which they do not have to compete. The size of animal and food quality are also related; larger-bodied animals have a relatively lower metabolic rate than small ones (metabolic rate $= KW^{0.75}$, where K is a constant and W is a body weight), so that they require relatively less food or can obtain their requirements from larger quantities of poor-quality food.

From these data it is clear that there is a correlation between body size, diet and degree of gregariousness. A grazing habit makes group living feasible because food is not a defendable resource and is not scattered in small pockets necessitating individual searching. Large antelopes, however, are not gregarious because they are grazers. The most probable explanation for the sociable habits of large grazing antelopes is that group herding has evolved as an anti-predator strategy, on the safety-in-numbers principle outlined earlier in this chapter.

Sexual dimorphism varies in the different groups and reaches its maximum in species with the highest degree of polygyny, where males live in a fixed home range and females are gregarious.

It has been found in some mammals that groups are flexible and may split into small foraging parties at times of food shortage or when food is scattered. In some species such as chimpanzees and bonobos the whole group assemble only at places where food is abundant, for example when a tree is in fruit or a semi-deciduous tree is covered in new leaves (see Reynolds and Reynolds, 1965; Goodall 1965; Nishida, 1968, for *P. troglodytes* and Kuroda, 1979, for *P. paniscus*).

A flexible grouping system is also found in some cetaceans. The common dolphin (*Delphinus delphis*) feeds in parties varying from 5–30, while bottlenosed dolphins are found in parties of 8–100. Schools of twenty or so individual pilot whales (*Globicephala melaena*) scatter to find prey solitarily. Saayman and Tayler (1979) observed groups of humpbacked dolphin (*Sousa sp.*) from a promontory, as it is an inshore species which hunts for fish among reefs. A school of twenty-five individuals split into small foraging parties but, when not feeding, they all assembled together. Hunting in small parties is the only practicable technique for catching isolated fish swimming among the reefs. The advantage of grouping together in a school relates to defence against large predators such as sharks. The flexible group structure of bonobos and humpbacked dolphins is illustrated in Figure 5.1.

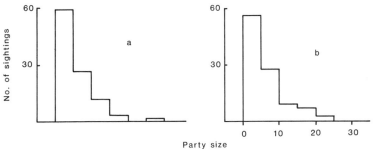

Figure 5.1 Species with flexible social organization. Sightings of parties of different sizes in (*a*) pygmy chimpanzees (*Pan paniscus*): number of sightings = 138, mean party size = 5.7, from Kuroda, 1979; (*b*) humpbacked dolphins (*Sousa* sp.): number of sightings = 211, mean party size = 6.5, from Saayman and Tayler, 1979.

Some mammals may move from one feeding area to another and this may lead to the formation of enormous aggregations or 'superherds'. This is true of the barren ground caribou which migrates north to the Canadian tundra in summer to take advantage of the rich supplies of lichen known as 'reindeer moss'. Vast herds of up to 700 000 wildebeest are found in the Serengeti in areas where rain has recently fallen and where grass shoots are present. After grazing, the herds move on, returning to the same area a few weeks later (Sinclair, 1977). During the dry season these superherds split up and smaller groups move to areas of permanent water supply; if rainfall has been exceptionally low, they take to the woodlands to feed. Thus patterns of opportunistic feeding may lead to the formation of vast aggregations of cursorial herbivores.

5.3.2 Climate as a determinant of social structure

Barash (1974) believed that the differences in the social behaviour of marmots (*Marmota*) can be explained by reference to the climatic conditions in which each species lives. The woodchuck (*M. monax*) lives solitarily in fields and forests at low altitudes; male and female make contact only at mating and weaned young leave their mother. The olympic marmot (*M. olympus*) of alpine meadows is highly sociable, living in colonies consisting of one male, several females and their yearling and two-year-old young. The habitat and social organization of the yellow-bellied

Table 5.6　Environmental and social data for three species of marmot (*Marmota*). (After Barash, 1974.)

	Woodchuck M. monax	Yellow bellied marmot (M. flaviventris)	Olympic marmot M. olympus
Growing season (days)	150	70–100	40–70
Age of dispersal (years)	0.5	1	2
Age of sexual maturity (years)	1	2	3
% of adult weight at 12 months old	80	60	30
Frequency of breeding (years)	1	1–2	2
Interadult aggression	+	+	−
Greetings per hour	0	0.1	1

marmot (*M. flaviventris*) are intermediate between those of the other two species. They are found in habitats where climatic conditions are midway between the alpine and woodland environments. Each female has her own living area but is intolerant of the young of other colony members. The colony contains yearlings, but no two-year-olds. Barash put forward the view that sociability in the three species reflected the length of growing season and the temperature conditions. The long growing season and plentiful food in the lowland habitat enabled woodchucks to become sexually mature within a year, while the olympic marmot took two years to reach breeding age; *M. flaviventris* is intermediate (see Table 5.6). Barash predicted that hoary marmots (*M. caligata*) which are found in alpine environments would resemble olympic marmots in social structure, and this proved to be the case (Barash, 1981). The European marmot (*M. marmota*) is also a highly sociable alpine species.

5.3.3 Primate social organization

Numerous attempts have been made to relate primate social structure to ecological factors (see Crook and Gartlan, 1966; Eisenberg *et al.*, 1972 (whose views have been summarized by Wilson, 1975); Clutton-Brock and Harvey, 1977a, b, and Chalmers, 1979). The wide variety of lifestyles and the vast range of forms within the order Primates have defied any overall explanation. Martin (1981) in a useful review has drawn attention to the major factors which are likely to be involved. He particularly emphasizes the relevance of metabolic rate to ranging pattern and the sociability of many small, primitive prosimians which, apart from group foraging, show behaviour which foreshadows that of higher primates.

The most useful data on the relationship between ecology and social structure in primates are those where closely-related species have been investigated. Hladik (1977) showed that the leaf eating purple-faced langur (*Presbytis senex*) had smaller groups and smaller home ranges than the common langur (*P. entellus*) which feeds on shoots, flowers and fruit.

5.4 Territorial behaviour

A territory is an area from which conspecifics are excluded by a combination of advertisement, threat or fighting. Territories may be defended by a single individual, a pair, a family or a social group or by individuals of either or both sexes. Males, however, are more commonly territorial than females. The size of mammalian territories varies; in some species, such as the rabbit, the female defends only her breeding burrow whereas in others the animal defends its whole home range. The shapes of territories are variable and usually relate to the distribution of resources within them. The European otter, for example, defends an elongated territory which follows the course of a river and provides both refuge and food for the animal.

Territorial behaviour will be considered under two broad headings; first, the economics of territorial defence and, secondly, by a series of examples which illustrate different forms of mammalian territoriality.

5.4.1 Economics of territorial defence

A territory generally contains some resource which is in limited supply, to which the owner thereby acquires exclusive use. This implies that adequate resources exist within the defended area, making it economical to defend. Individuals would not be expected to defend resources which were superabundant or highly unpredictable in time or space (Brown, 1975).

Some species are known to be territorial under one set of conditions, but not under another, as in the cases of black and white colobus monkeys (Oates 1977) and spotted hyaenas. Kruuk (1972) found that spotted hyaenas were territorial in the Ngorongoro crater, where there were large resident herds of their prey, but in the Serengeti, where ungulates are more mobile, hyaenas ranged over larger undefended areas. Territorial mammals will only defend their home range if it is sufficiently productive and, in species as diverse as shrews (*Blarina*), wildebeest and Grevy's zebra, individuals have been observed to abandon impoverished territories. There may be considerable variations in the productivity of different areas within the habitat, and individuals who can monopolize rich areas will need smaller territories than those in poorer regions. This situation is exemplified by waterbuck, where high-status males occupy small, rich territories adjacent to the river; as the lower-ranking males' home ranges increase in distance from the river, they become larger. Finally there comes a point where the territorial system breaks down and males occupy large undefended home ranges. Females show preferential mating with males whose territories are adjacent to the river. Male reproductive success is also related to territory quality in the American pronghorn, where the number of females within a male's territory is positively correlated with the forage available (see Fig. 3.4).

In all territorial species there will be some individuals who do not hold a territory. Such individuals may be nomadic, accept a subordinate status within a territory or, in the case of many male ungulates and some primates, join a bachelor herd of non-breeding males. They may lack a territory for one of three reasons: they may be too young to have yet acquired one, or they have abandoned it because it became impoverished, or they were driven off by a rival.

The two main costs incurred in holding a territory are those involved in patrolling it and in driving out intruders. As far as patrolling is concerned, in species which defend their home range, there might be expected to be a direct relationship between a mammal's locomotor ability and the size of its territory. Few relevant data are available, but Mitani and Rodman (1979) examined this problem in relation to primate territoriality. They postulated that the diameter of an idealized circle of equal area to that actually defended (d') should not be greater than the animal's daily movement path (d), defined as the average distance which it covers in a day. From this concept was derived a parameter which they termed the index of defendability (D) where $D = d/d'$. A survey of the published literature showed that, for all territorial primates, D was greater than one, so that the data supported Mitani and Rodman's hypothesis. A territorial mammal would be expected to make regular visits to the boundary of its home range. One of the few detailed studies of ranging behaviour in the field is that of Charles-Dominique (1977a) on Allen's bushbaby (*Galago alleni*), which showed that individuals tended to move out from the centre of the home range, travel out to the border and then loop back to the centre again (see Figure 5.2).

Sleeping refuges were near the centre of the range and as the animal moved around, it scent-marked by urinating. Using an ingenious attachment, Charles-Dominique was able to detect when and where individuals urinated. Each time they did so an electrical contact was made and a signal was emitted which could be detected by a receiver.

Some mammals may need to return to the centre of their territory to rest; this is unavoidable in the breeding season for species with altricial or semialtricial young such as wolves, spotted hyaenas and burrowing rodents such as marmots and prairie dogs. Where young are precocial, however, adults may carry them, as in the case of most primates, or they may be able to follow the herd. Such species can patrol a larger area because they need not return to the same base area every night.

Territories are not invariably exclusive; for example, in *Galago demidovii* male territories overlap (Figure 5.3). Nonetheless, males avoid confrontation in the common areas, and Leyhausen (1965) found that domestic cats share parts of their home ranges but travel through them at

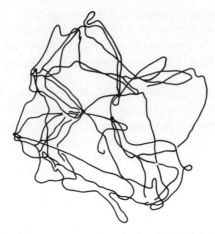

Figure 5.2 A sample of the movement paths of a female Allen's bushbaby (*Galago alleni*) within her territory. Notice the looping of the paths with frequent returns to the same locations (fruit trees). The diameter of the area traversed is approximately 400 m. Each major area has visited at least once a week. (After Charles-Dominique, 1977.)

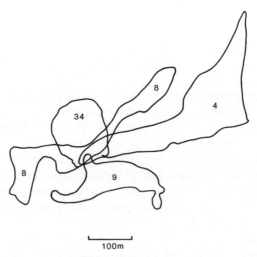

Figure 5.3 Territories of four male Demidoff's bushbabies (*Galago demidovii*) showing overlap. The individual males are numbered 4, 8, 9, and 34. (After Charles-Dominique, 1977a.)

different times of day, each individual having a recognized priority over a particular period.

One way in which both the costs of patrolling and the need for physical combat can be reduced is by advertisement and territorial display.

Harrington (1976) showed the importance of urine marking in the territorial behaviour of laboratory mice. He allowed the male mice to set up territories in a cage with a series of compartments, one of which formed the boundary. The arena had a moveable floor and when the floor was moved the boundary of the two territories changed with it.

Beliefs that scent-marking deters or intimidates intruders or enhances the confidence of residents have little unambiguous field evidence to support them, although Eaton (1970) found that cheetahs avoided the freshly-deposited scent-marks of strangers but ignored older ones. A number of authors have suggested that scent-marks provide intruders with information about the status of the resident (Mykytowycz, 1970). Various other functions of scent-marking, such as assistance in orientation and attraction of mates, have been suggested. Gosling (1983) suggested that territorial marking enables an intruder who has identified the scent marks to match them against any individual which it may meet and so determine whether it is the territory owner. If the two scents match, the intruder will generally withdraw. There are several lines of evidence which support this hypothesis. First, some mammals anoint themselves with urine, saliva or scent-gland secretion which could serve to facilitate matching. Secondly, territory owners often make themselves available for olfactory inspection by standing immobile when approached by a stranger, as in the case of hartebeest and impala. Finally, territory owners remove or replace scent marks which do not match their own odour; for example, male pronghorn defaecate and urinate over the faeces of another male, while male beavers overmark the scent of other males.

Gosling (1981) considered the economics of territorial advertisement in the male gerenuk, an African antelope which leaves conspicuous scent marks, secreted by the antorbital gland (see Figure 5.4). These scent marks were distributed in the form of a rough oval, well within the boundary of the territory, but with extending arms reaching towards the border. The secretion was deposited on food plants, particularly on projecting twigs which had been defoliated. This system is efficient because the scent marks are placed on food plants during feeding periods and detection by conspecifics is facilitated when they visit the same plant to forage. This pattern of scent-marking may, at first sight, seem curious but Gosling pointed out that it could be more economical than simple boundary

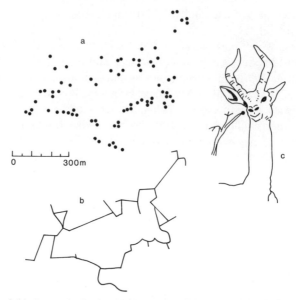

Figure 5.4   Orbital scent marking in the gerenuk (*Litocranius walleri*): (*a*) Pattern of scent marking in the male's territory, (*b*) interpretation of the pattern (using nearest-neighbour technique) as an oval polygon with radiating arms, (*c*) male scent-marking a branch. (After Gosling, 1981)

marking for several reasons. In the first place, the marks can be more closely set and, secondly, the radiating arms will serve to intercept intruders moving through the area. Marking food plants well within the territory is also less disruptive of general feeding activity than border marking would be.

Another economical method of marking is to concentrate marks on trouble spots where boundary confrontations are most likely to occur. Walther (1978*b*) found a pattern of this type in the male Thomson's gazelle, where dung piles were most frequent in sections of the border where agonistic encounters most commonly occurred. (Figure 5.5). As adjacent territories were not mapped it is not apparent why conflicts were restricted to certain parts of the border, but it may be that these areas were in dispute.

Some mammals advertise territorial ownership by vocal signals. While this method has the potential disadvantage of drawing the attention of predators, it has the compensating advantage of carrying over a considerable distance and providing intruders or territorial neighbours with information regarding an individual's precise location. Male prairie dogs (see King, 1955) indicate their territorial ownership by whistling, while large cats (*Panthera*) roar. Some small primates living in treetops have low-

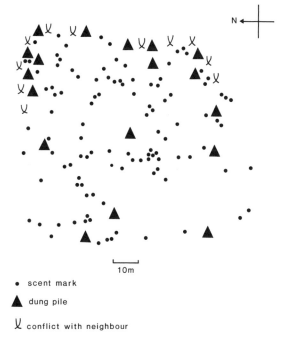

Figure 5.5 Marking system of a male Thomson's gazelle in his territory. (After Walther, 1978*b*.)

pitched calls produced by special resonators such as vocal sacs (siamangs) or inflated hyoid bones (howler monkeys); these allow the production of sounds between 100–500 Hz which undergo a minimum of attenuation. Gibbons (*Hylobates lar, H. pileatus*) may spend up to 4% of their activity period in calling. In some species, breeding pairs duet and unmated individuals, including nomadic individuals, also call and thus provide information regarding their whereabouts to potential mates. The time of day at which calling takes place has been shown to be of considerable significance. Gibbons, like many species of bird, have a dawn chorus and Henwood and Fabrick (1979), in an experimental study of sound transmission, found that sounds transmit 40 times further at 5am than they do at midday in the Borneo forest. In the Arizona desert the difference was 20 times. Elevation is also important, because a high calling station allows the animal to get well above the marked temperature gradients which may exist close to the ground and can result in an acoustic shadow effect.

The direct behavioural effect of calling on another individual varies from species to species (see Chapter 2). Robinson (1979*a*) found that calling groups of the monogamous Columbian titi monkey close to the territorial boundary attracted the neighbouring group, which then gave visual displays in the form of piloerection, arched posture, tail-lashing and occasional chases of members of the same sex. Ultimately, one of the groups quietly withdrew so that the function of this behaviour appears to be to determine the territorial boundary. Recorded playbacks of the group calling near their territorial boundary had a similar attractant effect on the neighbouring group. Wolf howling (see Harrington and Mech, 1979) attracts separated pack members while repelling other groups. Waser and Homewood (1979) however failed to detect any response to loud calls from neighbouring groups of mangabey (*Cerocebus galeritus* and *C. albigena*) and, in the former species, neighbouring groups sometimes mixed amicably.

Elaborate visual advertisement is uncommon but is shown by some large mammals living in habitats where visibility is good. A plains antelope, the blue wildebeest, shows at least 30 behaviour patterns in this context including cavorting, leaping, bucking, digging with the horns, head-shaking and stamping.

Display and advertisement commonly play an important role in territorial defence and the intimidation of opponents. Sometimes, however, two evenly matched individuals will meet and challenge one another. In this situation, the arbitrary rule 'resource holder wins' may be applied, so that damaging fighting is avoided (see Chapter 4). The cost of defence may also be reduced by the operation of the 'dear enemy' phenomenon, whereby the individual is much more tolerant towards neighbouring territory-owners than it is to unfamiliar transients. The former present far less threat than the latter in terms of complete territorial takeover. Quantitative data exemplifying this situation were obtained for deermice (*Peromyscus maniculatus*) by Healey (1967), who found statistically significant differences in the level of aggression displayed towards individuals with adjacent home ranges as compared with previously unfamiliar mice.

5.4.2 Territoriality: mammalian examples

A good example of a mammal which defends its individual home range is the short-tailed shrew (*Blarina brevicauda*) studied by Platt (1976). Using a radioisotope technique, Platt found that each shrew occupied a defended area of approximately 300m². Males and females held independent territories, although those of opposite sex overlapped in the breeding season. The boundaries were marked with secretions from the lateral and ventral glands. On meeting, shrews engaged in vocalization duels in which they screamed at one another and which sometimes led to physical assault and fighting. Most of the aggression which Platt recorded was between resident and nomadic shrews, not between territorial neighbours. Nomads were either the young of that year or residents emigrating from areas of low food density. Residents patrolled the boundaries of their territories but rarely intruded into those of their neighbours. The size of the shrew's territory was little larger than the area used daily but territory size was influenced by food resources, reflected in the density of field mice and invertebrates upon which the shrews preyed. As food supplies became less plentiful, so the territory increased in size until a critical point was reached when it became too poor to sustain the shrew, which then adopted a nomadic habit until it found a territory in a richer area. Nomads tended to remain on the boundaries of established territories, rarely intruding into occupied areas. They vocalized only when in the process of displacing a resident from its territory, so that the vocalization appears to be a form of offensive threat. In the laboratory, shrews sometimes had vocalization duels which did not involve attack but simply led to the two animals dividing an area between them.

In the majority of mammals individuals of the opposite sex are tolerant of one another with the result that territories are defended only against members of the same sex. Where male and female territories are of the same size with complete overlap, the species are monogamous. Examples are known from a variety of mammalian orders, including elephant shrews, klipspringers, coyotes and gibbons. In this situation, each partner drives out members of its own sex (see Chapter 3). Where male territories are larger than those of females, a polygynous situation may exist if a male can totally include the territory of more than one female within his own. Male common tree shrews have been found (Kawamichi and Kawamichi, 1979) to defend a territory which usually included that of a single female, but occasionally males had larger territories which included those of two or three females.

The sportive lemur (*Lepilemur mustelinus*) is a territorial, tree-living, nocturnal mammal where both sexes hold territories. Male territories are larger (average 0.30 hectares) than those of females (0.18 hectares). Defence is most marked in the male who uses surveillance posts in trees from which he can see his rivals, and both vocal and visual displays are given. The latter consist of shaking the head from side to side, leaping and shaking branches. Such a visual display is unusual in a nocturnal mammal. Neighbours display to one another and may even vocalize together, forming duets or trios. Male territories contain those of several females; up to five have been recorded and males appear to mate opportunistically with any female in heat (see Hladik and Charles-Dominique, 1974).

Frequently female mammals have an undefended home range, the selection of their living area being mainly dependent upon suitable breeding sites such as burrows; males, on the other hand, are territorial and a male territory may contain several female home ranges. This situation has already been described for mustelid carnivores in Chapter 3 (see Erlinge, 1968), and Carl (1971) suggested that mate selection in a ground squirrel, the long-tailed souslik (*Spermophilus undulatus*), results from two independent factors, first the female's selection of a suitable burrow system, which she defends against other females, and secondly a male's dominance over a particular district. To obtain maximum mating success a male should acquire a territory which includes several suitable sites in which females can breed.

In the species so far described, non-territorial individuals are nomadic, avoiding occupied territories unless challenging the owner. In some species, however, non-territorial males may be tolerated and occupy subordinate status within a territory. Bearder and Martin (1979) found this situation in the lesser bushbaby (*Galago senegalensis mohohi*) where a territorial male associated with females and young, while subordinate and juvenile males lived peripherally and did not breed.

A similar hierarchical system also operates in prairie dogs, studied by King (1955). Each social group or 'coterie' is confined to a territory held by a dominant male, who displays by leaping and rearing up on the hind legs while uttering a trisyllabic call. The coterie boundary is traditional and may be maintained over many generations even though the territorial males may change. Females defend their breeding burrow when rearing families. The young learn the boundaries of the coterie and males tend to emigrate to take over other coteries, while females remain in the area of their birth.

The male white rhinoceros is territorial and his breeding success depends on holding a territory (see p. 128). Two-thirds of adult males (alphas) hold territories, while females are more mobile and move through the males' territories. A territorial male actively attempts to prevent an oestrous female from leaving his territory by standing between her and the border. Alpha males tolerate subordinate males (betas) which live in their territory and, on meeting, the beta emits a submissive shriek or snarl. Unfamiliar males are attacked. Alpha males meet very occasionally at the territorial border, on average once every two weeks. Sometimes the two males charge and wrestle horn-to-horn. Trespassing alpha males, often on the way to a water hole, give the submissive snarl and retreat on meeting the territory owner. Alpha males mark the territory with dung, which the animal kicks and spreads out, and also spray urine. Beta males and females defaecate on dung heaps approximately half of the time but do not spray urine. Dung heaps are especially prominent on territorial boundaries and spray-urinating by alpha males occurs both on the boundary and on well-marked trails.

Territorial takeover occurs when a male is successfully challenged by a beta male from another area. The former alpha is tolerated and remains in his territorial area but ceases to kick dung and spray-urinate. The new alpha male takes over the old territorial boundaries but also attempts to increase his territory size. Juvenile white rhinoceros are driven away by the mother at 2–3 years of age on the birth of a new offspring, when they join subadult groups of up to six individuals. Cows separate from these groups at 9–10 years old and bulls at 11–12, when they become fully-grown and sexually mature.

In more social species it is common for non-breeding males to join bachelor herds. Breeding males may hold year-round territories, with females moving into these areas during the rut, but in other cases males are only territorial during the breeding season. Sometimes males defend very small areas which are used solely for breeding, a situation which is common in eared seals (Otariidae) and some true seals (Phocidae).

Male Steller sea lions defend an area of the beach which includes a group of females; as the females are relatively mobile, individuals may come and go at will (but see Figure 5.6). A similar situation was recorded from the grey seal by Fogden, 1971. Weddell's seals (*Leptonychotes wedelli*)breed on ice and the females congregate near an ice hole around which a male defends an underwater territory. Males (unusually for a polygynous species) are actually smaller than females.

Another example of male territorial behaviour restricted to the breeding season is that of the lek. Females appear to mate selectively with males holding certain territories within the lek. Bradbury (1977b) laid down certain criteria for defining a lek breeding system which he divided into primary and secondary features. Primary criteria which are present in all leks are as follows: absence of male parental care, existence of a mating arena, male territories which contain no resources other than access to a female, and finally female selection of mating partners. Secondary criteria, which may be present, are: strong sexual dimorphism, males maturing later than females, traditional locations for arenas, extreme ritualization of male displays, mating restricted to a small number of males in the arena and a region in the arena where the most successful males aggregate. Lek mating systems with all these criteria are found in the hammer-headed bat (*Hypsignathus monstrosus*) and the Uganda kob and these will be briefly described.

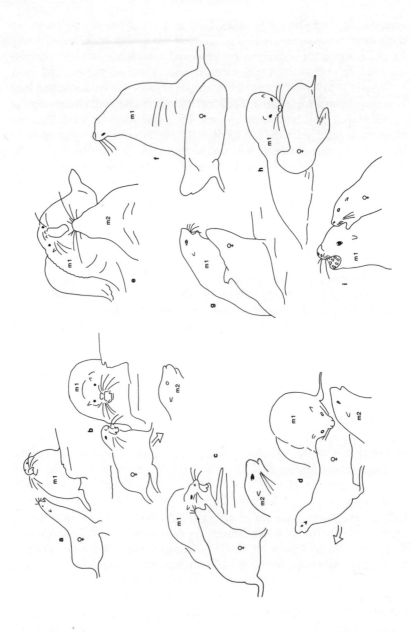

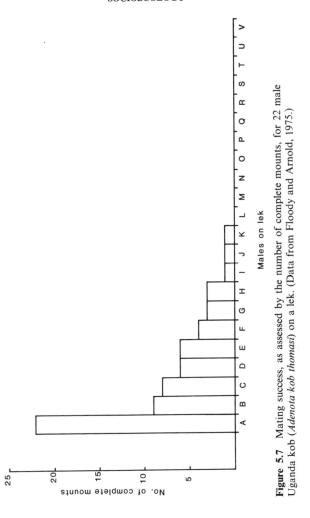

Figure 5.7 Mating success, as assessed by the number of complete mounts, for 22 male Uganda kob (*Adenota kob thomasi*) on a lek. (Data from Floody and Arnold, 1975.)

← **Figure 5.6** Steller sea lion (*Eumetopias jubata*) territorial behaviour and courtship: (*a*) female moving to boundary male (m1) blocking her; (*b*) female moves towards second male (m2); (*c*) female near territory boundary, male 1 stretches his neck; (*d*) male 1 herds female away from male 2, who vocalizes; (*e*) males give boundary display with erected vibrissae; (*f*) female prostrate; (*g*) female shows positive orientation to male 1 with body contact and female mounting; (*h*) female shows positive body contact; (*i*) female bites male 1, male with relaxed open mouth. (Drawings from photographs by Sandegren, 1976).

The hammer-headed bat was studied by Bradbury (1977b) in Gabon, Central Africa. In the biennial breeding seasons males assemble at traditional breeding sites where each male defends an area by hanging from a branch uttering loud display calls and flapping the wings. Each male is separated from his neighbour by 13–18 m, on average with as many as 84 others in a single lek area. Males attack other males who approach them, and the females approach and inspect the males; 6% of males were responsible for 40 out of 50 recorded copulations and the successful males were found in mating centres within the lek. Males leave the lek to forage up to 10km away during the day but return to the same branch to display at night. The species is highly sexually dimorphic; males are 1.79 times heavier than females and are mature at 18 months as compared with six months for the female.

An antelope, the Uganda kob (*Adenota kob thomasi*) also shows lek behaviour. The males defend small territories 15–30m in diameter in a traditional breeding ground where they advertise to females by whistling and visual display. A relatively small number of males are responsible for the majority of copulations and these males hold territories near the centre of the lek (Figure 5.7). Leks are of particular interest because territories apparently contain no particular resource. It has generally been asserted that males compete for particular locations but Bradbury and Gibson (1983) cast doubt on this and considered that the criteria for female choice are still unidentified.

Some gregarious mammals defend group territories. Both sexes co-operate for defence purposes in wolves, hyaenas and common marmosets, but defence is the prerogative of the male in lions and chimpanzees. Matrilineal groups of common langurs defend territories, while a male simply defends the group of females against rival males.

5.5 Summary

1. The factors which determine the nature of mammalian social organization are mating strategy, gregariousness, intolerance of conspecifics, non-sexual affectional bonds, complexity of communication, mechanism of inbreeding avoidance, group mobility, fecundity and longevity, and ecological factors such as food, climate and spatial restrictions.

2. Mammalian social organizations have been classified, according to sociability, mating strategy and territoriality, into 23 major types which are described in the text and listed in Table 5.2.

3. The forms taken by social organization have been shown to be influenced by diet, feeding strategy and climate.

4. A solitary way of life is generally adopted by mammals whose food is scattered in small rich packets.

5. Group-living mammals usually seek food which is found in large rich concentrations.

6. Pack-hunting enables carnivores to kill larger prey, and is associated with the occurrence of large prey or large herds of prey.

7. Herbivores are generally found in small groups if they are browsers, while grazers form the largest social groups and include the largest-bodied mammals.

8. Group size in closely related herbivores is also related to food selectivity. The largest group sizes are found in the least selective grazers e.g. social kangaroos and wallabies and African antelopes. Some mammals are gregarious; in some instances this habit results from restrictions in resting or breeding sites. There are, however, a number of advantages which may be derived from living in groups, such as protection against predators, increased feeding efficiency as a result of cooperative feeding strategies, or gains in inclusive fitness as a result of altruistic behaviour towards relatives. Any or all of these may be applicable in a particular case.

9. Mammals as diverse as dolphins and chimpanzees have flexible groups which can adapt their party size to the nature and abundance of clumped food resources.

10. Alpine rodents, such as marmots, because of the short grazing season and the slow rate of maturity, may form longer-lasting family associations than solitary congenerics living in lowland regions.

11. Attempts to provide a single ecological explanation for the varieties of form taken by primate social organization have been unsuccessful. It is doubtful whether such an approach is valid.

12. A territory is a defended area occupied by an individual or group. Three types of territory are found in mammals, defended home range, breeding territory and mating territory.

13. A mammal only defends a home range if it is economical to do so. The territory must contain adequate food for its existence, otherwise the system breaks down. The economics of territorial defence depend upon the cost of excluding others and the value of exclusive ownership. There is a relation between size of home range, length of daily ranging path and territorial defence.

14. Breeding territories are found in the highly mobile bats and pinnipeds. Females settle in the area to give birth to young while males defend them to acquire exclusive mating rights.

15. Mating territories may vary in size from the male's entire home range to a small defended area or a lek. Females only mate with territorial males, so that breeding success for the male depends upon his ability to retain an exclusive area.

16. Forms of territorial advertisement are discussed. (i) The pattern and economics of scent-marking are considered. The view that an intruder compares the territorial scent mark with the odour of any individual whom it meets within the area seems to accord well with the facts. (ii) Vocal advertisement has the advantage that it can carry over a considerable distance and save energy by decreasing the need for patrolling. (iii) Visual displays are generally typical of diurnal species with relatively small territories in open habitats.

CHAPTER SIX

AN ORDER-BY-ORDER SYNOPSIS OF SOCIAL BEHAVIOUR

For each order of mammals the range of social structure, reproductive strategies, parental behaviour and communication systems together with any other factors of special interest will be outlined. In classifying social organization the system devised in Chapter 5 will be followed (see Table 5.2).

6.1 Monotremata

Field data for the three genera are largely anecdotal, but platypus (*Ornithorhynchus anatinus*) have been described as particularly intolerant to conspecifics of both sexes outside the female's oestrous period, so it seems probable that they are solitary and exclusively spaced. Spiny anteaters (*Tachyglossus, Zaglossus*) are believed not to be territorial but to live solitary lives; their organization involves independent dispersal of the two sexes.

In captivity the male platypus courts for several weeks while several male *Tachyglossus* have been observed in the field to congregate around an oestrous female and may compete for her. Monotremes are *K*-selected. *Tachyglossus* produces a single egg carried by the female in her pouch, while *Ornithorhynchus* lays 1–2 eggs in a nest. The young are weaned by 4–5 months and may accompany their mother on foraging excursions. They have been known to live for between 14 (platypus) and 50 (*Tachyglossus*) years in captivity.

Chemical communication utilizes the cloacal gland; vocalizations include growling and hissing in the platypus and sniffing in *Tachyglossus*. The platypus appears to have a wider behavioural repertoire, which includes rubbing, crawling over, nibbling and allogrooming. In *Tachyglossus*, aggression consists of butting and pushing.

Platypus behaviour has been described by Burrell (1927), Fleay (1944), Strahan and Thomas (1975) and Griffiths (1978), and that of *Tachyglossus* by Dobruka (1960), Griffiths (1968), Brattstrom (1973), and Augee *et al.* (1975). Nothing appears to be known of the behaviour of *Zaglossus*, the New Guinea spiny anteater.

6.2 Marsupialia

The majority of marsupials are solitary-living in independent home ranges, as is the case of the American opossum *Didelphys* (see Chapter 5) and the Tasmanian devil (*Sarcophilus harrissii*) (see Guiler, 1970a, b). The sugar glider *Petaurus breviceps*, according to Schultze-Westrum (1965), lives in family groups and male and female live in the same nest so it is possible that this species may be monogamous. The most sociable of the marsupials are certain members of the genus *Macropus* (kangaroos and wallabies) such as *M. rufus* and *M. parryi* which live in multimale/multifemale herds or mobs (see Kaufman, 174b, and Chapter 5).

Young marsupials are born at an extremely premature stage, necessitating a long period of maternal care (see Chapter 3). After the young become detached from the mother's nipple some species continue to carry them around for a considerable period, for example *Marmosa*, the mouse opossum (Hunsaker and Shupe, 1977); others such as *Antechinus* leave them in an underground nest (Settle and Croft, 1982). During the later part of lactation young *Macropus* follow their mother on foot. Marsupial maternal behaviour resembles that of other mammals and includes allo-grooming, licking and ingesting the young's excrement and urine; some species (e.g. *Marmosa, Antechinus*) retrieve young who have strayed. The weaned young of carnivorous or insectivorous marsupials may accompany their mother on foraging excursions before becoming fully independent.

Some marsupials such as *Didelphys, Marmosa* and *Antechinus* are short-lived with a lifespan of 1–2 years and produce up to 12 offspring (*r*-selected), while at the other extreme (*K*-selected) are the wombats (*Vombatus*) and *Macropus*, which are long-lived and produce only a single offspring at a time.

The communication system in marsupials has been reviewed by Eisenberg and Golani (1977), Eisenberg (1981), Croft (1982). Scent-marking through the deposition of saliva, urine and faeces, and cloacal, chin, cheek, ventral and sternal rubbing have all been observed. Olfactory investigation of mouth, nasal region and cloacal area all occur in dasyurids. Vocalizations include alarm calls (chatter, huff, bark), agonistic calls (hiss, churr, pant-hiss, chatter, snort, cough, moan, whine, shriek) and contact calls between young and mother (chirp) and members of the opposite sex (click or cluck). In some Dasyurids e.g. the tiger quoll (*Dasyurus maculatus*) there is a mating call; males and females call to one another at dawn and dusk, alternately calling and listening (duetting); see Fanning (1982), Croff (1982). Some marsupials emit soft calls during copulation.

Agonistic behaviour includes open-mouth threat, upright, facing and lateral postures and submissive crouching and lying on the back. Copulation is often long-lasting, two hours being common, but as long as five hours in *Marmosa* (see Croft, 1982).

The communication system of marsupials appears to be of a similar order of complexity to that of eutherian mammals of similar lifestyle.

Further information on marsupial behaviour and biology can be found in Tyndale-Biscoe (1973), Hunsaker (1977), Stonehouse and Gilmore (1977) and Archer (1982).

6.3 Insectivora

The majority of Insectivora are believed to be solitary, like the short-tailed shrew whose social organization is described in Chapter 5. The only species known to be social is the streaked tenrec (*Hemicentetes semispinosus*) which is colonial, living in complex burrow systems. Eisenberg (1981) has indicated that the species may be polygynous, with a colonial harem system. The fact that the female will tolerate the presence of a male in her burrow after the young are two weeks old lends support to the view that he is probably their father.

The young of Insectivora are all altricial. Some species give birth to one or two young (eg *Solenodon*), while the majority produce between two and eight (e.g. *Sorex, Blarina, Neomys*) and are *r*-selected, some temperate species being semelparous. The record litter size is found in the tailless tenrec (*Tenrec ecaudatus*) which gives birth to as many as 32 offspring! There is extensive parental care and weaned young spend a period following the mother on hunting expeditions. In shrews (*Crocidura*) the phenomenon of 'caravanning' has been observed where a nest has been disturbed. The mother leads the young away to safety and each individual holds the tail of the animal in front.

Social communication is largely by chemicals and vocalization. Territorial marking with faeces is common and communication includes mutual sniffing of scent glands on meeting. Hedgehogs (*Erinaceus*) anoint themselves with saliva. Vocalizations associated with aggression, contact, lost young and mating have all been observed. Visual signals are few but many species show open-mouth threat and lordosis. Various upright, sideways or prone postures are adopted in agonistic encounters but it is not known whether these are visual signals *per se*. Social communication in insectivores has been reviewed by Poduschka (1977), but the behaviour of these common animals has tended to be neglected.

6.4 Macroscelidea (elephant shrews)

Two of these small cursorial African mammals, whose diet consists mainly of invertebrates, have been studied in the field by Rathbun (1979). Both the small (58 g) *Elephantulus rufescens* and the larger (450 g) *Rhynchocyon chrysopygus* are monogamous and territorial, and aggression is directed towards same-sex conspecifics. Contact between the pair is only intermittent, consisting of nose-to-nose greeting and, at times presumably when the female is in oestrus, the male follows her and attempts to mount.

The mother gives birth to 1–2 precocial young and operates an absentee parental system, visiting the litter at daily intervals to suckle. The young may play together and are capable of locomotion within hours of birth. (Mean interbirth intervals are 61 days for *Elephantulus* and 82 for *Rhynchocyon*. Young *E. rufescens* are driven out of the parental territory about ten days after weaning, when six weeks old; by contrast, the young of *Rhynchocyon*, at two weeks old, follow their mother on foraging expeditions over a five-day period.) They remain in the parental territory until they find a territory of their own when between 32 and 200 days old. In one territory a pair of *R. chrysopygus* and three consecutive young, ranging from 11–108 days post-nest emergence, lived in one territory.

Paternal investment is restricted to mobbing predators and, in *E. rufescens*, clearing trails. The pair bond in *E. rufescens* is life-long (2–3 years) and the two sexes are of similar adult size. The female appears to be dominant. In this species both parents defended termite concentrations against same-sex conspecifics.

Detailed social communication has not been studied, but territorial boundaries were scent-marked with the subcaudal gland in *R. chryosopygus*; *E. rufescens* used perineal and sternal glands and also marked the boundary with faeces and urine. Aggressive territorial defence in both species was acompanied by a display (tail-slapping on the substrate) in *Rhynchocyon* and drumming with the rear feet to produce a 'prrr prrr prrr' sound in *Elephantulus*.

6.5 Scandentia (tree shrews)

The tree shrew (*Tupaia glis*) was found by Kawamichi and Kawamichi (1979, 1982) to be monogamous and territorial. Male territories generally overlapped that of a single female but some males, which had larger territories, were polygynous and had territory including those of up to three females. Sometimes two generations of offspring coexisted in the parental territory but sexually mature males were driven out before females, usually when their mother was approaching oestrus.

In *T. glis* (= *belangeri*), twin young are born in a nursery nest which the mother visits every 48 hours for lactation (see Martin, 1968). The young are relatively altricial, being naked and blind at birth. Their eyes open at three weeks old but they are homoiothermous from birth and are capable of grooming themselves from the first day of life. Maternal care consists only of lactation and the ingestion of the infant's urine and faeces. They leave the nest at 7–8 weeks old and littermates typically remain together, sometimes playing socially until they reach sexual maturity at nine weeks.

The communication system of tree shrews has been described by Martin (1968), Sorensen (1970) and Kawamichi and Kawamichi (1979). They are aggressive to same-sex conspecifics. Males use chin, anal and sternal glands to scent-mark their territory on conspicuous objects such as tree trunks, fallen trees and roots above the ground surface.

Six vocalizations have been described for *Tupaia longipes*: warning, threat, aggression, fear, excitement and infant calls. Other species may have fewer. An open-mouth defensive threat is recognized and receptive females present their genitalia to a male. Nuzzling, allogrooming and sleeping in contact all occur and social play has been identified by Sorensen (1970).

6.6 Pholidota (pangolins)

The ecology of these mammals has been studied by Pages (1965, 1970, 1972a, b, 1976). They are arboreal and solitary, males occupying large exclusive territories (20 hectares) which overlap those of several females (3.5 hectares). Males distinguish territorial neighbours from transients to whom they show aggressive behaviour and unreceptive females are hostile to males.

The single precocial young is born in a nest, but after two weeks clings to its mother's neck or the base of her tail; on occasions where two females meet, their offspring may play together.

Pangolins scent-mark their home range with the anal glands; they defaecate in the ground and bury the faeces. Males are highly aggressive to one another, while females are not. The male has a single aggressive display which involves standing on the hind legs in a tripoidal stance and attempting to claw the opponent. As these animals have reduced dentition, they do not use biting in aggression, and the absence of allogrooming relates to the scaly nature of their coat.

6.7 Edentata

This order is comprised of three distinct groups, the anteaters, sloths and armadillos. The majority are solitary species living spaced out in a home range. Armadillos of the genus *Dasypus*, however, often nest in colonial burrows, although nothing is known of their mating strategy or social organization.

Sloths and anteaters have a long gestation period of between six months and one year and produce a single precocial offspring, which is left in a nest in the case of anteaters, but carried by the mother in sloths. Female anteaters are known to carry their young when moving them from one nest site to another (Montgomery and Lubin, 1977, 1978). In contrast to other edentates, armadillos generally produce more than one semialtricial offspring. The genus *Dasypus* is remarkable in giving birth to up to five offspring all derived from a single egg. Any signs of exceptional altruism between these sibs, which might be expected by kin selection theory, has so far been undetected, but the species has not been well studied. Young armadillos of the genus *Euphractus* are suckled and groomed by their mother for two months and any which stray are retrieved. The young are highly vocal, uttering squeals and clicks. The group as a whole is *K*-selected and it may be that the polyembryony of *Dasypus* is one way of adopting a more *r*-selected strategy.

Montgomery and Sunquist (1974, 1978) found that the two-toed sloth *Choloepus hoffmani* marks its home range with secretions from its cloacal gland and nostrils (from the orbital gland). The only forms of sound communication known are the distress calls of the young, clapping of the jaws and hissing and puffing. The anteaters *Myrmecophaga* and *Tamandua* also growl in addition to the hissing and puffing and distress calls. Armadillos have a slightly larger repertoire, producing up to six sound types (see Eisenberg, 1981). The communicative value of these various sounds is not clear but it is apparent that the edentates have a very restricted vocal repertoire. Nothing appears to be known about their visual displays or tactile communication.

Like pangolins, armadillos of the genus *Dasypus* and the sloth *Bradypus* are known to bury their faeces (Montgomery and Sunquist, 1975), but the significance of this behaviour is not known.

6.8 Lagomorpha (rabbits, hares and pikas)

Three different types of social organization have been identified in this order. Hares (e.g. *Lepus*) are solitary animals with precocial hider young who assemble to be fed every 24 hours. Pikas (*Ochotona*) are colonial animals and a male's territory may include one or more females. Rabbits (*Oryctolagus*) are also colonial but live in multimale/multifemale colonies which are female bonded. There may be distinct male and female dominance hierarchies; the dominant male and female are responsible for most of the breeding (see Chapter 5).

The offspring of lagomorphs are precocial in hares, but altricial in pikas and rabbits. In all species, feeding the young occurs infrequently at 24- or 48-hour intervals. Hares produce between three and five young but rabbits may have up to fifteen in a litter.

Lagomorphs have a well-developed chemical communication system, using chin marking, cheek marking, paw scraping, urine and faeces to mark their territories. Dominant male rabbits are responsible for 80% of marking (see Bell, 1980). Rabbits and hares are not very vocal, but pikas have a wide vocal repertoire; short calls are a response to a territorial intrusion, while territorial males produce a song which lasts up to 30 seconds (see Jones, 1973). Rabbits are aggressive to same-sex adults and dominant and submissive postures can be recognized; they also have a greeting ceremony with naso-chin and naso-genital contact. Males may enurinate by squirting or spraying urine onto a female.

Although this is a small order of mammals there is a large literature on it because of the importance of rabbits as pests (see Southern, 1948; Mykytowycz, 1958, 1959, 1960, 1968; Myers and Schneider 1964; Mykytowycz and Dudzniski, 1972; Kawamichi, 1976).

6.9 Rodentia

The large majority of rodents are solitary and some are territorial while others, such as field mice (*Apodemus*), have undefended home ranges. Elliott (1978) observed that male Eastern chipmunks (*Tamias striatus*) actively competed for an oestrous female by forming a loose dominance hierarchy even though they are normally territorial and solitary.

Some rodents are colonial; for example, the male yellow-bellied marmot defends a territory which includes a female-bonded harem. While female burrow-mates have a 90% overlap in their territories and 74% of their interactions have been observed to be amicable, 86% of interburrow confrontations were agonistic. Some rodents such as the cursorial South American agouti (*Dasyprocta punctata*) are usually facultatively monogamous. Male and female territories completely overlap and each member of the pair defends it against intrusion by like-sex conspecifics. A minority of males are, however, polygynous. Defence of territory is related to food abundance, being most intense when food is short (see Smythe, 1978). Grade II monogamy has been identified in a number of rodents such as the beaver and is also believed to exist in the prairie vole (*Micotus ochrogaster*) and the old field mouse (*Peromyscus polionotus*).

Prairie dogs (*Cynomys ludovicianus*) and Belding's ground squirrels live in multimale/multifemale colonies made up of territorial female-bonded clans. Males emigrate to breed. Ewer (1971), found that black rats (*Rattus rattus*) live in bisexual colonies with independent male and female hierarchies; also females generally bred in their natal group.

Some rodents may have variable social organization dependent on the nature of their environment and population density. The house mouse (*Mus musculus*) ranges from being solitary and territorial to forming multimale/multifemale colonies (Reimer and Petras, 1967; Berry 1970, 1981). The yellow-bellied marmot is generally colonial but in areas where suitable burrow sites are not clumped together they may be widely distributed (Johns and Armitage, 1979).

The only known eusocial vertebrate is the rodent *Heterocephalus glaber* whose social behaviour is described in Chapter 3. It possesses a female reproductive caste and three other castes, non-workers, occasional workers and frequent workers. Female members of these castes appear to be sterile and it is probable that the male non-workers mate with the fertile female (see Jarvis, 1981).

Most rodents have altricial young apart from the spiny mouse (*Acomys cahirhinus*) and South American cursorial histricomorph rodents, such as guinea pigs (*Cavia spp*) and agouti (*Dasyprocta*) whose young are precocial.

Maternal care in most rodents with altricial young is extensive and, in some species (*Microtus ochrogaster, Peromyscus polionotus* and *Meriones ungiculatus*), there is also paternal care (see Elwood, 1977).

Many rodents are highly r-selected, especially those in latitudes where there may be great varieties in environmental conditions, making this strategy an adaptation which allows the animal to respond rapidly to the arrival of favourable environmental conditions. Mace and Eisenberg (1982) related reproductive rate, longevity and brain size in the genus *Peromyscus*; they found that reproductive rate and brain size were negatively correlated and that brain size was positively correlated with the number of sympatric species.

Social signals in rodents have been described for a wide variety of species. Grant and Mackintosh (1963) provided the first comparative description, classifying behaviour into acts and postures in rats, mice and guinea pigs. Barnett (1958) described the behaviour of the brown rat and Eisenberg (1968) that of deermice (*Peromyscus*).

There is a very extensive literature on the communication systems of rodents; they have a chemical signalling system which utilizes urine, faeces and glandular secretions (see Chapter 2). Vocal signals range into the ultrasonic (Noirot, 1969) and are used largely in an agonistic context but the young also utter an ultrasonic distress call. Berryman (1976) described eleven different vocalizations in five functional categories for the guinea pig. Tactile behaviour includes allogrooming, crawling under and biting. Many species of rodent play socially, and the social play of the Columbian ground squirrel (Steiner, 1971) and the laboratory rat (Poole and Fish, 1975, 1976) have been described in detail. A useful bibliography of the literature on social organization in mice is given by Bronson (1979).

6.10 Hyracoidea

Hyraxes are rodent-like mammals which are believed to be related to ungulates. They are colonial grazers or browsers. *Procavia* has a colonial harem system in which the dominant males defend groups of females. Hoeck (1982) studied hyrax colonies on rock outcrops (kopjes) in the Serengeti. *Procavia johnsoni* and *Heterohyrax brucei* were found in the same habitat islands, with colonies ranging in size from 2–16 in *P. johnsoni* and 5–78 in *H. brucei*. Male dispersal is usual, so that females are closely related. Peer groups of juveniles are found in crèches, with subadults and adults acting as sentries.

There is a long gestation period of $7\frac{1}{2}$ months, after which the female produces between one and four precocial young (Mendelssohn, 1965). Both species have territorial calls and the arboreal *Dendrohyrax* also appears to use vocalization to ensure spacing.

6.11 Tubulidentata (aardvarks)

The African aardvark (*Orycteropus afer*) which feeds on ants, termites and fruit, leads a solitary existence in a large home range. Little is known of aardvark ecology and behaviour but Melton (1976) stated that males are nomadic while females are stationary. They nest in burrows and produce a single young after a long gestation period (seven months). No quantitative data are available on the social behaviour of these mammals.

6.12 Perissodactyla (odd-toed ungulates)

Perissodactyls range in social structure from the solitary browsing tapirs through the slightly more sociable rhinoceroses to the highly social zebras and horses.

The South American tapir is a solitary browsing mammal which has a long gestation period (13 months) and, like all perissodactyls, gives birth to a single precocial young.

Breeding male rhinoceroses are generally spaced out or territorial. When younger, however, they may be more sociable, and sub-adult male Indian rhinoceroses (*Rhinoceros unicornis*) and African black rhinoceroses (*Diceros bicornis*) form dominance hierarchies. Breeding males are spaced in both species, but male ranges overlap in *D. bicornis* and adult males are hostile to one another and compete for oestrous females. Related females of *D. bicornis* may form long-term associations (see Goddard 1966, 1967). The social organization of the white rhinoceros (*Ceratotherium simum*) has been described in Chapter 5 and takes the form of male territories with sub-adult and subordinate adult males coexisting peacefully with the alpha male (see Owen Smith, 1975).

The horse family (Equidae) contains the most social species of perissodactyls (see Klingel, 1975). Two types of social organization exist. In one (Klingel's type II) breeding males are territorial and oestrous females mate only with these males. Territorial males allow non-territorial males to enter their territory and permit them to approach and sniff anal and nasal regions before chasing them off for 50–100m. Non-breeding males and females may be sociable and form herds, but there are no permanent associations between individuals. Examples of this type of social structure are found in equids living in arid and semi-arid environments, e.g. asses (*E. hemionus, E. africanus*) (see Klingel, 1977a) and Grevy's zebra (*E. grevyi*). Territorial ownership is advertised by roaring and by scent-marking with dung piles and urine.

The second type of social organization in equids is one in which there are permanent groups of females and young who are probably closely related. These are taken over by a male who defends the group against other males; non-breeding males live in hierarchically-organized bachelor herds. Young female plains zebras (*E. burchelli*) are abducted at the age of 13–15 months by an adult male who challenges the harem owner, in contrast to the mountain zebra (*E. zebra*), where some female foals are driven out by their mothers; in feral horses (*E.caballus*) young mares leave spontaneously. Stallions, in all species, leave the harem of their own accord. Harem owners abandon their females if successfully challenged by a younger male (see Klingel, 1974). Berger (1977) in a study of feral horses in the Grand Canyon found that band sizes (harems) varied from 3–5, with a single male; other stallions were solitary. There was a hierarchy among band stallions which was unrelated to harem size. Aggression between stallions took the form of rearing, kicking with the forefeet, biting while rearing and during pursuit, and kicking with the hind feet.

Perissodactyls give birth to a single precocial follower-type offspring which is usually rejected by its mother when a second offspring is born.

There is a whole repertoire of communicative signals in Perissodactyla (see Klingel, 1977b). In addition to the use of urine and faeces for territorial marking, personal recognition appears to involve perineal, anal and circum-oral scent glands. Females produce chemical signals which indicate their oestrous condition. Auditory communication includes contact calls (the bray) distress calls, and vocalizations expressive of excitement or submission. Seven calls have been described for the white rhinoceros: aggressive snorting, bellowing, bass bellowing and shrieking, submissive squealing or distress call, courtship grunting and, when rejected by a female, trumpeting. There are few visual signals in tapirs and rhinoceroses, but equids have a rich repertoire involving head, tail, legs, ear positions, and lips and also flehmen. These are found in the contexts of threat, greeting, courtship, play, contact and territorial display. Tactile communication includes play biting and allogrooming.

6.13 Proboscoidea (elephants)

The female herd with young forms the stable group in elephants. These groups are believed to be matriarchal, i.e. females remain in their natal herd to breed while males are driven out at puberty or leave of their own accord. Females form kinship groups which, on meeting, show elaborate greeting ceremonies and much excitement.

When a male African elephant (*Loxodonta africanus*) leaves the nursery herd he may join other males in a bull group, usually of 2–3 individuals, but occasionally larger. Bull groups appear to be temporary aggregations but there is evidence that the bulls in an area know one another and have a hierarchical organization. Sexually inactive male African elephants associate together and exhibit low levels of aggression. High-ranking males, however, have intermittent periods of heightened sexual activity known as 'musth' (see p. 14). During this period they leave the male group and compete for females which are in oestrus. Only one male from any bull area is in musth at any one time so that direct sexual competition occurs only between bulls from different areas. Moss and Poole (1983) suggested that bulls from the same area are related, if so, this pattern of reproductive behaviour will serve to reduce direct competition between kin. While 35–40% of African bull elephants are solitary, this way of life is typical of bull Asiatic elephants (*Elephas maximus*), although an older male may sometimes be accompanied by a younger one. Each bull has his own home range which is undefended, while herds cover much larger areas; if a cow is in oestrus, bulls in the area through which the herd passes attach themselves to it. The highest-ranking male mates with the oestrous female (see Eisenberg *et al.*, 1971; Douglas-Hamilton, 1973; Douglas-Hamilton and Douglas-Hamilton, 1975; Leuthold, 1977).

Female elephants give birth after 22 months' gestation to a single precocial follower young. Parental care is long and extensive and the calf is suckled for over a year. Calves may suckle from females other than their mother and are protected by all members of the cow herd.

Male elephants have an orbital gland which produces a copious secretion during the period of musth, which is rubbed on trees. They also produce a variety of vocal signals which include contact calls and aggressive trumpeting. Visual displays include movements of the ears, trunk, head and 'standing tall', sometimes with the front feet on a raised object. The trunk may also have a function in tactile signalling. Male elephants fight using their tusks, sometimes killing their rival by penetrating its brain or chest cavity. Fighting is primarily a pushing match. Redirected aggression includes thrashing and breaking of bushes. Most of the elephant fights which have been observed, however, were between young bulls and were probably only playfighting (Leuthold, 1977).

6.14 Artiodactyla (even-toed ungulates)

This order shows an extremely wide range of social organization, from solitary species such as the mouse deer (*Tragulus*) to highly social animals such as the African buffalo which lives in bisexual herds.

Wild pigs (*Sus scrofa*) are among the most primitive artiodactyls; males are spaced out in undefended home ranges while females form small groups with their young. Each female retires to a nest to give birth and when the young are old enough they join the nursery herd. It seems likely that females in these groups are related. Males, on the other hand, are unsociable and hostile to other males and associate with a female only when she is in oestrus.

The collared peccary (*Tayassu tajacu*) lives in social bisexual herds of 5–15 individuals (mean 7.7). Relations between the herd members are extremely amicable with a great deal of overt affectional behaviour; males do not compete for females. Eleven per cent of males emigrate to breed, and Byers and Bekoff (1981) who studied this species concluded that there must be strong family relationships; they could find no evidence of male or female dominance hierarchies. Females give birth to between one and three precocial young, leaving the herd only for a few hours.

Camels and llamas are harem-forming. The Bactrian camel (*Camelus ferus*) is migratory and, in the rut, each male attempts to defend a group of females. The South American vicuña has by contrast a year-round harem system where each breeding male has a territory and bachelor herds exist outside territorial areas.

The types of social organization found in African ruminants have already been outlined in Chapter 5. These include facultatively monogamous species such as Kirk's dikdik (see Hendricks 1975b), where males alone defend the breeding territory which is demarcated by dung piles; the klipspringer, where both defend it; the Bohor reedbuck where male territories include the home ranges of several females (1–5) and thus form a dispersed harem, although females sometimes move around in groups (mean size 2.09, $n = 228$). Male fawns are driven off before reaching puberty, but females remain with the mother after the next young is born and may sometimes stay in the mother's territory for life. Sub-adult and non-breeding males live in areas between territories in undefended home ranges (see Hendricks, 1975a).

Many artiodactyls show territorial polygyny, where females are herd-living and move through the territories of a number of males. In Coke's hartebeest Gosling (1974) found that 38% of males were territorial, marking their boundaries with dung piles. They attempted to prevent oestrous females from leaving their territory. Juvenile males of 10 months old began to behave submissively to the territorial male, and at 20 months joined a bachelor group with a linear hierarchy partially determined by age. Dominant bachelor group males of 3–4 years attempted to take over territories, usually by entering them when the territorial male was away and challenging him when he returned.

The Uganda kob (see Chapter 5) may adopt a social organization like the Coke's hartebeest, or it may show lek behaviour (see Leuthold, 1966).

African buffalo live in bisexual or bachelor herds with dominance hierarchies, sexual access to females being restricted to dominant males. Mother-offspring bonds are persistent for 2–3 years.

The offspring of all artiodactyls are precocial. Some, such as wildebeest are followers while others, such as red deer are hiders and some members of the pig family such as the warthog nest in burrows. Where the dispersal mechanism has been identified, in most cases it is the male sex which disperses, while females remain in their natal group or find territories close to their mother.

Social communication is very well developed in members of this order and readers are referred to two excellent reviews of artiodactyl social signalling by Leuthold (1977) and Walther (1977). Scent glands on the body for example the perineal, anal and antorbital glands, are sniffed by conspecifics. Many artiodactyls such as gerenuk and Thomson's gazelle leave conspicuous secretions from the antorbital glands on vegetation (see Gosling; 1972, 1981; Walther, 1978b). Territories are frequently marked by dung piles and urine; some species (e.g. eland) mark themselves with urine while others (e.g. lechwe) mark themselves and their females. Gosling (1983) interprets this as a means by which an intruder can compare the identity of a male with the marks left on his territory (see Chapter 5).

Artiodactyls commonly vocalize, and calls have been recorded in the following contexts: contact, mother-young, mating, territorial advertisement, alarm, aggression and distress. Visual displays may be extremely conspicuous in ruminants, in threat, courtship, submission, territorial advertisement and alarm; the head, horns, tail, legs, or whole body may be used and may involve a static posture or a ritualized movement (see Walther, 1978a).

Artiodactyls show some tactile social signals such as licking the genitalia, nudging or prodding with the forefoot or horns, while the courtship of some species involves laying the head on the female's rump or holding the foreleg between the female's hind legs (see Chapter 3).

6.15 Carnivora

Their differences in lifestyle make it essential to consider the two suborders of Carnivora independently.

6.15.1 Fissipedia (terrestrial carnivores)

The social organization of carnivores covers a wide spectrum. Solitary terrestrial species include most of the cat family, bears and civets. Males and females each have a system of home ranges, males overlapping females. The American black bear is an example of a mammal showing this type of social organization.

The weasel family are solitary hunters but each male's territory includes the home ranges of one or more females, making this essentially a dispersed harem (see Lockie, 1966; Erlinge, 1968, 1974, 1977a; King, 1975; Powell, 1979; Gerell, 1970). By contrast male coatis are spaced, with females living in small packs (see Kaufmann, 1962).

The social organization of the dog family has been discussed in Chapter 5, so further detailed accounts will not be given. Fox (1975) classified the Canidae into three types. Type 1 canids are temporarily monogamous, with the pair separating after the young have become independent, for example the red fox (*Vulpes vulpes*). Type 2 are permanently monogamous canids where the pack includes one or two generations of offspring which hunt co-operatively with the parents, for example the golden jackal and coyote. Type 3 canids are permanently social and groups contain several adults of both sexes; there are male and female dominance hierarchies, and breeding is usually restricted to the alpha male and female. This is what I have termed 'status-determined monogamy' and represents the highest level of social organization in carnivores; examples are the wolf, the African hunting dog and the dhole. Status-determined monogamy is also found in the social mongooses (e.g. *Helogale parvula*) (see Rasa 1973a,b; 1977, 1979).

There are two other types of pack-living carnivores which have already been mentioned in Chapter 5. The lion pride contains a group of closely-related female bonded lionesses which is taken over by a group of 1–7 males who may or may not be closely related, depending on whether they originated from the same pride. This type of social organization, is, far as we know, unique to lions.

The other apparently unique type of social grouping is that found in the brown hyaena where packs include both sexes but females breed only with extra-group nomadic males. Female hyaenas are larger than, and do-minant to, male pack-members (see Mills, 1981, 1982). Kruuk (1972) suggested that the reason for female dominance in the spotted hyaena (*Crocuta crocuta*) may be that the large dominant females were more easily able to defend their offspring from possibly cannibalistic males.

Most fissipede carnivores have a relatively short gestation period and give birth to between two and five semi-altricial young (see Chapter 3). Pack-hunting carnivores such as mongooses, wolves, hunting dogs and lions leave their young at the den with a babysitter. There is a relationship between hunting strategy and babysitting: in the case of lions, the females hunt while the males guard the young, and weaned young are allowed to share the carcases of large prey; in a pack of hyaenas, each female produces only one or two young which she leaves in a burrow too small for a large predator to enter; wolves and hunting dogs confine breeding to a single female who produces a large litter (mean size 6.5 for wolf, 7 for *Lycaon*) and herself acts as babysitter.

The ability of canids to bring home excess food which can be regurgitated (see Chapter 3 and Malcolm and Marten, 1982) allows early weaning of the pups at three months. The socioecology of some African carnivores has been reviewed by Bertram (1979).

Communication systems in terrestrial carnivores have been reviewed by Fox and Cohen (1977), Wemmer and Scow (1977) and Pruitt and Burghardt (1977). The repertoires of different carnivores vary so greatly that it is not possible to summarize them briefly, only to draw attention to the major studies and stress the high level of complexity of the communication systems in the Felidae and Canidae.

All carnivores employ scent-marking and most also use faeces and urine to mark their home ranges. The large cats (*Panthera*) may spray urine for a distance of several metres. Cats commonly rub the head and neck on the substrate and may also roll over; clawing and scuffing are probably also forms of social communication. Wemmer and Scow (1977) describe scent-marking patterns in the snow leopard (*Panthera uncia*). Mustelids such as polecats perform anal dragging and rolling on the substrate, and bears rub the body on inanimate objects. Kleiman (1966) reviewed scent-marking in canids, and Peters and Mech (1975) made a study of scent-marking in wolves and came to the conclusion that raised-leg urination marked the pack territory, particularly its boundaries (see Chapter 2).

Many carnivores of the cat and dog families have a wide repertoire of acoustic signalling. These are found in agonistic, territorial, courtship, affectional, playful, fearful, submissive, contact, separation, and defensive contexts. Fox and Cohen (1977) give eight sound-types for canids while Wemmer and Scow (1977) enumerate 6–13 graded calls in felids. Vocal communication is often combined with visual display. Leyhausen (1979) described the visual repertoire in cats and Fox and Cohen (1977) reviewed visual communication in canids (see also Chapter 4). The more social members of the genus *Canis* have a wider repertoire of visual signals than more solitary fox-like canids. As these signals appear to be graded it is difficult to enumerate them but they involve the mouth, ears, tail and bodily postures such as erect stance, bow and rolling on the back. Tactile behaviour includes nuzzling, licking, pawing, butting, chin resting, holding the partner's head in the mouth and allogrooming. Comparative studies of behavioural development in canids have been published by Bekoff (1974), Fox (1975) and Biben (1983).

The foregoing account has been mainly concerned with Canidae and Felidae; the social behaviour of Hyaenidae (*Crocuta crocuta*) has been outlined by Kruuk (1972). The social behaviour of bears has been reviewed by Pruitt and Burghardt (1977) and the behaviour of the American black bear described by Henry and Herrero (1974). The most detailed studies of social behaviour in Mustelidae are those on the weasel (Erlinge, 1977*a*) and the stoat (*Mustela orminea*) (Müller, 1970) and polecat (*M. putorius*) (Herter, 1959; Poole, 1966, 1967). Vocalizing has also been described for various species by Gossow (1970), Huff and Price (1968) and Channing and Rowe-Rowe (1977).

6.15.2 Pinnipedia (seals, sea lions and walruses)

The data for this suborder are a most entirely derived from breeding aggregates. All pinnipeds come ashore to breed and, during this period, show a rich repertoire of social behaviour. After leaving the breeding grounds they return to the sea and, while many species appear to be gregarious, little is known of their behaviour during this, the greater part of their lifetime. This survey of the sociobiology of pinnipeds will be confined to the period when the animals are on land.

Jouventin and Cornet (1980) have attempted to correlate ecological conditions and breeding strategy for the true seals or Phocidae. They rate two factors to be of paramount importance; these are the richness of food supply and choice of breeding site. Arctic and antarctic cold waters provide the richest food sources so that the largest populations of phocids are found in these areas and there is a tendency for species with the highest density of population to be the most highly polygynous. The second factor which influences reproductive strategy is the extensiveness of the breeding grounds. Pack ice provides plentiful breeding sites with ready access to the sea in channels between floes; solid ice, however, offers less access to water so that the breeding area is more restricted and leads to the animals crowding together. Finally, species which breed on islands are most restricted in terms of access to sea and availability of suitable breeding sites and these are the most polygynous of all seals, with very large harems (see Table 6.1).

The ringed seal (*Pusa hispida*) breeds on pack ice and is monogamous,

Table 6.1 Mating strategy, age of maturity, and sexual dimorphism in four species of seal (Phocidae).

Species	No. of females per male	Male/female Age of maturity	Male/female Body weight
Pusa hispida	1	?	1.0
Phoca vitulina	1–4	1.3	1.2
Halichoerus grypus	1–10	1.8	1.3
Mirounga leonina	3–55	2.6	4.0

females being scattered on floes over a large area. The common seal is a wider-ranging, largely temperate species with low population density and it is either monogamous or has a small harem of 1–4 females; mating occurs in the sea. The grey seal breeds on rocky coasts and islands and has a harem of 1–10 females. In poorer areas, such as the Argentinian Valdes Peninsula, the Southern elephant seal has small harems, 50% of which contain only 2–3 females, whereas in rich areas with restricted breeding sites, such as Kerguelen Island, harems are much larger and may contain up to 55 females (see Le Boeuf and Petrinovich, 1974). In different species the degree of sexual dimorphism is also generally related to harem size; the larger the harem, the relatively larger the male seal is and the longer its reaching sexual maturity is delayed (see Table 6.1).

The eared seals (Otariidae) and walruses (Odobenidae) are all polygynous. The Steller sealion can be taken as an example of a polygynous pinniped. The male defends a territory which includes a group of females. Males challenge one another at boundaries of the territory and attempt to prevent oestrous females from leaving (see Chapter 3). Gentry (1974) found that males have a dominance hierarchy, while females are hostile to one another but seldom attack. There is a high premium on stamina for breeding males, since they do not feed for the entire breeding season of $2–3\frac{1}{2}$ months. Subadult males and females playfight in areas away from the breeding sites. Young pups join peer groups (pup pods) at the age of 2–3 weeks when their mothers are foraging. Pup pods are of mixed sex and a great deal of playfighting takes place (Farentinos, 1971; Gentry, 1974).

Female pinnipeds give birth to a single precocial young (see Chapter 3). Female phocids do not feed during lactation but produce a very rich milk derived from stored fat. Their lactation period is short for so large an animal, being only 9–10 days in the harp seal (*Phoca groenlandicus*), 16–21 days in the grey seal and 23–28 days in the Southern elephant seal (see Bonner, 1984). In marked contrast, female eared seals (Otariidae) and walruses (Odobenidae), which forage during the lactation period, may nurse the young for two to three years.

Pinnipedia show a wide repertoire of social signals. Olfaction probably plays a minor role, although it may be involved in sexual behaviour and mother-offspring recognition. Vocalizations occur in aggression, territorial display, threat, submission, alarm, mother-infant contact, distress call of young and courtship (see Winn and Schneider, 1977). Visual displays are involved in agonistic and courtship behaviour. Sandegren (1976) described the male Northern elephant seal's aggressive behaviour, which included proboscis erection, rearing up, neck-raising, head-tossing and shoving with the forequarters; the Steller sealion has a submissive grin, relaxed open mouth, lateral head sway, lateral neck-shake and vibrissa erection. Females in oestrus indicate their sexual receptivity by displaying the pink inside of the vulva. Aggressive behaviour involves biting the head, neck, flippers and anterior part of the opponent's body. Tactile signals appear to be of significance in courtship, for example mounting of the male by the female and gentle biting. The male also nuzzles the female's vulva, presses his head on her back, nips, pokes and lifts her abdomen (see Farentinos, 1971; Gentry, 1974; Sandegren, 1976). Mating in the spotted seal has already been described in some detail in Chapter 3.

Social play of the Steller sealion has been described by Gentry (1974) and that of the common and grey seals by Wilson (1973a). An excellent review of social behaviour in pinnipeds is that of Winn and Schneider (1977).

6.16 Sirenia (sea cows)

There are two living genera of these aquatic herbivores, the manatees (*Trichecus*) and dugongs (*Dugong*). Both may form herds, but the only social tie is between mother and offspring.

The Florida manatee (*T. manatus*) is long-lived, surviving for up to 26 years. An oestrous female is competed for by anything up to seventeen males known as 'the oestrous herd', members of which may have an age-dependent rank order. The dugong browses on marine algae in herds which travel together, and has been observed to show some anti-predator behaviour towards sharks (Andersson, 1982). The young of Sirenia are precocial followers which may sometimes be carried on their mother's back.

The communication system of this order is poorly known but Hartman (1979) in his monograph on *T. manatus* gave some behaviour descriptions which are summarized here. Mating is ventro-ventral (see Chapter 3) and homosexual behaviour was observed between males. Vocalizations included squeals, chirp-squeaks, screams and groaning. Tactile signals appeared to be important and included kissing, mouthing, embracing and rubbing the genital area on a partner.

6.17 Cetacea (whales)

The social organization of whales is poorly understood, not only because studies in their natural habitat are few, but also because the age/sex composition of natural groups is difficult to determine in species without pronounced sexual dimorphism. The sociobiology of whalebone whales (Mysteceti) and toothed whales (Odontoceti) will be considered independently.

6.17.1 Mysteceti

The humpbacked whale (*Megaptera novae angliae*) generally lives alone or in groups of two or three individuals; large breeding assemblies of up to 500 individuals, however, come together in the area off Hawaii. The mother-calf bond is strong and often a mother with young is accompanied by an adult escort who may play some role in defending them.

The best-known behaviour of this species is the whale 'song' (see Chapter 3). The sex of the singers is not known but they generally avoid one another and Tyack (1981) has suggested that the song contains information about species, sex, location and readiness to attack or mate. Hermann and Tavolga (1980) put forward the opinion that the singers are males and that the song functions as a communal display by males to attract females. The sex ratio of two males to each female in this species would be expected to lead to male-male competition and, as singing is confined to the breeding season, this suggestion is plausible. Females appear to leave the breeding grounds as soon as they are pregnant. Apart from their songs, Mysteceti have a wide repertoire of vocal signals, including tonal pulses such as moans (15–500 Hz), grunts (45–200 Hz), chirps and cries (up to 1 KHz) and clicks (3 Hz–3 KHz); their context and significance are, however not known. Visual displays such as leaping, waving the forelimbs and releasing strings of airbubbles have been observed. Courtship includes waving tail flukes and forelimbs, and tactile signals such as rubbing and patting with the forelimbs and rubbing heads, which may stimulate the bristles on the jaws.

Table 6.2 Relation between habitat, group size, group composition and predation pressure in toothed whales

| Species | Habitat | Group size | | Predators | Types of group | | | | | Adult size (m) |
		Typical	Max.		Mixed sexes	Pairs	Nursery	All Male		
I Riverine										
Ganges dolphin (*Platanista gangetica*)	R	1	10	–	–	–	–	–		2.3
Amazon dolphin (*Inia geoffroyensis*)	R	1	4	–	–	?	–	–		2.5–3
Tucuxi (*Sotalia fluviatilis*)	R + C	1	3	–	–	–	–	–		1.2
II Coastal										
Humpbacked dolphin (*Sousa* spp.)	C + R	1–2	25	SK	+	–	–	–		2.4
Harbour porpoise (*Phocaena phocoena*)	C + R	2–10	50	SK	–	–	+	+		1.5–1.8
Beluga (*Delphinapterus leucas*)*	C + R	5–10	>10	SKB	–	+	+	+		4–5
Narwhal (*Monodon monoceros*)*	C + R	3–15	>15	SKW	+	–	+	+		5

III Pelagic

Species								
Bottle-nosed dolphin (*Tursiops truncatus*)	C + R + P	2–20	100s	S	+	–	–	+	2.4–3.7
Dall's porpoise (*Phocaenoides dalli*)*	C + P	3–15	100s	K	+	–	–	–	2.1
Killer whale (*Orcinus orca*)	C + R + P	1–40	>100	–	F	–	–	–	7–10
Long-finned pilot whale (*Globicephala melaena*)*	C + P	20–85	–	K	+	–	–	+	6.2
Short-finned pilot whale (*G. macrorhynchus*)*	C + P	5–60	100s	K	+	–	–	+	4.7–6
Spinner dolphin (*Stenella longirostris*)	C + P	6–250	–	S	–	–	?	–	2.1

Key: C = Coastal, P = Pelagic, R = Riverine, S = Shark, K = Killer whale, B = Polar bear,
W = Walrus, F = Family group,
* = migratory forms.
+ = observed
– = not recorded
? = possible positive sighting

6.17.2 Odontoceti

While little is known of group composition, some data are available on group size in toothed whales (see Table 6.2). Riverine odontocetes such as the Ganges river dolphin are solitary, or found in very small groups, and it is possible that this species may also be territorial. Species found in both riverine and coastal environments, such as the common porpoise live in slightly larger groups and in several species all-male and nursery herds have been observed. Belugas (*Delphinapterus leucas*) form male-female pairs in the breeding season and large males are often seen leading travelling groups.

Pelagic species typically form large groups, usually of mixed sex and age. Sometimes, during migration, groups separate according to age and sex. In the killer whale the stable group appears to be an adult male and a group of females with young, thus suggesting a mobile harem structure. School structure and size is undoubtedly related to hunting techniques. Killer whales hunt co-operatively, feeding on other species of whales and pinnipeds (see Chapter 5). They have been observed to adopt a crescent formation when chasing California sea lions (*Zalophus californiacus*), with individuals rushing in to make a kill. Both common dolphins (*Delphinus delphis*) and *Tursiops* spp. have been observed to round up fish and drive them ashore.

Pelagic species such as the common dolphin, spotted dolphin (*Stenella attenuata*) and spinner dolphin (*S. longirostris*) travel in large schools which are broader than they are long. Such schools cut a path approximately 1 km wide through the ocean and travel at 5 kph, so that they search five square kilometres per hour. Dolphins feed on shoaling fish, such as anchovies, sprats and squids; they co-ordinate their hunting by diving in unison, breaking up the prey shoal so that individuals are easier to catch.

Another function of schooling is protection against predators, both through increased vigilance and co-operative defence. Humpbacked dolphins have been observed to chase off sharks, and variations in school size in pelagic species appear to bear a good relation to predator pressure. Larger species are rather solitary, apart from breeding and migration, while smaller pelagic species which suffer from shark and killer whale predation show strong schooling tendencies.

Wells *et al.* (1980) studied group structure in bottle-nosed dolphins and found it to be extremely fluid; however, some long-term associations appeared to exist between adult males and also between subadult males (see also Chapter 5).

Like the Mysteceti, Odontoceti give birth to a single precocial follower young, and the mother-offspring bond is of long duration. The infant whale remains close to its mother's side. There have been no reports of male parental care, but allomothering is observed by other females, who may assist the newborn young to the surface after birth to enable it to fill its lungs with air. Altruistic behaviour between adults can include supporting an injured companion which is unable to reach the surface. There have even been anecdotal reports of dolphins assisting human swimmers who were in difficulties.

The social behaviour of odontocetes has been observed mainly in marine oceanaria. Detailed ethograms have been provided for the bottlenosed dolphin by Caldwell and Caldwell (1977*b*) and the killer whale, including some data from the wild, by Martinez and Klinghammer (1978). The literature has been reviewed by Caldwell and Caldwell (1977*a*) and Defran and Pryor (1980). Odontocetes have a rich repertoire of pulsed vocalizations (such as cracks and pips), squawks, squeaks, and whistles; whistles appear to be commoner in the more gregarious species, but they are graded signals so that estimates as to their number in the repertoire may be subjective. Isolated dolphins connected via hydrophones will whistle alternately to one another (see Herman and Tavolga, 1980).

In captivity, dominance hierarchies have formed in *Tursiops truncata*. The dominant male shows jaw-snapping, ramming, biting and chasing. Open-mouth threat and a submissive posture, which involves turning the head away with mouth closed and head up, have also been observed. When courting, the white ventral surface is displayed; leaping, inverted swimming and a sigmoid posture are adopted by the male. Head-nodding and shaking are usually associated with disturbance or aggression. Tactile signals include flank-rubbing and contact with forelimbs, flukes and dorsal fin. Heterosexual affiliative behaviour includes gentle nudging, stroking of fins and genitals and mild tooth-raking. Play has been observed between both adults and mothers and young. Major reviews of whale biology and behaviour have been provided by Slijper (1962); Norris (1966); Evans and Bastian (1969); Tayler and Saayman (1972); Caldwell and Caldwell (1972, 1977*b*; Ridgway and Benirschke (1977); Winn and Olla (1979); Herman (1980).

Some authors have suggested that dolphins have a language which enables them to exchange ideas. There is, to date, no convincing objective evidence that this is the case. Currently, bottle-nosed dolphins are being taught to comprehend *our* language and it is claimed that they can understand eleven nouns, nine verbs, two proper names and respond to three signals indicating 'yes', 'no' and 'ready'. For a discussion of this interesting question of language comprehension, see Herman and Tavolga (1980).

6.18 Chiroptera

The bats are extremely diverse in their social behaviour, ranging from solitary to highly gregarious forms. Solitary bats such as *Micropteropus pusillus, Pipistrellus nanus* and *Lasiurus borealis* have independent hunting territories and roost in isolation. In temperate species mating may be opportunistic in the autumn, with females storing sperm but delaying gestation until spring. As a female could be mated a number of times over a period of months, male competition for mating opportunities would not appear to be productive. The noctule bat (*Nyctalus noctula*), however, has a vaginal plug and male/male competition, including the formation of a harem defended by the male, has been observed in this species.

Four main types of social organization have been recorded for bats, namely, monogamy, harems, bisexual groups and leks.

A number of species of bat are believed to be monogamous on the grounds that they usually occur in pairs. In the false vampire (*Vampyrum spectrum*), a carnivorous South American bat which preys on small vertebrates (Vehrencamp *et al.*, 1977), the male provisions the female and young and also guards them. The Australian grey-headed flying fox (*Pteropus poliocephalus*) (Nelson, 1965) is a colonial bat; some males are polygynous, but surprisingly males which mate with a female who already has an infant are monogamous. The colonial *Saccopteryx bilineata* from Trinidad has a restricted breeding season but year-round harems of between one and eight females; the male defends a breeding territory on a vertical tree trunk, and male/male competition is intensive. The male attracts the females by singing a loud, complex, stereotyped song and also employs visual and olfactory displays. Whereas some females remain consistently with a particular male, others change roosts frequently. *Saccopteryx* have colonial foraging territories and harems generally hunt together within a territory, chasing out members of other harems. If a female changes her harem she also changes her foraging area. In this species, female dispersal is the rule.

Phyllostomus discolor harems consist of 1–15 females per male, though there are also all-male clusters. Like *Saccopteryx* there is no consistent harem structure. Males and females both display and allogroom. To enter the group, an individual must give a specific display which includes wing-shaking, a piping call and smelling the axillary region of the soliciting individual. Young bats which are offspring of harem females show this display by two weeks of age.

The South American *Phyllostomus hastatus*, an omnivorous, colonial bat which roosts in caves has harems of 10–100 females per male (mean 17.9 ± 5.1). While there is considerable male/male competition, males do not display to females. Harems have a consistent structure and a single male fathers most of the offspring of harem females, so it appears that this species has female-bonded harems. Supernumary males form loose bachelor aggregations. Juvenile one male/multifemale groups and juvenile all-male groups have also been identified. Harems and bachelor groups forage in different areas; the latter appear to be nomadic (McCracken and Bradbury 1981).

The lek behaviour of *Hypsignathus monstrosus* has already been described in Chapter 5. In this species there is male territoriality and female choice. It also displays the highest degree of sexual dimorphism known in any bat (Bradbury, 1977*b*).

The Indian flying fox (*Pteropus giganteus*) forms bisexual societies, both sexes being highly integrated. There is a male hierarchy which confers breeding success on high-ranking individuals. At parturition, females become segregated and form all-female nursery groups.

Some species of bat show seasonally variable social structure. *Mormoops megalophylla* and *Pteronotus parnelli* live in sexually segregated colonies; the Australian vespertilionid *Myotis adversus* which breeds twice a year has female unisexual groups and males are either territorial or live in small sexually segregated groups. In the autumn, females join the males within a territory, forming harems of 1–12 individuals with a high turnover of females which may be promiscuous, moving from harem to harem. The females regroup in the winter but join males again in spring to have their young and mate again; the offspring of the spring mating are born in the female group and not a harem.

In some species the sexes segregate at parturition, forming nursery colonies; this is common in temperate bats but also occurs in a number of tropical forms. The segregation is ended in *Antrozous pallidus* by the invasion of males; in *Miniopterus schriebersii* females leave their young behind at weaning, while in *Chalinolobus dwyeri* the weaned young leave before their mothers.

Maternal care is extensive in bats. Some young (e.g. *Saccopteryx*) are born in a precocial state, while the others such as *Hipposideros commersoni* are relatively altricial. The young have an isolation cry which attracts the mother. Often young are creched in large groups with one to ten adults remaining behind, e.g. *Miniopterus*. In general, returning mothers call and their own young replies and is recognized by its mother, but in *Miniopterus schreibersii* and *Tadarida brasiliensis*, there is apparently indiscriminate nursing.

Young bats fly before they are weaned and may accompany their mother on foraging excusions. Bats have a wide repertoire of social communication. Aggressive displays include vocalization, wing-flapping and scent spreading. Males of some species e.g. *Pteropus poliocephalus* often mark their territories with the scent glands. Breeding behaviour includes male singing in *Epomops franqueti* and *Saccopteryx bilineata* or loud trumpeting in *Hypsignathus monstrosus*.

In most cases females respond to male courtship displays by calling. Some male bats (e.g. *Vespertilio murinus*) give an aerial vocal display to the female. Nelson (1965) describes three threats, two territorial displays and an appeasement display by the female, plus two sounds emitted during fighting in *Pteropus poliocephalus*.

Affiliative behaviour takes the form of allogrooming and rubbing, or spraying one another with secretions from the scent glands, in addition to displays permitting entry to the group after foraging. The extent to which ultrasonic cries are utilized in social communication is not known, and further investigation is desirable.

Some bats are sexually dimorphic; male phyllostomatids and pteropids are larger than females, while male emballonurids and vespertilionids are generally smaller than females.

It is apparent that bats show a wide range of social structure and sexual strategies, and while many species are bird-like in their feeding habits, few are monogamous like birds (see Chapter 3). An excellent review of bat behaviour was given by Bradbury (1977a); see also Bradbury and Vehrencamp (1976a, b; 1977a, b), and Nelson (1965).

Bradbury and Vehrencamp (1976a, b; 1977a, b) studied the social organization of five species of emballonurid bats in Trinidad and Costa Rica and attempted to relate sociobiological parameters to ecology and feeding strategies. The data are interesting and a series of models for group size, mating structure and parental investment patterns are considered by the authors. Their social system and ecology is compared with the model devised by Jarman (1974) for African antelopes.

6.19 Dermoptera (galagos or flying lemurs)

Little is known of the biology of this order. *Cynocephalus* appears to be solitary and to give birth to altricial young (see Wharton, 1950).

6.20 Primates

Primate social structure ranges from solitary dispersed prosimians to the most complex societies in the animal kingdom. Because of their close affinity to man there is a vast literature on this group which includes studies in the laboratory, in semi-natural environments and in the wild. Several textbooks have been published which provide useful outlines of primate social behaviour, for example those of Jolly (1972), Rowell (1972), and Chalmers (1979). In the survey which follows, detailed treatment will be confined to species which have been the subject of extensive field studies and illustrate distinctive types of social organization. The consideration of primate sociobiology will be made under three headings: prosimians, simians and hominids.

6.20.1 Prosimians (suborder Strepsirhini or Prosimii)

Where prosimians and simians occur in the same area, the former occupy a noctural insectivore/frugivore/carnivore niche. In Madagascar, however, where there are no simians, there has been an adaptive radiation of lemurs; some of these lemurs occupy equivalent ecological niches to monkeys and lesser apes and have evolved complex forms of social organization.

Two types of social organization have been identified in small noctural prosimians. The potto (*Perodicticus potto*) is a slow-moving creature whose diet is mainly fruit. Males have large territories which include the home ranges of several females. A male regularly contacts the females in his territory but, when one is in oestrus, consorts with her throughout the whole fertile period. Non-territorial males are nomadic and males ge-nerally avoid one another, so that males whose home ranges overlap are not usually simultaneously present in the area of overlap (see Charles-Dominique, 1977*b*).

Demidoff's bushbaby (*Galago demidovii*) and the mouse lemur (*Microcebus murinus*) have a system of dispersed polygyny (see Charles-Dominique and Bearder, 1977; Bearder and Martin, 1979). Some males are territorial and encompass within their territory the home ranges of several females; non-territorial males are peripheral and subordinate, or nomadic. Females congregate together in the daytime to form sleeping clusters which are matriarchal groups (see Chapter 5) but forage inde-pendently at night. Male *G. demidovii* visit their females at intervals of between one and four days and, if a female is approaching oestrus, the male consorts with her. There is some male territorial overlap but males avoid one another. The sociality of the higher primates is foreshadowed in this system, for females show affectional bonds with their close female relatives and males are known by the females in whose territories they live. What is missing is group foraging, which presumably is not practical because of the scattered nature of food items.

Among the lemurs of Madagascar the indri (*Indri indri*) is monogamous. A pair defend a territory and families of 2–5 individuals forage together. The male has a loud territorial call which advertises his presence. Mature young leave the family group before breeding so that each territory contains only a single breeding pair.

Bisexual groups are found in a number of lemurs, the best studied from the viewpoint of social behaviour being the diurnal ringtailed lemur (*Lemur catta*). Jolly (1966) found that there were hierarchies in both sexes but that females were dominant to males. Only the most dominant males associate with the females and juveniles, while subordinates straggle behind the main group in what Jolly termed a 'drones club'. Groups range between five and 24 individuals and one-third of the males transfer to another group in the breeding season. Thus the social arrangement appears to be a female-bonded multimale grouping. *L.catta* is territorial and when neighbouring groups confront one another at territorial boundaries, they display aggressively.

As in all primates, the gestation period is long for the size of animal (60 days for the 70 g mouse lemur, 130 days for the 220 g *Galago*). The majority of prosimians give birth to a single, clinging, precocial young, but the mouse lemur produces two semi-altricial infants born with their eyes closed and incapable of locomotion. Young mouse lemurs are left in a nest and, should their mother wish to move them, they are carried in her mouth. The dwarf lemur (*Cheirogaleus*) produces 2–3 offspring. Allomothering is common in the ringtailed lemur.

Chemical communication plays an important role in the social behaviour of prosimians. The small nocturnal species mark their home ranges with urine, faeces and direct rubbing of scent glands on the substrate. *Lemur catta* has wrist glands which it rubs on its tail. Jolly (1966) described aggressive interactions between groups of this species in which scent is wafted towards the opponents with the tail; she termed these 'stink fights'. The role of chemical communication in prosimians has been reviewed in considerable detail by Schilling (1979).

Vocal communication (see Petter and Charles-Dominique, 1979) includes territorial songs (in *Indri*), agonistic, affiliatory and anxiety calls. Jolly described 15 different call types in *L. catta*, with numerous intermediates.

Visual signals include bodily postures and movements such as head swaying and changes in tail position: the latter are particularly con-spicuous in *L. catta*, where the tail is ringed with black and white.

The facial muscles of diurnal prosimians are more complex than those of nocturnal species and raising and puckering the snout, open mouth and movements of the eyelids all occur in social interactions (see Pariente, 1979).

6.20.2 Simians (suborder Haplorhini)

Monogamy is an uncommon form of social organization in primates, but is found in a number of New World monkeys (*Platyrrhinae*); the titi monkeys (*Callicebus*) conform to this pattern and are territorial, with a long-distance call which advertises their presence. They form small groups with one or two immature offspring (see Mason 1966, 1968; Kinzey *et al.*, 1977; Robinson, 1979*a, b*). The marmosets and tamarians (Callitrichidae) live in bisexual groups with status-determined monogamy (see Abbott and Hearn, 1978; Rothe, 1975; Poole, 1978*b*; Evans and Poole, 1983). Field studies have confirmed the existence of a dominant pair and a single breeding female in *Saguinus oedipus, Callithrix jacchus jacchus* and *C. humeralifer intermedius* (Neyman, 1978; Dawson, 1978; Stevenson and Rylands, in press). Group transfer by both adults and juveniles has been noted in *Saguinus oedipus* by Neyman (1978) and Dawson (1978). Non-breeding members of the group assist the parents in carrying and caring for infants.

The Hylobatidae (gibbons and siamangs) are small, obligately mono-gamous, territorial apes (see Chapter 5). Sub-adult offspring are driven out of the family group. In *Hylobates pileatus* in south-east Thailand, Srikosamatara and Brockelmann (pers. comm.) found only one group out of twelve groups studied which had two breeding females, all others being monogamous. Status in the family group is directly related to age, and in some species (e.g. *Hylobates lar*), the female is dominant to her mate.

Some species of monkey have a harem or 'one-male group' system, where a single male dominates a group of females and has exclusive sexual rights over them. The social behaviour of three species has been particularly well studied under natural conditions, namely the common langur, the gelada baboon and the hamadryas baboon (*Papio hamadryas*).

The langur (see Hrdy, 1977) is a territorial species with a matrilineal female-bonded group structure, typically each breeding unit has a single alpha male. Females remain in their natal group, while males are generally driven out on reaching sexual maturity and join hierarchically organized bachelor groups. Male sexual strategies take four forms: first, they may 'haunt' a bisexual troop by lurking and attempting to mate with females if their dominant male is distracted; secondly, bachelor groups may make attacks on a one-male group and attempt to snatch copulations; thirdly, they may join a one-male group and may have some breeding success as they outnumber the alpha male, and may co-operate in attacking and driving him out. Finally, the dominant male of a bachelor group may attack and displace the alpha male of a breeding group.

These forms of behaviour are especially prevalent if a female is in oestrus. On takeover, a new alpha male may attempt to kill unweaned infants, which will enhance his own reproductive success (see Chapter 4), and force out of the group sub-adult males who are the offspring of his predecessor. On average, a new male takes over a harem every 2–3 years.

Females tend to oppose takeover unless they are in oestrus, when they may solicit males in a bachelor group or even neighbouring alpha males. Females born after a male takeover will avoid mating with an alpha male who might be their father, and hence solicit males outside the group. It is ironic that the seeds of a male's downfall, in the shape of his daughter's efforts to solicit other males, are sown in his own reproductive success!

Male langurs protect their offspring and often rescue them from danger; there is also a great deal of allomothering (see Chapter 3), and the close genetic relationship of the females is undoubtedly a factor which promotes this behaviour through kin selection. Alpha males rarely succeed in acquiring two harems because the two groups of females are quarrelsome and hostile to one another. In fact, aggression between two alpha males and their harems is normally much less than that between those of breeding units and bachelor groups; the juveniles of different harems often play together on meeting (see Dolhinow, 1972; Hrdy, 1974, 1977).

Two further species with a harem type of breeding unit will be discussed, namely, the gelada baboon (*Theropithecus gelada*) and the hamadryas baboon (*Papio hamadryas*). These two species, however, differ from langurs in that the harem structure exists within a multimale/multifemale troop. They also differ from each other in social structure, for the gelada has strongly matrilineal harems while hamadryas baboon males collect a group of unrelated females.

Thanks to the researches of Dunbar and Dunbar (1975) and Dunbar (1979 *a, b*, 1980 *a, b*, 1982) and a monograph edited by Kawai (1979), our knowledge of the behaviour of this species under natural conditions is considerable. Gelada baboons are unusual among primates in being grazers and, like many other species which adopt this way of life, they form large

Figure 6.1 Two harems of gelada baboons (*Theropithecus gelada*) in close proximity. (Photograph R. I. M. Dunbar.)

herds. Within these herds are what Dunbar has termed 'bands'—Ohsawa (1979) uses the term 'troops' for these groups (see Figure 6.1). Within the bands are breeding units which consist of a group of related females, a dominant male and, sometimes, a follower. Dunbar and Dunbar found that one-male groups averaged 8.6 individuals, with 3.3 females and 4.3 juveniles; two-male groups were larger. Two-male groups were formed when a younger 'follower' male attached himself to the breeding unit. The two males behaved amicably and the younger one built up relationships with the juvenile females in the group. These young females and the satellite male may, in due course, leave the harem to form a one-male unit. As time goes on the females become less submissive to the new male and develop strong bonds among themselves. As a male reaches the end of his reproductive prime his female group is likely to be taken over, either by a male an all-male group or by a follower. In the latter case, the displaced male remains at the edge of his old group until his death.

The behaviour of females is of crucial importance in group takeover (cf. the langur) and a male needs female support to be successful. A male attempting takeover threatens the alpha male while calling to females. The cohesion of the breeding unit is influenced by the strength of female bonds, which determine whether or not a group is likely to split. Alpha males are reluctant to mate with females who may be their daughters, so that these females are most likely to mate with a follower or split off from the group.

Female harems are organized into between one and seven matrilines, with high-ranking females producing the most offspring. Young females may join peer groups, but ultimately return to their natal group. Males, by contrast, leave the breeding unit when $2\frac{1}{2}$–3 years old and join an all-male group which usually consists of sub-adults with one adult leader who controls the group. All-male groups are loosely tied together and may even move from one band to another; there is considerable hostility between these males and those in breeding units.

Studies by Kummer (1968) showed that the harem group is also the basic social structure in the hamadryas baboon (*Papio hamadryas*). In this species, however, harem females are unrelated and leave their breeding unit on maturity. The male hamadryas baboon adopts one of two reproductive strategies; he either joins a breeding unit as a sub-adult satellite male and gradually takes over the group of females as the alpha male ages, or he kidnaps a late infant female and cares for her until she becomes the first member of his harem on reaching maturity. Males may acquire extra females which have spontaneously left their one-male units or may attempt to steal one from another breeding unit. Where a satellite male has taken over a group of females, relations remain good between the two males and the older male tends to determine group movements. The basis of social organization in this species is the male/female non-sexual bond (see Chapter 4), all females in a harem being attracted to the male. Grooming relationships are centripetal; females mainly groom the male, but Stammbach (1979) found that in captive all-female groups of hamadryas baboons there was still a tendency to centripetal grooming relations, with all other females grooming the alpha. Unlike langurs and gelada baboons, hamadryas females do not form a cohesive group and the male herds them, if they stray, by biting the neck, which makes the female move towards him.

The breeding units are organized into a band structure and there appear to be strong social bonds between the alpha males in different breeding units (see Figure 6.2). Band movement appears to result from the concerted action resulting from communication between male harem leaders. At night, bands of baboons join together and form sleeping aggregations or troops which are real social groups because strangers cannot gain entry to them.

A number of species of primate live in multimate/multifemale groups and the social behaviour of two genera namely *Macaca* and *Papio* has been

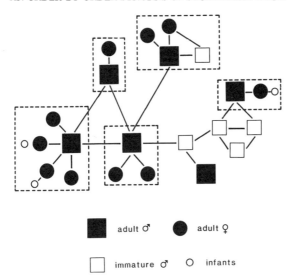

adult ♂   adult ♀

immature ♂   O   infants

Figure 6.2   Hamadryas baboon (*Papio hamadryas*) schematic sociogram showing relations between and within one-male units (enclosed in dotted lines). Males are both unit leaders and band members, whereas females are only unit members. (After Kummer, 1968)

particularly well investigated. Both have female-bonded bisexual societies with males emigrating from their natal group to breed.

The sociobiology of *Macaca sinica* has already been discussed on a number of occasions (Chapters 3, 4) and, because of the interesting contrast with *P. hamadryas*, *Papio* will be used as the example to be considered. Two species have been investigated in depth in the field, i.e. *Papio anubis* (see Packer, 1975, 1977, 1979 *a*, *b*, 1980) and *P. cynocephalus* (Altmann, 1980; Altmann and Altmann, 1970; Hausfater, 1975). In these species, both males and females are ranked and, as in *Macaca*, the status of an offspring is correlated with that of its mother. Males are dominant to females for every age/class. In the natal group, dominance is positively correlated with age but immigrant males compete with one another for status. Natal males, some of which may be high-ranking adults, rarely copulate and yield females to immigrants, for whom females also show preference. Males only show interest in females at oestrus and then consort with them; rank and reproductive success in immigrant males are positively correlated.

The social structure of *Papio anubis* contrasts markedly with that of *P. hamadryas*, yet these species are closely related because hybrids between them occur in nature (see Nagel, 1971). Both live in troops, but *P.*

hamadryas forms permanent harems while *P. anubis* males only show interest in females when they are in oestrus. The real differences between the two societies lie in dispersal and social bonds. In *P. hamadryas*, females disperse and the strongest bond is the non-sexual male/female bond; males (who may be related) are more loosely bonded. In *P. anubis* and *P. cynocephalus*, the stable non-sexual bonds are between females who form the persistent core of society, while most males emigrate to breed; there is no non-sexual male/female bond.

Eisenberg *et al.* (1972) regarded the multimale/multifemale society of primates as the highest form of social organization but introduced the term 'age-graded male groups' for certain primate societies, arguing that this form of social structure was intermediate between a harem and a true multimale/multifemale society. He defined an age-graded society as one which lacked fully adult males of equivalent age and gave the Indian langur and *Gorilla* as examples. It is now known that these two species have very different types of social organization. 'Age-graded male groups' only occur in the female-bonded harem-forming langur, when a male has had a long tenure of a harem and sons remain in the group until expelled by the next alpha male. Gorillas, by contrast, form groups from which females emigrate to breed, thus giving a male-bonded society with the oldest male holding the harem. In view of this new insight into primate social organizations it seems advisable to drop the term 'age-graded male society' on the grounds that it is a heterogeneous category, the basic social bonds and type of dispersal being more fundamental factors.

Because of the close affinity of the chimpanzee with *Homo sapiens*—it has been estimated that 98.9% of their genes are shared (Benveniste and Todaro, 1976)—there has been a great deal of interest in the social organization of the Pongidae and the four living species are therefore considered in detail.

The mountain gorilla (*Gorilla gorilla beringei*) has been studied in the wild by Schaller (1963), Harcourt (1978, 1979), and Harcourt *et al.* (1976, 1981). Males are generally found to remain in their natal group to breed, while females usually emigrate twice. The organization is essentially a non-female-bonded harem, with only a single breeding male in the group. Females which have reached maturity transfer to another group when two groups are in proximity. There is an age-graded dominance hierarchy and males adopt one of two strategies for reproduction, either remaining in their natal group until they become the oldest and most dominant male, or leaving the group, becoming solitary and attempting to acquire an oestrous female (possibly the group leader's daughter) from an established group.

This second strategy involves challenging the leader and occasionally actual fighting. Group females solicit copulation from males, but the dominant has priority of access to all females in his group and copulates with them in peak oestrus. There are always more sexually mature females than males in gorilla society because males are much larger and take longer to mature. In this species female choice of mate may be of some significance.

Wild chimpanzees (*Pan troglodytes*) have been studied by Reynolds and Reynolds (1965); Goodall (1965, 1967, 1968a, b, 1975); Tutin (1979, a, b, 1980); Tutin and McGinnis (1981); Wrangham (1979); Wrangham and Smuts (1980) and Nishida (1968). Males are the more sociable of the sexes in this species, travelling in parties most of the time, although group composition is extremely variable. Each male belongs to a territorial band and lone members of other bands are attacked. Females are less sociable, spending most of their time alone. There is a male dominance hierarchy, and males show very considerable affiliative behaviour to one another. Males and females only consort when a female is sexually receptive. There are long-lasting social bonds between a mother and her offspring, but females emigrate to breed and so lose contact. Males very rarely mate with their mothers when the latter are their only female relatives remaining in the group area.

Three mating strategies are employed by male chimpanzees (Tutin 1979b), namely opportunistic or promiscuous mating, guarding an oestrous female, or consortship (see Chapter 3). If a male has a choice of forming an exclusive relationship with either of two oestrous females he chooses the elder. Male chimpanzees belonging to the same territorial band are likely to be closely related.

The bonobo or pygmy chimpanzee (*Pan paniscus*), like the common chimpanzee, shows a flexible social structure. Bands of *P. paniscus* live in fixed areas but move around in small parties (mean size 16.9). Eighty per cent of the groups contain both sexes and it is in this respect that this species differs from *P. troglodytes* (Kuroda, 1979, 1980). The main social bond in *P. paniscus* is between male and female though, unlike common chimpanzees, there is some affiliative behaviour between females in the form of genital/genital rubbing. As in the common chimpanzee, males are dominant to females. Interestingly this species commonly shows ventro-ventral copulation.

Bonobos appear to be unaggressive and, while each band occupies a home range, there is considerable overlap and Kuroda (1979) did not directly observe any interband conflict. Clearly studies of this species are in their infancy and more data are required before detailed comparisons can be made between the two species of chimpanzee. Enough is known, however, to show that there are marked differences in the social bonding of the two species. In chimpanzees there are only male/male bonds; in bonobos there are male/female, male/male and even female/female bonds.

The orang utan (*Pongo pygmaeus*) has a social structure which is most unusual for a higher primate. Light has been thrown on its behaviour by the field studies of MacKinnon (1974), Horr (1977), Rijksen (1978), Rodman (1973), Galdikas-Brindamoor and Brindamoor (1975), Galdikas (1981, 1982) and Schürmann (1982). The species is sexually dimorphic, adult males being nearly twice the adult female weight. Males live solitarily, ranging over undefended home ranges. They advertise their presence by loud calls. Adult males rarely come into contact and appear to avoid one another. The home range is relatively small (0.5–0.6 km²) compared with that of the chimpanzee (4 km²). Adult females, as in the common chimpanzees, are largely solitary, accompanied by an infant and sometimes an adolescent as well. Females may travel together for periods of time, when there may be contact between their infant and adolescent offspring.

As the orang utan becomes adolescent, it seeks contact with peers or sub-adults, who travel in small parties of 2–5 and play together during positive social contacts. Adolescents of both sexes may join mother-infant parties and show interest in the infant. Sub-adults retain the sociability of the adolescent, but sub-adult males attempt to mate forcibly with oestrous females if they meet them. Rijksen (1978) Galdikas (1981) and Schürmann (1982) found that females presumed to be in oestrus seek out an adult male, presumably attracted by his long call. The female solicits the male and forms a consort relation with him throughout her oestrous period; there is thus a large element of sexual selection by the female. Male sexual strategies change with age. As a sub-adult, the male attempts to mate with unwilling oestrous females, while as an adult he advertises to attract females.

In spite of the unsociable way of life of adult orang utans, the species has a rich repertoire of social signals (see Maple, 1980) presumably inherited from more social ancestors. It seems likely that the solitary way of life of this species may be regarded as a form of dispersed sociality, in contrast with the hostility and indifference characteristic of the social interactions of primitive solitary mammals. The sociability of adolescent and sub-adult orang utans support this contention.

The reason why orang utans have adopted this isolated existence has been the subject of much speculation (see, for example, Wrangham, 1979).

Possibly the slow locomotion, scattered food sources and arboreal nature of the animal militate against a gregarious way of life. In fact, females behave rather like chimpanzees, but the very large size of male orang utans is presumably related to strong female sexual selection.

Most simians produce a single offspring but the South American marmosets and tamarins (Callitrichidae) normally produce twins. Parental care is the preserve of the mother in the majority of primates, although paternal care has been observed in siamangs (see Chapter 3) and among callitrichid monkeys. In some species, especially those with female-bonded social organization, allomothering is common (e.g. *Presbytis entellus*), while older juvenile and sub-adult males and females assist in the carrying, protection and grooming of callitrichid young. Females of some species such as the pigtailed macaque (*Macaca nemestrina*), however, are extremely protective of their offspring and will not allow other females to handle them. Young simians have a long period of dependence on their mothers and in many cases lifelong social bonds between mother and daughter are forged.

There is a very large literature on the social signals of simians, which are the most complex in the animal kingdom. Scent appears to play a rather minor role in the Catarrhinae (Old World monkeys, apes and man) although some monkeys certainly detect the oestrous condition of a female by her scent (see Michael and Keverne, 1970). Scent also plays an important role in communication in South American monkeys such as Callitrichidae (see Epple, 1974a, b, 1979; Sutcliffe and Poole, 1978) which use anal and sternal scent glands and urine for marking their home range. Scent-marking in one catarrhine (*Cercopithecus neglectus*) has been observed in captivity by Oppenheimer (1979). Vocal communication includes territorial calls, alarm calls, contact calls, threat, submission, courtship, parent-infant contact calls and excitement calls. Many of the calls are graded (see Chapter 2) and often there is more than one vocal variation in each context, each with a slightly different meaning. Visual communication includes a rich repertoire of facial expressions, bodily posture, tail positions, piloerection displays and body movements. Allogrooming is a particularly important form of tactile contact but some species shake hands, kiss, put an arm round one another, touch genitalia or make playful contact by slapping or rough-and-tumble play.

Communication in simians has been reviewed by Andrew (1963a, b); Altmann (1967); Van Hoof (1962, 1967); Redican (1975); Oppenheimer (1977); Gautier and Gautier (1977); and Marler and Tenaza (1977).

6.20.3 *Hominidae*

Any comparison between mankind and other species of mammals is fraught with pitfalls. The following account attempts to be objective and follows the line of previous descriptions of mammalian sociobiology in the chapter. To draw any comparison with other species may be invalid, and social behaviour may not be homologous to apparently similar behaviour in other species. It is the reader's privilege to draw what conclusions he will.

Human beings live in multimale/multifemale societies; the mating strategy may be monogamous, polygynous or, rarely, polyandrous. Both matriarchal and patriarchal societies exist, and dispersal may be through the emigration of daughters or sons to another social group. Incest is generally infrequent and taboos against it exist in many societies. Human beings appear to have some difficulty in forming sexual relationships with individuals with whom they have been reared from an early age. The male/female bond, which is not dependent upon the stage of oestrous cycle, is an important factor and both male/male and female/female social bonds may also be important. Parent/offspring bonds are long-lasting and nepotism is prevalent.

Human beings are sexually dimorphic, males being larger than females. In some societies males are dominant to females. Dominance hierarchies are common amongst males, and female rank may be dependent upon that of the mate.

In many societies a monogamous pair bond is an important feature; its duration may be brief or lifelong.

Maternal care is of long duration, the human infant being one of the most helpless of all primate neonates. Human infants are unique among other primates in being unable to cling to their mother (although chimpanzee infants need to be supported during the first 2–3 weeks) and the scantiness of human body hair also makes clinging more difficult. The fact that the human infant requires support during the mother's locomotion may reduce group mobility; unlike the males of most other primate species, males may go further afield to forage than females and offspring. Like pack-living carnivores, many human beings have evolved a co-operative hunting strategy and bring excess food back to the home base.

Allomothering is common in humans, in some cases even to the extent of lactation (wet nursing). The principles inherent in communication systems, and the factors which have influenced the expression of social behaviour in other species of mammal, have clearly played a role in the evolution of human social behaviour. *Homo sapiens* has inherited a wide repertoire of relatively stereotyped behaviour patterns from a primate ancestry. Its rich repertoire of facial expressions include typical primate patterns such as grinning, frowning, pouting, staring and vocalizations such as screaming. Like other mammals, humans use non-verbal communication in playing, fighting, mating, and affectionate behaviour. Powers of olfactory communication, like those of the apes, are somewhat restricted.

The development of language, making it possible to exchange ideas and make long term plans, provided a potential for creativity on a scale unprecedented in other mammals. For this reason any serious consideration of human social behaviour is outside the scope of this book, because the emphasis has been on a comparative approach. Nonetheless, an understanding of the fundamentals of human social behaviour may be facilitated by a knowledge of social behaviour in other mammals.

6.21 Summary

The social organization of the different orders of mammals can be described as follows.

1. Monotremata: solitary, laying 1–2 eggs.

2. Marsupialia: solitary, or multimale/multifemale herd, or possibly monogamous; r- or K-selected; premature young (usually 1–4 but in some species up to 12).

3. Insectivora: solitary or, in one case, colonial; r or K-selected; 1–32 altricial young.

4. Macroscelidea: monogamous; 1–2 precocial young.

5. Scandentia: monogamous, or dispersed harem; 1–2 altricial young.

6. Pholidota: solitary or dispersed harem; 1 precocial young.

7. Edentata: solitary; 1 precocial young (armadillos solitary or colonial, more r selected, 1–5 semi-altricial young (polyembryony in *Dasypus*)).

8. Lagomorpha: solitary; monogamous or in multimale/multifemale colonies; young precocial (3–5) or altricial (5–15).

9. Rodentia: solitary, monogamous; colonial harem or multimale/multifemale colony; young 1–32, usually altricial but a few precocial (all hystricomorphs). One eusocial rodent.

10. Hyracoidea: multimale/multifemale colonies; 1–2 precocial young.

11. Tubulidentata: probably solitary, with precocial young.

12. Perissodactyla: solitary; harem-forming or with territorial breeding males; 1 precocial young.

13. Proboscoidea: females in matriarchal herds, males solitary or in small loose groups; 1 precocial young.

14. Artiodactyla: solitary, monogamous; harem-forming, with territorial males, multimale/multifemale herds or loose aggregates; 1 precocial young, but Suidae have 3–5 precocial young.

15. Carnivora: (a) Fissipedia: solitary, monogamous; spaced males and pack of females, or multimale/multifemale groups; 1–7 semi-altricial young (b) Pinnipedia: solitary, monogamous or harem-forming; precocial offspring.

16. Sirenia: ephemeral aggregates; 1 precocial young.

17. Cetacea: solitary or pairs, harems or multimale/multifemale groups; 1 precocial offspring.

18. Chiroptera: solitary, monogamous, with territorial males; harem-forming or multimale groups; 1–2 precocial or semi-altricial young.

19. Dermoptera: solitary with precocial young.

20. Primates: solitary, harem, monogamous, or multimale/multifemale groups. 1 or 2 precocial young (may be 2–3 semi-altricial young in some prosimians).

21. The socioecology of Monotremata, Dermoptera and Tubulidentata is virtually unknown and there is a dearth of data on solitary mammals.

22. More data are needed on the mating strategies of Cetacea and the behaviour of Pinnipedia outside their breeding season.

CHAPTER SEVEN

FUTURE DEVELOPMENTS

Having provided a synthesis of mammalian sociobiology, I shall now try to identify some areas where further research could clarify major points of theoretical importance.

While there are many partial descriptions of the behavioural repertoire of a variety of mammals, and even a few very detailed ones, there is still a need for careful detailed ethograms of the social behaviour of a wider diversity of species, with well analysed quantitative data on the context and the responses of the recipient. Such research may not result in revolutionary findings, but could undoubtedly throw light on the current controversy over the predictive value of displays and the advantages which they confer on signaller and recipient. The signalling function of different scent glands and complex visual and vocal displays are also poorly understood.

Extended consortship may enable a male mammal to assure the paternity of offspring. Consortship, however, incurs costs to the male which must be offset against the genetic benefit; factors such as the interruption of feeding patterns, risk of injury by rivals and the restriction of mating to the consort female all need investigation and must vary from species to species. An obviously significant factor is the duration of the period during which the female is fertile, but order of mating may be equally important. It is known that in some species it is the male who mates first who leaves the most offspring, while in others it is the one who is last. The female's behaviour may also play a decisive role in the male's reproductive success; she may find a superior male and use his presence as a means of fending off mating attempts by other males. It is possible, however, that in some environmental situations, in species which produce large litters, a female may gain from multiple paternity for her offspring because of their genetic diversity. This must be offset against the value of having a litter of more closely-related young (sibs as opposed to half-sibs) who may be less competitive. So little is known of these factors that the field is wide open for further research, and there are insufficient data on the reproductive strategies of solitary mammals. The great variability in patterns of copulation cannot, at present, be interpreted in any meaningful way but they must surely have a strong bearing on the overall reproductive strategy of the species. Associated with this problem are variations in the probability that a single copulation will result in conception.

The costs associated with inbreeding need more assessment under natural conditions; the advantages of mating and co-operation with close relatives must be balanced against risks involved in emigration or the inheritance of deleterious gene combinations. Recent research on Japanese quails and rodents has revealed that individuals of some species can assess their genetic relationship with an unfamiliar conspecific, and that this may influence their choice of mate. More data are needed to discover how common this phenomenon may be and whether, for example, physical family resemblances such as facial appearance in higher primates are perceived as such and to what extent they may influence social relationships. Wolves are believed to be highly inbred, and it would be interesting to have more information about the closeness of genetic relationships in the pack and whether any other species are similarly inbred.

Modern techniques of blood typing make it feasible to investigate the paternity of infants in naturally-occurring social groups. Further research would not only throw light on mating systems but would also allow assessment of the success of different male reproductive strategies.

From a male standpoint the acquisition of a harem of females would appear to be an optimal reproduction strategy; the existence of multimale/multifemale groups seems therefore to be contrary to the alpha male's interests because of the risk of subordinates mating. More data are needed on paternity in multimale groups.

The question of the frequency of male infanticide in natural social groups is of considerable theoretical interest. Females might be expected to develop counter-strategies to prevent it, and recent evidence has suggested that former dominant males in multimale/multifemale groups may protect their offspring against infanticidal attempts by a high-ranking immigrant males. Thus the multimale group may be of benefit to the reproductive success of both sexes.

In harem-forming species, if an alpha male's tenure is sufficiently long, his daughters may, to avoid inbreeding, solicit unrelated males and thus endanger his position as leader. One way of avoiding this is for a male to tolerate a satellite male who can mate with his daughters and will allow him, as he gets older, to remain in the group to protect his own infants. Infanticide has not been recorded in situations where a satellite male ultimately takes over a group. More data are needed on all these points, both suitable hypotheses and relevant facts (such as length of male tenure, number of mature daughters in the group, paternity of offspring and number of females with young infants in relation to those in oestrus) need to be determined for a range of species.

In general, the influence of females on mammalian social organization may have been greatly underestimated. In a number of species it is clear that female choice determines which male has the opportunity to mate, but the criteria applied are far from clear; such factors as dominance, quality of territory and vigour of display may all be indicative of male superiority and used in mate selection.

Social play is believed to occur in all three mammalian subclasses, but its functional significance is inadequately understood. More studies are needed to provide detailed information on the structure of play in a wider variety of species, particularly under natural conditions. Data on play in monotremes and marsupials are likely to be of particular importance.

The forms taken by mammalian social organization are determined by the existence and relative strengths of non-sexual social bonds, as indicated by mutual proximity and co-operative interactions. Information is needed on the way in which these bonds develop and are maintained, and the extent to which they are developed in different types of grouping, for example, nursery herds and bachelor groups. Most mammalian societies are female-bonded with males emigrating to breed, and more data are needed on non-female bonded groups and the factors which may be of relevance to this type of social structure.

Most of the data currently available on mammalian mating strategies, kin selection and reproductive success under natural conditions are derived from a small number of long-term studies of single species, most of which are primates. There is a pressing need for long term field studies to be extended to a wider range of species from different mammalian orders, especially where closely allied species have very distinctive types of social organization. More socioecological studies of solitary mammals are needed; while most of them are nocturnal, modern methods of radio tracking and night viewing equipment make such investigations practicable. Mammal groups which have been sorely neglected are Monotremata, Marsupialia, Insectivora, Edentata, Tubulidentata, Dermoptera and

Cetacea, while little is known of the social behaviour of Pinnipedia outside their breeding season.

Game theory has provided an important theoretical insight into agonistic behaviour but there is a dearth of hard data on real-life fighting techniques. Much more needs to be known of the costs and payoffs, in terms of lifelong reproductive success, of competing for more than one female, and more comparative data should be acquired for males of the same species adopting monogamous and polygynous mating strategies.

Finally, the costs and benefits of territorial defence need more assessment in terms of food distribution and daily ranging patterns; there is also a need for further evaluation of the effectiveness of advertisement, by chemical or auditory means, as a substitute for actual confrontation. Recent ideas on the role of chemical messages in territorial behaviour need to be tested on a variety of mammals, and for the pattern and economics of scent-marking to be examined in situations where several individuals have adjacent territories.

In addition to these fields of mammalian sociobiology, which seem likely to prove productive in the immediate future there is also a scope for a combined behavioural-physiological approach, particularly in the field of reproductive biology where hormones, signalling systems and mating strategies are all closely interlinked. The social behaviour of mammals seems likely to remain a challenging and intellectually stimulating discipline for the research worker for many years to come.

APPENDIX

Table 1 Species of mammal mentioned in the text classified into orders. English names follow those used by the authors or those quoted by Corbet and Hill, 1980, Leuthold, 1977, or Sebeok, 1977. (It must be realized that some English names, especially those of bats, are sometimes not in common use.)

Class: Mammalia

Sub-Class Prototheria (egg-laying mammals)
Order: Monotremata

Ornithorhynchus anatinus	platypus
Tachyglossus aculeatus	short-nosed echidna
Zaglossus bruijni	long-nosed echidna

Sub-Class Metatheria (pouched mammals)
Order: Marsupialia

Marmosa sp.	Mouse opossum
Didelphys virginiana	Virginian opossum
Antechinus flavipes	yellow-footed marsupial mouse
A. stuartii	brown marsupial mouse
Dasyuroides byrnei	kowari
Myrmecobius fasciatus	numbat or banded anteater
Dasyurus maculatus	tiger quoll
Sarcophilus harrisii	Tasmanian devil
Petaurus breviceps	sugar glider
Vombatus cristatus	common wombat
Hypsoprimnodon moschatus	musk rat kangaroo
Setonyx brachyurus	quokka
Lagostrophus fasciatus	banded hare wallaby
Wallabia bicolor	swamp wallaby
Macropus eugenii	tamar, or scrub wallaby
M. parryi	whiptailed wallaby
M. giganteus	great grey kangaroo
M. robustus	wallaroo (hill kangaroo)
M. rufogriseus	Bennett's wallaby
M. rufus	red kangaroo

Sub-Class Eutheria (placental mammals)
  Order: Insectivora (insectivores)
  Tenrec (Centetes) ecaudatus   tail-less tenrec
  Hemicentetes semispinosus   streaked tenrec
  Echinops telfairi   lesser hedgehog tenrec
  Setifer setosus   greater hedgehog tenrec
  Solenodon solenodons   solenodon
  Neomys fodiens   water shrew
  Erinaceus europaeus   European hedgehog
  Blarina brevicauda   short-tailed shrew
  Sorex araneus   common shrew
  Crocidura flavescens herero   Herero musk shrew
  Order: Macroscelidea (elephant shrews)
  Elephantulus rufescens   rufous elephant shrew
  Rhyncyon chrysopygus   yellow-rumped elephant shrew
  Order: Scandentia (tree shrews)
  Tupaia glis (belangeri)   common tree shrew
  T. longipes
  Order: Pholidota (pangolins)
  Manis tricuspis   pangolin
  Order: Edentata (edentates)
  Dasypus   long nosed armadillo
  Euphractus   hairy armadillo
  Choloepus hoffmani   two-toed sloth
  Bradypus tridactyla   three-toed sloth
  Myrmecophaga tridactyla   giant anteater
  Tamandua   Collared anteater
  Order: Lagomorpha (rabbits and hares)
  Lepus europaeus   common hare
  Oryctolagus cuniculus   rabbit
  Ochotona hyperborea   Japanese pika
  O. princeps   American pika
  Order: Rodentia (rodents)
  Marmota caligata   hoary marmot
  M. olympus   olympic marmot
  M. flaviventris   yellow-bellied marmot
  M. marmota   European or alpine marmot
  M. monax   woodchuck
  Cynomys ludovicianus   black-tailed prairie dog
  Tamias striatus   Eastern chipmunk
  Spermophilus columbianus   Columbian ground squirrel
  S. beldingi   Belding's ground squirrel
  S. undulatus   long tailed souslik
  Castor fiber   beaver
  Peromyscus maniculatus   deer mouse
  P.m. gracilis
  P.m. bairdii
  P. polionotus   oldfield mouse
  P. leucopus   white-footed deer mouse
  Cricetus   hamsters
  Mesocricetus auratus   golden hamster
  Dicrostonyx groenlandicus   collared lemming
  Lemmus   true lemmings

Order: Rodentia (rodents) (continued)

Meriones unguiculatus	Mongolian gerbil or jird
	Central Asian clawed jird
Clethrionomys glareolus	bank vole
Microtus ochrogaster	prairie vole
Heterocephalus glaber	naked mole rat
Cricetomys gambianus	giant rat
Acomys cahirinus	spiny mouse
Rattus norvegicus	brown rat (laboratory rat)
R. rattus	black rat
Mus musculus	house mouse (laboratory mouse)
Apodemus	field and wood mice
Hystrix crassispinis	Bornean rattle porcupine
Octodon	S. American bush rats
Cavia porcellus	guinea pig
Dolichotis (Pediolagus)	mara
Cuniculus	agoutis
Dasyprocta punctata	agouti
Myoprocta pratti	green acouchi
Geocapromys ingrahami	Bahamian hutia

Order: Hyracoidea (hyraxcs)

Procavia johnsoni	large-toothed rock hyrax
Heterohyrax brucei	small-toothed rock hyrax
Dendrohyrax	tree hyrax

Order Tubulidentata (aardvarks)

Orycteropus afer	aardvark

Order: Perissodactyla (odd-toed ungulates)

Ceratotherium simum	white rhinoceros
Diceros bicornis	black rhinoceros
Rhinoceros unicornis	Indian rhinoceros
Equus africanus (asinus)	African wild ass, domestic ass
E. hemionus	Asiatic wild ass
E. caballus	feral and domestic horse
E. grevyi	Grevy's zebra
E. burchelli	plains zebra
E. zebra	mountain zebra

Order: Proboscidea (elephants)

Loxodonta africana	African elephant
Elephas maximus	Indian elephant

Order: Artiodactyla

Sus scrofa	wild pig, domestic pig
Phacochoerus aethiopicus	warthog
Tayassu tajacu	collared peccary
Choeropsis liberiensis	pygmy hippopotamus
Hippopotamus amphibius	hippopotamus
Camelus ferus	Bactrian or two-humped camel
Vicugna vicugna	vicuña
Tragulus sp.	mouse deer or chevrotain
Moschus moschiferus	musk deer
Cervus elaphus	red deer
Cervus canadensis	elk
Dama dama	fallow deer

Order: Artiodactyla (continued)

Odocoileus hemionus hemionus	mule deer
O.h. columbianus	black-tailed deer
Rangifer arcticus	caribou
Giraffa cameloparadalis	giraffe
Antilocapra americana	pronghorn
Syncerus caffer	African buffalo
Tragelaphus strepsiceros	greater kudu
T. imberbis	lesser kudu
T. scriptus	bush buck
Taurotragus oryx	eland
Cephalophus sp.	duikers
C. maxwelli	Maxwell's duiker
Redunca redunca	Bohor reedbuck
R. arundinum	Southern reedbuck
Kobus ellipsiprymnus	waterbuck
K. lechwe	lechwe
Adenota (Kobus) kob thomasii	Uganda kob
Oryx gazella	oryx, gemsbok
O. beisa	Beisa oryx
Connochaetes taurinus	blue wildebeest
Alcelaphus sp.	hartebeests
A. busephalus cokei	Coke's hartebeest
Damaliscus dorcas dorcas	bontebok
D. korrigum	topi
Aepyceros melampus	impala
Gazella granti	Grant's gazelle
G. thomsoni	Thomson's gazelle
Litocranius walleri	gerenuk
Oreotragus oreotragus	klipspringer
Madoqua kirki	Kirk's dikdik
M. phillipsi	Phillips' dikdik
Ourebia ourebi	oribi
Raphicerus sp.	steinbok and grysbok
Capra hircus	mountain goat, domestic goat
C. ibex	ibex
C. waalie	Walia ibex
Ovis aries	domestic sheep
O. ammon	Marco Polo sheep
O. canadensis	mountain sheep
O. dalli	Dall sheep
Ovibos moschatus	musk ox

Order: Carnivora (carnivores)
Sub-order Fissipedia (land carnivores)

Mustela erminea	stoat
M. nivalis	weasel, least weasel
M. vison	American mink
M. putorius	European polecat, ferret
Lutra lutra	otter
Meles meles	European badger
Mephitis mephitis	striped skunk
Gulo gulo	volverine
Nasua narica	coati

Sub-order Fissipedia (land carnivores) (continued)

Ursus americanus	American black bear
Suricata suricatta	meerkat
Helogale parvula (*H. undulata*) (*rufula*)	dwarf monogoose
Mungos mungo	African banded mongoose
Civettictis civetta	African civet
Crocuta crocuta	spotted hyaena
Hyaena brunnea	brown hyaena
Proteles cristatus	aardwolf
Canis aureus	golden jackal
C. adustus	side-striped jackal
C. mesomelas	black-backed jackal
C. latrans	coyote
C. lupus	wolf
C. familiaris	domesticated dog
Lycaon pictus	African hunting dog
Cuon alpinus	dhole, Asian wild dog
Otocyon megalotis	bat-eared fox
Fennecus zerda	fennec fox
Speothos venatica	bush dog
Vulpes vulpes	red fox
Felis catus	domestic cat
F. viverrinus	fishing cat
F. bengalensis	leopard cat
Acinonyx jubatus	cheetah
Panthera leo	lion
P. tigris	tiger
P. uncia	snow leopard

Sub-order Pinnipedia (seals, sealions and walruses)

Odobenus rosmarus	walrus
Eumetopias jubata	Steller sea lion
Zalophus californianus	Californian sea lion
Arctocephalus gazella	(Antarctic) fur seal
A. galapagoensis	Galapagos or Kerguelen fur seal
A. pusillus	fur seal
Phoca groenlandicus	harp seal
P. vitulina	common or harbour seal
P. largha	spotted seal
P. (Pusa) hispida	ringed seal
Halichoerus grypus	grey seal
Mirounga leonina	Southern elephant seal
M. angustirostris	Northern elephant seal
Leptonychotes wedelli	Weddell's seal

Order: Sirenia (sea cows)

Dugong dugong	dugong
Trichecus manatus	Northern manatee

Order: Cetacea (whales)

Sub-order Mysteceti

Megaptera novaeangliae	humpback whale

Sub-order Odontoceti

Platanista gangetica	Ganges dolphin
Inia geoffroyensis	Amazon dolphin

Sub-order Odontoceti (continued)

Sotalia fluviatilis	tucuxi
Delphinus delphis	common dolphin
Tursiops truncatus	bottle-nosed dolphin
Stenella longirostris	spinner dolphin
S. attenuata	spotted dolphin
Monodon monoceros	narwhal
Orcinus orca	killer whale
Globicephala melaena	long-finned pilot whale
G. macrorhynchus	short-finned pilot whale
Phocoena phocoena	common or harbour porpoise
Phocenoides dalli	Dall's porpoise
Delphinapterus leucas	beluga
Sousa sp.	humpbacked dolphin

Order: Chiroptera (bats)

Sub-order Megachiroptera (fruit bats)

Pteropus giganteus	Indian flying fox
P. poliocephalus	greyheaded flying fox
Hypsignathus monstrosus	hammer-headed bat
Micropteropus pusillus	dwarf epauletted-fruit bat
Epomops franqueti	Franquet's fruit bat

Sub-order Microchiroptera (inectivorous bats)

Saccopteryx bilineata	greater white lined bat
Hipposideros commersoni	Commerson's leaf-nosed bat
Pteronotus parnelli	Parnell's moustached bat
Mormoops megalophylla	Peter's ghost-faced bat
Phyllostomus hastatus	spear-nosed bat
P. discolor	pale spear-nosed bat
Vampyrum spectrum	American false vampire bat
Myotis adversus	large footed bat
Pipistrellus nanus	Banana bat
Nyctalus noctula	noctule bat
Vespertilio murinus	particoloured bat
Chalinolobus dwyeri	large-eared pied bat
Lasiurus borealis	red bat
Miniopterus schreibersii	Schreiber's long-fingered bat
Antrozous pallidus	pallid bat
Tadarida brasiliensis	Brazilian free-tailed bat

Order: Dermoptera (colugos or flying lemurs)

Cynocephalus sp.	colugo or flying lemur

Order: Primates (primates)

Sub-order Strepsirhini (prosimians)

Lepilemur mustelinus	sportive lemur
Lemur catta	ring-tailed lemur
Lemur fulvus	brown lemur
Microcebus murinus	mouse lemur
Chirogaleus	dwarf lemur
Indri indri	indri
Perodicticus potto	potto
Galago senegalensis moholi	lesser bushbaby
G. alleni	Allen's bushbaby
G. crassicaudatus	greater bushbaby
G. demidovii	Demidoff's bushbaby

Sub-order Haplorhini (tarsiers and simians)
Infraorder Platyrrhina (New World monkeys)

Callicebus moloch	titi monkey
Saimiri sciureus	squirrel monkey
Cebus sp.	capuchins
Alouatta sp.	howler monkeys
Cebuella pymaea	pigmy marmoset
Callithrix jacchus jacchus	common marmoset
C. humeralifer intermedius	
Saguinus oedipus oedipus	cotton-topped tamarin
S. o. geoffroyi	Geoffroy's tamarin
S. fuscicollis	saddle-backed tamarin
S. labiatus labiatus	white-lipped red-bellied tamarin

Infraorder Catarrhina (Old World simians)

Macaca fuscata	Japanese macaque
M. fascicularis	long tailed or crab-eating macaque
M. radiata	bonnet macaque
M. sinica	toque macaque
M. nemestrina	pig-tailed macaque
M. mulatta	rhesus monkey, rhesus macaque
M. sylvana	barbary ape
M. (Cynopithecus) niger	Celebes black ape
Papio anubis	olive baboon
P. cynocephalus	yellow baboon
P. ursinus	chacma baboon
P. hamadryas	hamadryas baboon
Mandrillus sphinx	mandrill
Theropithecus gelada	Gelada baboon
Cercocebus albigena	grey cheeked mangabey
C. atys	sooty mangabey
C. galeritus	agile mangabey
C. torquatus	collared mangebey
Cercopithecus ascanius schmidti	red tailed monkey
C. pogonias	crowned guenon
C. aethiops	vervet monkey
C. neglectus	De Brazza's monkey
Miopithecus talapoin	talapoin monkey
Erythrocebus patas	patas monkey
Presbytis entellus	common or hanuman langur
P. johni	Nilgiri langur
P. senex	purple faced langur
P. obscura	dusky leaf monkey
P. cristatus	silvered leaf monkey
Colobus guereza	black and white colobus monkey
Symphalangus syndactylus	siamang
Hylobates lar	white banded gibbon
H. pileatus	pileated gibbon
Pongo pygmaeus	orang utan
Gorilla gorilla beringei	mountain gorilla
Pan troglodytes	chimpanzee
P. paniscus	bonobo or pygmy chimpanzee
Homo sapiens	human beings

Table 2 Glossary

Affectional or affiliative behaviour: friendly interactions between individuals, usually including allogrooming, close proximity, body contact and sometimes mutual defence.

Aggregation: a number of conspecifics which are in close proximity, but show no co-operation or consistent personal relations. An aggregation normally lacks a fixed composition and can be entered by any individual (cf. *society*).

Agonistic behaviour: that concerned with attack, defence and submission.

Allogrooming: grooming another individual.

Allomothering (or 'aunting'): assisting another female in the care of her offspring.

Alloparental care: care of an infant by an individual who is not its parent.

Alpha male/female: the highest-ranking member of a dominance hierarchy or an individual whose status confers exclusive rights to a limited resource.

Altricial: young of placental mammals which are naked, blind, deaf and incapable of locomotion (see *Precocial*) after birth.

Altruism: behaviour which benefits another individual at the expense of the animal carrying it out (the altruist).

Anthropomorphism: the attribution of human motives and emotions to animals.

Bachelor herd: a group of non-breeding males which may be hierarchically organized.

Band: a group of individuals personally known to one another which show concerted movement.

Beta male/female: a high-ranking adult who is subordinate to an alpha male or female.

Binaural: using two ears, each acting as an independent receptor.

Bond (non-sexual bond, social bond): a close friendly relationship between two individuals (see *Affectional behaviour, Pair bond*) which is unrelated to female oestrous condition.

Breeding unit: a group of individuals where one or more males have exclusive sexual access to one or more females. Males may or may not be competitive.

Browser: an animal which feeds on browse, i.e. leaves, shoots and young branches.

Buccal cavity: the mouth cavity from throat to lips.

Coefficient of relationship (r): the degree of relatedness of two individuals expressed as the fraction of genes which are identical by direct descent, e.g. an offspring inherits half of its genes from each parent so that r (for parent and infant) $= \frac{1}{2}$.

Communication: behaviour of one individual which has evolved to influence that of another (cf. *Social communication*).

Consort: a male consorts with a female when he remains in close proximity to her and prevents other males from mating. Consorting normally occurs around the female's oestrous period.

Conspecific: a member of the same species.

Core area: the central part of an animal's home range in which it spends most of its time. Core areas are often exclusive to a particular animal or group of animals.

Cursorial: a running animal, usually with elongated distal limb joints, such as deer and dog.

Dispersal: the movement made by an animal from one group or site to another place or group in which it reproduces. It is a mechanism which promotes inbreeding avoidance. Usually adolescents or sub-adults leave their natal group or area but adults may also disperse one or more times. In mammals, males generally disperse while females remain in their natal area or group.

Display: a behavioural act, or sequence of communicative value.

Dominance hierarchy: a group of individuals which, considered as dyads, show unidirectional aggression–submission relationships. (A may be dominant to B who is subordinate to A but dominant to C, etc.) In any conflict the dominant individual normally wins; subordinates seldom fight back, but may sometimes show threat as a response.

Ecological niche: the way of life of an animal in a particular habitat. This important concept is best illustrated with an example, e.g. the 'small cursorial herbivore niche' is occupied by rodents in South America, antelopes in Africa and wallabies in Australia.

Embryon: the newborn young of a marsupial which is capable of locomotion but is naked, blind and of an embryonic appearance.

Ethogram: a description of the behaviour repertoire of the species in terms of units such as 'open-mouth threat', 'whine', 'anal scent mark', etc.

Eusocial: social animals in which distinct reproductive and non-reproductive (worker) castes are found in a colony; there is also co-operative care for young and an overlap of at least two generations.

Evolutionarily stable strategy (ESS): a strategy which, if adopted by most members of a population, gives higher reproductive fitness than any other strategy. A mixed ESS is a situation where particular proportions of two or more strategies in a population would result in equal payoffs for each strategy.

Female-bonded group: one in which males disperse to breed and the remaining females show strong personal relationships with one another, usually based on kin (see *matriarchy*).

Fitness: genetic success measured in terms of an individual's contribution to the next generation (see also *Inclusive fitness*).

Flehmen: curling of the upper lip when exposed to an odour. It occurs commonly in male mammals exposed to the urine of an oestrous female. It is believed that flehmen is associated with olfactory perception by the vomero-nasal organ (Jacobson's organ).

Gallivanting: a term coined by Barash (1981) to describe the behaviour of a male who has acquired exclusive sexual access to one or more females by guarding, but makes excursions to mate opportunistically with any other females he may encounter.

Game Theory: a mathematical analysis of conflicts (usually applied to war, economics and games of skill).

Graded signal: one which varies in intensity, frequency or both and is therefore capable of conveying quantitative information about the mood of the sender.

Grazer: an animal which feeds mainly on grass.

Gregarious: individuals which seek the company of conspecifics and form groups. Gregariousness varies seasonally in some species.

Harem: a group of females guarded by a male, who, prevents other males from mating with them.

Home range: the area over which an individual or group of individuals forage, and come to know, thoroughly (see *territory, core areas*.)

Inclusive fitness: the animal's production of adult offspring stripped of all components resulting from the help or hindrance of its neighbour, plus fractions of the quantities of harm and benefit which the individual personally causes to his neighbours. The fractions are based on the coefficients of relationship appropriate to the neighbours who are affected, (i.e. $\frac{1}{2}$ for full sibs, $\frac{1}{4}$ for half sibs, 1/8 for cousins, zero for those whose relationship is negligibly small—see p. 5).

Intromission: the entry of the male's penis into the female's vagina.

Iteroparous: producing young more than once in a lifetime (see *Semelparous*).

K-selected: species which are long-lived, producing few, well-cared-for offspring at a time. This type of selection is typical of predictable, stable environments where population growth is very restricted (see *r-selected*).

Kin selection: the selection of genes which promote the survival and reproduction of close relatives other than offspring (see *Inclusive fitness*).

Kinship: the possession of a recent common ancestor. Kinship can be measured by the coefficient of relationship *r* (q.v.).

Lactation: the secretion of milk.

Lek: an area used for communal courtship displays where each male defends a small territory into which he attempts to attract females. Certain of the territories in the lek are favoured by the females, so that males holding them show the highest reproductive success.

Matriarchy: a social group in which adult females continue to behave altruistically towards their daughters even after they attain maturity (see *Female-bonded group*).

Matriline: a group of females all descended from the same mother.

Monogamy: where the breeding unit consists of a single male and female. Grade I: male and female may not remain in contact, the maximum sized group is the pair and unweaned offspring. Grade II: a family group typically includes more than one generation of offspring. Grade III (status determined): a multimale/multifemale group in which alpha male and female alone breed.

Multimale/multifemale groups (often referred to simply as multimale groups): breeding groups containing more than one adult male; usually there is a male hierarchy and often a female one as well; status reproductive success are commonly associated.

Natal group: the social group in which an individual is born.

Natal male, natal female: adult members remaining in the group in which they were born.

Neonate: newborn individual.

Nepotism: behaviour benefiting a close relative as opposed to an unrelated individual.

Non-female bonded group: one where females disperse from their natal group to breed. (see *Female-bonded group*).

Nulliparous: not previously having given birth.

Nursery herd: a mobile group of adult females with juvenile and infant offspring of both sexes.

Oestrus (*adj.* **oestrous**): restricted period of maximal sexual receptivity in a female mammal, usually associated with ovulation and maximum fertility.

Ovulation: release of the female gamete (the ovum) from the ovary. Ovulation may be spontaneous, or induced by copulation.

Peer group: a group of individuals of approximately the same age or at the same stage of development (e.g. juvenile peer group, infant peer group).

Play group: a group of young individuals (not litter-mates) who play together. Social species giving birth to single or twin young often form play groups (e.g. sheep, monkeys).

Pair bond: the close and persistent affectional tie which exists between adult male and female in monogamous species.

Parental investment: anything done by the parent for the offspring that increases the offspring's change of surviving while decreasing the parent's ability to invest in other offspring.

Parturition: the act of giving birth.

Polyandry: having several male mates at a time.

Polygamy: having more than one mate.

Polygyny: having several female mates at a time.

Presenting: directing the ano-genital region towards another individual.

Precocial young: those born fully-furred with the eyes open and capable of locomotion.

Proceptive behaviour: sexual soliciting by a female.

Promiscuous (promiscuity): indiscriminate or opportunistic mating.

r-**selected**: species which are short-lived and produce large numbers of young. Typical of species which colonize short-lived environments or undergo large fluctuations in population size (see *K-selected*). This strategy of reproduction is characteristic of species which live in environments with wide fluctuations in availability of resources, or situations where young are subjected to a high mortality rate. It enables a species to colonize short-lived favourable environments.

Resource holding potential (RHP): an individual's ability to control a contested resource such as food, females or territory. It is a measure of strength, size, weapons etc., which would enable an animal to win an escalated contest.

Semelparous: breeding only once in a lifetime (see *Iteroparous*).

Sexual dimorphism: where adults of the two sexes are typically different either in gross body form, in the possession of special organs (such as antlers or manes) or in colouring, but excluding the normal differences in external genitalia.

Sexual selection: The differential ability of individuals of different genetic types to acquire mates. Sexual selection acts on secondary sexual characters based on choices made between males and females. Intrasexual selection occurs when there is competition between members of the same sex.

Sibling, sib: offspring of the same parent(s); half-siblings have one parent in common (half brother, half sister), full siblings have both parents in common (brother, sister).

Society or social group: a group of individuals of the same species which is organized co-operatively, is of a stable composition and presents barriers to the entry of non-group members (is impermeable). There is reciprocal communication and usually distinctive, and often asymmetrical, social relationships between adult group members.

Status: position in a dominance hierarchy.

Strategy: a course of behaviour which optimizes fitness.

Sub-adult: a young, but sexually mature, individual which is non-breeding and often has not achieved full adult size.

Sympatric species: those which have overlapping geographical ranges.

Territory: an area of exclusive use by an individual or group which is defended against conspecifies by patrolling, overt aggression and/or advertisement.

Troop: a mobile group of mammals (usually applied to primates) which assemble together for resting or sleeping, there is usually hostility to non-troop members.

Ungulate: a convenient collective noun which refers to all hooved mammals; they do not necessarily represent a natural phylogenetic grouping.

Vaginal plug: a post-copulatory obstruction in the female's reproductive tract which is derived from coagulation of a component of the seminal fluid.

BIBLIOGRAPHY

Abbott, D. and Hearn, J. P. (1978) Physical, hormonal and behavioural aspects of sexual development in the marmoset monkey (*Callithrix jacchus*). *Primates* **16**, 155–174.

Albone, E. S., Eglinton, S., Walker, J. M. and Ware, C. S. (1974) The anal sac secretion of the red fox *Vulpes vulpes*: its chemistry and microbiology. A comparison with the anal sac secretion of the lion *Panthera leo*. *Life Sci.* **14**, 387–400.

Aldis, O. (1975) *Play Fighting*. Academic Press, New York.

Alexander, R. D. (1974) The evolution of social behaviour. *Ann. Rev. Ecol. Syst.* **5**, 325–383.

Altmann, M. (1963) 'Naturalistic studies of maternal care in moose and elk', in *Maternal Behaviour in Mammals*, Rheingold, H. L. (ed.) John Wiley & Sons, New York, pp. 233–253.

Altmann, S. A. (1974) Baboons, space, time and energy. *Amer. Zool.* **14**, 221–248.

Altmann, S. A. (ed.) (1967) *Social Communication among Primates*. Chicago University Press, Chicago.

Altmann, S. A. and Altmann, J. (1970) *Baboon Ecology*. University of Chicago Press, Chicago.

Altmann, J. (1980) *Baboon Mothers and Infants*. Harvard University Press, Cambridge, Mass.

Altmann, S. A., Wagner, S. S. and Lenington, S. (1977) Two models for the evolution of polygyny. *Behav. Ecol. Sociobiol.* **2**, 397–410.

Anderson, P. K. (1982) Studies of Dugongs at Shark Bay, Western Australia. II. Surface and subsurface observations. *Aust. Wildl. Res.* **9**, 85–99.

Andersson, M. (1982) Female choice selects for extreme tail length in a widowbird. *Nature* **299**, 818–820.

Andrew, D. L. and Settle, G. A. (1982) 'Observations on the behaviour of species of Planigale (Dasyuridae, Marsupialia) with particular reference to the narrow nosed planigale (*Planigale tenuirostris*)', in *Carnivorous Marsupials*, Archer, M. (ed.) Royal Zoological Society of New South Wales, pp. 311–323.

Andrew, R. J. (1963*a*) Evolution of facial expression. *Science* **142**, 1034–1041.

Andrew, R. J. (1963*b*) The origin and evolution of the calls and facial expressions of primates. *Behaviour* **20**, 1–109.

Archer, J. E. (1968) The effect of strange male odour on aggressive behaviour in male mice. *J. Mammal.* **49**, 572–575.

Archer, M. (ed.) (1982) *Carnivorous Marsupials*. Royal Zoological Society of New South Wales, Sydney.

Arnold, S. J. (1983) 'Sexual selection: the interface of theory and empiricism', in *Mate Choice*, Bateson, P. (ed.), Cambridge University Press, Cambridge, pp. 53–66.

Aron, C. (1979) Mechanisms of control of the reproductive function by olfactory stimuli in female mammals. *Physiol. Rev.* **59**, 229–284.

Augee, M. L., Ealey, E. H. M. and Price, I. P. (1975) Movements of echidnas *Tachyglossus aculeatus* determined by marking, recapture and radio tracking. *Australian Wildl. Res.* **2**, 93–101.

212

Baldwin, J. D. and Baldwin, J. I. (1974) Exploration and social play in squirrel monkeys (*Saimiri*). *Amer. Zool.* **14**, 303–315.

Baldwin, J. D. and Baldwin, J. I. (1976) Effects of food ecology on social play: a laboratory simulation. *Z. Tierpsychol.* **40**, 1–14.

Barash, D. P. (1973) The social biology of the olympic marmot. *Animal Behaviour Monographs* **6** (3), 171–245.

Barash, D. P. (1974) The evolution of marmot societies: a general theory. *Science* **185**, 415–420.

Barash, D. P. (1981) Mate guarding and gallivanting by male hoary marmots (*Marmota caligata*). *Behav. Ecol. Sociobiol.* **9**, 187–193.

Barnett, S. A. (1958) An analysis of social behaviour in wild rats. *Proc. Zool. Soc. Lond.* **130**, 107–152.

Barrett, P. and Bateson, P. (1978) The development of play in cats. *Behaviour* **66**, 106–120.

Bateson, G. (1955) A theory of play and fantasy. *Psychiatric Research Reports* **2**, 39–51.

Bateson, P. P. S. (ed.) (1983) *Mate Choice*. Cambridge University Press, Cambridge.

Beach, F. A. (1968) 'Factors involved in the control of mounting behaviour by female mammals', in *Perspectives in Reproduction and Sexual Behaviour*, Diamond, M. (ed.) Indiana University Press, Bloomington, Indiana, pp. 83–131.

Beach, F. A. (ed.) (1974) *Sex and Behaviour*. Krieger, New York.

Beach, F. A. (1976) Sexual attractivity, proceptivity and receptivity in female mammals. *Hormones and Behaviour* **7**, 105–138.

Beach, F. A. and Le Boeuf (1967) Coital behaviour in dogs 1. Preferential mating in the bitch. *Anim. Behav.* **15**, 546–558.

Bearder, S. and Martin, R. D. (1979) 'The social organization of a nocturnal primate revealed by radio-tracking', in *A Handbook on Biotelemetry and Radio-tracking*, Amlaner, C. J. and Macdonald, D. W. (eds.) Oxford, Pergamon Press, pp. 623–648.

Beauchamp, G. K. (1973) Attraction of male guinea pigs to conspecific urine. *Physiol Behav.* **10**, 589–594.

Beauchamp, G. K., Criss, B. R. and Willington, J. L. (1979) Chemical communication in *Cavia*: responses of wild (*C. aperea*), domestic (*C. porcellus*) and F_1 males to urine. *Anim. Behav.* **27**, 1066–1072.

Beier, J. C. and Wartzok, D. (1979) Mating behaviour of captive spotted seals (*Phoca largha*). *Anim. Behav.* **27**, 772–781.

Bekoff, M. (1972) Development of social interactions, play and metacommunication in mammals: An ethological perspective. *Biol. Rev.* **47**, 412–434.

Bekoff, M. (1974) Social play and play soliciting in infant canids. *American Zoologist* **14**, 323–340.

Bekoff, M. (1977) Social communication in canids: evidence for the evolution of a stereotyped mammalian display. *Science* **197**, 1097–1099.

Bekoff, M. (1978a) 'Social play: structure, function and evolution of a cooperative social behaviour', in *The Development of Behaviour: Comparative and Evolutionary Aspects*, Burkhardt, G. M. and Bekoff, M. (eds.), Garland Press, New York, pp. 367–383.

Bekoff, M. (1978b) 'Behavioural development in coyotes and eastern coyotes', in *Coyotes, Biology, Behaviour and Management*, Bekoff, M. (ed.), Academic Press, New York, pp. 97–126.

Bekoff, M. and Byers, J. A. (1981) 'A critical reanalysis of the ontogeny and phylogeny of mammalian social and locomotor play: a methodological hornet's nest', in *Issues in Behavioural Development: The Bielefeld Interdisciplinary Conference*, Immelmann, K., Barlow, G., Main, M. and Petrinovich, L. (eds.), Cambridge University Press, Cambridge.

Bekoff, M. and Wells, M. C. (1980) Social ecology in coyotes. *Sci. Am.* **242**, 130–148.

Bell, D. J. (1980) Social olfaction in lagomorphs. *Symp. zool. Soc. Lond.* **45**, 141–164.

Bell, D. J. (1983) 'Chemical communication in the European rabbit: urine and social status', in

Proceedings of the World Lagomorph Conference, Guelph, Canada, 1979, Myers, K. and MacInnes, J. C. (eds.)

Bennett, G. (1835) Notes on the natural history and habits of the *Ornithorhynchus paradoxus*, Blum. *Trans. Zool. Soc. Lond.* **1**, 229–258.

Benveniste, R. E. and Todaro, G. J. (1976) Evolution of type C viral genes: evidence for an Asian origin of man. *Nature* **261**, 101–108.

Berger, J. (1977) Organizational systems and dominance in feral horses in the Grand Canyon. *Behav. Ecol. Sociobiol.* **2**, 131–146.

Bernstein, J. S. (1981) Dominance: the baby and the bath water. *The Behavioural and Brain Sciences* **4**, 419–457.

Berry, R. J. (1970) The natural history of the house mouse. *Field. Stud.* **3**, 219–262.

Berry, R. J. (1981) Population dynamics of the house mouse. *Symp. zool. Soc. Lond.* **47**, 395–425.

Berryman, J. (1976) Guinea-pig vocalizations: their structure, causation and function. *Z. Tierpsychol.* **41**, 80–106.

Bertram, B. C. R. (1975*a*) The social system of lions. *Scientific American* **232**, 54–65.

Bertram, B. C. R. (1975*b*) Social factors influencing reproduction in wild lions. *J. Zool., Lond.* **177**, 463–482.

Bertram, B. C.R. (1976) 'Kin selection in lions and in evolution', in *Growing Points in Ethology*, Bateson, P. P. G. and Hinde, R. A. (eds.), Cambridge University Press, Cambridge, pp. 281–301.

Bertram, B. C. R. (1978) 'Living in groups: predators and prey', in *Behavioural Ecology: an Evolutionary Approach*, Krebs, J. R. and Davies, N. B. (eds.), Blackwell, Oxford, pp. 64–96.

Bertram, B. C. R. (1979) 'Serengeti predators and their social systems', in *Serengeti, Dynamics of an Ecosystem*, Sinclair, A. R. E. and Norton-Griffiths, H. (eds.), University of Chicago Press, Chicago, pp. 221–248.

Bertram, B. C. R. (1983) Cooperation and competition in lions (with a reply by Packer and Pusey). *Nature* **302**, 356.

Beruter, J., Beauchamp, G. K. and Muetterties, E. L. (1973) Complexity of chemical communication in mammals: urinary components mediating sex discrimination in male guinea pigs. *Biochem. Biophys. Res. Comm.* **53**, 264–271.

Biben, M. (1979) Predation and predatory play behaviour of domestic cats. *Anim. Behav.* **27**, 81–94.

Biben, M. (1983) Comparative ontogeny of social behaviour in three South American canids, the maned wolf, crab eating fox and bush dog: implications for sociality. *Anim. Behav.* **31**, 818–826.

Bonner, W. N. (1984) Lactation strategies in pinnipeds: problems for a marine mammalian group. *Symp. zool. Soc. Lond.* **51**, 253–272.

Bradbury, J. W. (1977*a*) 'Social organization and communication', in *Biology of Bats*, **3**, Wimsatt, W. A. (ed.), Academic Press, New York, pp. 1–72.

Bradbury, J. W. (1977*b*) Lek mating behaviour in the hammer-headed bat. *Z. Tierpsychol.* **45**, 225–255.

Bradbury, J. W. and Gibson, R. M. (1983) 'Leks and mate choice', in *Mate Choice*, Bateson, P. (ed.), Cambridge University Press, Cambridge, pp. 109–138.

Bradbury, J. W. and Vehrencamp, S. L. (1976*a*) Social organisation and foraging in emballonurid bats. I. Field studies. *Behav. Ecol. Sociobiol* **1**, 337–381.

Bradbury, J. W. and Vehrencamp, S. L. (1976*b*) Social organisation and foraging in emballonurid bats. II. A model for determination of group size. *Behav. Ecol. Sociobiol* **1**, 383–404.

Bradbury, J. W. and Vehrencamp, S. L. (1977*a*) Social organisation and foraging in emballonurid bats. III. Mating systems. *Behav. Ecol. Sociobiol* **2**, 1–19.

Bradbury, J. W. and Vehrencamp, S. L. (1977*b*) Social organisation and foraging in emballonurid bats. IV. Parental investment patterns. *Behav. Ecol. Sociobiol* **2**, 19–31.

Braithwaite, R. W. (1974) Behavioural changes associated with the population cycle of *Antechinus stewartii* (Marsupialia). *Australian J. Zool.* **22**, 45–62.

Bramblett, C. A. (1976) *Patterns of Primate Behaviour*. Mayfield Publishing Co., California.

Brattstrom, B. H. (1973) Social and maintenance behaviour of the echidna *Tachyglossus aculeatus*. *J. Mammal.* **54**, 50–71.

Broekhuizen, S. and Maaskamp. F. (1980) Behaviour of does and leverets of the European hare (*Lepus europaeus*) whilst nursing. *J. Zool., Lond.*, **191**, 487–501.

Bronson, F. H. (1979) The reproductive ecology of the house mouse. *Q. Rev. Biol.* **54**, 265–299.

Brooks, R. J. and Banks, E. M. (1973) Behavioural biology of the collared lemming (*Dicrostonyx groendlandicus* (Trais)). An analysis of vocal communication. *Animal Behaviour Monographs* **6** (1) 1–83.

Brown, J. H. and Lasiewski, R. C. (1972) Metabolism of weasels, the cost of being long and thin. *Ecology* **53**, 939–943.

Brown, J. L. (1975) *The Evolution of Behaviour*. W. W. Norton, New York.

Brown, P. (1976) Vocal communication in the pallid bat *Antrozous pallidus*. *Z. Tierpsychol* **41**, 34–54.

Bruce, H. M. (1960) A block to pregnancy in the mouse caused by proximity of strange males. *J. Reprod. Fert.*, **1**, 311–312.

Buchman, O. L. K, and Guiler, E. R. (1977) 'Behaviour and ecology of the Tasmanian devil *Sarcophilus harrisii*', in *The Biology of Marsupials*, Stonehouse, B. and Gilmore, D. (eds.), Macmillan, London, pp. 155–168.

Budnitz, N. and Dainis, K. (1975) '*Lemur catta* ecology and behaviour', in *Lemur Biology*, Tattersall, I. and Sussman, R. W. (eds.), Plenum, New York, pp. 219–235.

Buechner, H. K. and Roth, H. D. (1974) The lek system in the Uganda Kob antelope. *Amer. Zool.* **14**, 145–162.

Burghardt, G. M. and Bekoff, M. (eds.) (1978) *The Development of Behaviour: Comparative and Evolutionary Aspects*. Garland, New York.

Burghardt, G. M. and Burghardt, L. S. (1972) 'Notes on the behavioural development of two female black bear cubs: the first eight months', in *Bears – their Biology and Management*, Herrero, S. (ed.), IUCN 23, Morges.

Burrell, H. (1927) *The Platypus*. Rigby, Adelaide.

Busse, C. and Hamilton, W. J. III (1981) Infant carrying by male chacma baboons. *Science* **212**, 1281–1283.

Byers, J. A. (1977) Terrain preferences in the play behaviour of Siberian Ibex kids (*Capra ibex sibirica*). *Z. Tierpsychol.* **45**, 199–209.

Byers, J. A. and Bekoff, M. (1981) Social spacing and cooperative behaviour of the collared peccary *Tayassu tajacu*. *J. Mamm.* **62**, 767–785.

Bygott, J. D., Bertram, B. C. R. and Hanby, J. P. (1979) Male lions in large coalitions gain reproductive advantages. *Nature* **282**, 839–841.

Caldwell, D. K. and Caldwell, M. C. (1977*a*) 'Cetaceans', in *How Animals Communicate*, Sebeok, T. E. (ed.), Indiana University Press, Brookfield, pp. 794–868.

Caldwell, M. C. and Caldwell, D. K. (1972) 'Behaviour of marine mammals', in *Mammals of the Sea*, Ridgeway, S. H. (ed.), Thomas, Springfeld, Illinois, pp. 409–465.

Caldwell, M. C. and Caldwell, D. K. (1977*b*) 'Social interactions and reproduction in the Atlantic bottlenosed dolphin', in *Breeding Dolphins, Present Status and Suggestions for the Future*, Ridgeway, S. H. and Benirschke, K. W. (eds.) U. S. Marine Mammal Commission Report MMM-76/07, Washington, pp. 133–142.

Carl, E. (1971) Population control in arctic ground squirrels. *Ecology* **52**, 395–413.

Caro, T. (1980) Effects of the mother, object play and adult experience on predation in cats. *Behav. Neurol. Biol.* **29**, 29–51.

Caro, T. M. (1981*a*) Sex differences in the termination of social play in cats. *Anim. Behav.* **29**, 271–279.

Caro, T. M. (1981*b*) Predatory behaviour and social play in kittens. *Behaviour* **76**, 1–24.

Carpenter, C. R. (1940) A field study in Siam of the behaviour and social relations of the gibbon (*Hylobates lar*). *Comp. Psychol. Monogr.* 1–212.

Caryl, P. G. (1979) Communication by agonistic displays: what can games theory contribute to ethology? *Behaviour* **68**, 136–169.

Caryl, P. G. (1981) Escalated fighting and the war of nerves: games theory and animal combat. *Perspectives in Ethology* **4**, 199–224.

Caryl, P. G. (1982) Animal signals: a reply to Hinde. *Anim. Behav.* **30**, 240–244.

Chalmers, N. (1968) The social behaviour of free living mangabeys in Uganda. *Folia Primatol.* **8**, 263–281.

Chalmers, N. (1979) *Social Behaviour in Primates*. Edward Arnold, London.

Chalmers, N. (1980) The ontogeny of play in feral olive baboons (*Papio anubis*). *Anim. Behav.* **28**, 570–585.

Chance, M. R. A. (1962) An interpretation of some agonistic postures: the role of 'cut off' acts and postures. *Symp. zool. Soc. Lond.* **8**, 71–89.

Channing, A. and Rowe-Rowe, D. T. (1977) Vocalizations of South African mustelines. *Z. Tierpsychol.* **44**, 283–293.

Chapman, G. and Hausfater, G. (1979) The reproductive consequences of infanticide in langurs: a mathematical model. *Behav. Ecol. Sociobiol.* **5**, 227–240.

Charles-Dominique, P. (1977*a*) Urine marking and territoriality in *Galago alleni* (Waterhouse, 1837 Lorisoidea, Primates). A field study by radio telemetry. *Z. Tierpsychol.* **43**, 113–138.

Charles-Dominique, P. (1977*b*) *Ecology and Behaviour of Nocturnal Prosimians*. Duckworth, London.

Clarles-Dominique, P. and Bearder, S. K. (1979) 'Field studies of Lorisid behaviour: methodological aspects', in *The Study of Prosimian Behaviour*, Doyle, G. A., and Martin, R. D. (eds.), Academic Press, New York, pp. 567–629.

Cheney, D. L. (1978) Interactions of immature male and female baboons with adult females. *Anim. Behav.* **26**, 389–408.

Cheney, D. L. and Seyfarth, R. M. (1980) Vocal recognition in free ranging vervet monkeys. *Anim. Behav.* **28**, 362–363.

Cheney, D. L. and Seyfarth, R. M. (1981) Selective forces affecting the predator alarm calls of vervet monkeys. *Behaviour* **78**, 25–61.

Chepko-Sade, B. D. and Oliver, T. J. (1979) Coefficient of genetic relationship and the probability of intragenealogical fission in *Macaca mulatta*. *Behav. Ecol. Sociobiol.* **5**, 263–278.

Chevalier-Skolnikoff, J. and Poirier, F. E. (eds.) (1977) *Primate Biosocial Development: Biological, Social and Ecological Determinants*. Garland, New York.

Chiarelli, A. B. and Corruccini, R. S. (eds.) (1982) *Advanced Views in Primate Biology*. Springer-Verlag, Berlin.

Chivers, D. J. (1972) The siamang and the gibbon in the Malay peninsula, in *Gibbon and Siamang*, Rumbaugh, D. M. (ed.), Karger, Basel, pp. 103–135.

Chivers, D. J. (1974) The Siamang in Malaya: a field study of a primate in a tropical rain forest. *Contributions to Primatology* **4**, 1–335. Karger, Basel.

Chivers, D. J. and Joysey, K. A. (eds.) (1978) *Recent Advances in Primatology. 3. Evolution*. Academic Press, London.

Clutton-Brock, T. H. (ed.) (1977) *Primate Ecology: Studies of Feeding and Ranging Behaviour in Lemurs, Monkeys and Apes*. Academic Press, London.

Clutton-Brock, T. H. (1977) 'Some aspects of intraspecific variation in feeding and ranging behaviour in Primates', in *Primate Ecology*, Clutton-Brock, T. H. (ed.), Academic Press, London, pp. 539–556.

Clutton-Brock, T. H. (1982) The functions of antlers. *Behaviour* **79**, 108–125.

Clutton-Brock, T. H. and Harvey, P. (1977*a*) Primate ecology and social organisation. *J. Zool., Lond.* **183**, 1–39.

Clutton-Brock, T. H. and Harvey, P. H. (1977b) 'Species differences in feeding and ranging behaviour in primates', in *Primate Ecology*, Clutton-Brock, T. H. (ed.) Academic Press, London.

Clutton-Brock, T. H. and Guinness, F. E. (1975) Behaviour of red deer (*Cervus elaphus* L.) at calving time. *Behaviour* **55**, 287–300.

Clutton-Brock, T. H., Albon, S. D. and Guinness, F. E. (1979) The logical stag: adaptive aspects of fighting in Red deer (*Cervus elaphus* L.). *Anim. Behav.* **27**, 211–225.

Clutton-Brock, T. H. Albon, S. D. and Guinness, F. E. (1984) Maternal dominance, breeding success and birth sex ratio in red deer. *Nature* **308**, 358–360.

Clutton-Brock, T. H., Greenwood, P. J. and Powell, R. P. (1976) Ranks and relationships in highland ponies and highland cows. *Z. Tierpsychol.* **41**, 202–216.

Clutton-Brock, T. H., Guinness, F. E. and Albon, S. D. (1982) *Red Deer, the Behaviour and Ecology of Two Sexes*. University of Chicago Press, Chicago.

Corbet, G. B. and Hill, J. E. (1980) *A World List of Mammalian Species*. British Museum, London.

Cox, C. R. and Leboeuf, B. J. (1977) Female incitation of male competition: a mechanism of mate selection. *Amer. Nat.* **111**, 317–335.

Croft, D. B. (1982) 'Communication in the Dasyuridae (Marsupialia): a review', in *Carnivorous Marsupials*, Archer, M. (ed.), Royal Zoological Society of New South Wales, Sydney, pp. 291–309.

Crook, J. H. (1966) Gelada baboon herd structure and movement. A comparative report. *Symp. zool. Soc. Lond.* **18**, 237–258.

Crook, J. H., Ellis, J. E. and Goss-Custard, J. D. (1976) Mammalian social systems, structure and function. *Anim. Behav.* **24**, 261–274.

Crook, J. H. and Gartlan, J. S. (1966) Evolution of primate societies. *Nature, Lond.* **210**, 1200–1203.

Cullen, J. M. (1966) Reduction in ambiguity through ritualization. *Phil. Trans. Roy. Soc. Lond.* **251**, 363–374.

Dagg, A. I. and Foster, J. B. (1976) *The Giraffe*. Van Nostrand Reinhold, New York.

Dagg, A. I. and Windsor, D. E. (1971) Olfactory discrimination limits in gerbils. *Can. J. Zool.* **49**, 283–285.

Daly, M. (1979) Why don't male mammals lactate? *J. Theor. Biol.*, **45**, 325–345.

Darwin, C. (1871) *The Descent of Man and Selection in Relation to Sex*. John Murray, London.

Darwin, C. (1973) *Expression of the Emotions in Man and Animals*. D. Appleton, New York.

Davies, N. B. (1978) 'Ecological questions about territorial behaviour', in *Behavioural Ecology: an Evolutionary Approach*, Krebs, J. R. and Davies, N. B., (eds.), Blackwell, Oxford, pp. 317–350.

Dawkins, R. (1976) *The Selfish Gene*. Oxford University Press, Oxford.

Dawkins, R. and Carlisle, T. R. (1976) Parental investiment, mate desertion and a fallacy. *Nature* **262**, 131–133.

Dawkins, R. and Krebs, J. R. (1978) Animal signals: information or manipulation, in *Behavioural Ecology*, Krebs, J. R. and Davies, N. B. (eds.), Blackwell, Oxford, pp. 282–309.

Dawson, G. A. (1978) 'Composition and stability of group of the tamarin *Saguinus oedipus geoffroyi* in Panama: Ecological and behavioural implications', in *The Biology and Conservation of the Callitrichidae*, Kleiman, D. G. (ed.), Smithsonian Institute Press, Washington, pp. 23–27.

Deag, J. M. (1977) Aggression and submission in monkey societies. *Anim. Behav.* **25**, 465–474.

Deag, J. M. (1980) Interactions between males and unweaned barbary macaques: testing the agonistic buffering hypothesis. *Behaviour* **75**, 54–81.

Deag, J. M. and Crook, J. H. (1971) Social behaviour and 'agonistic buffering' in the wild barbary macaque *Macaca sylvana* L. *Folia Primat.* **15**, 183–200.

de Boer, L. E. M. (ed.) (1982) *The Orang Utan, its Biology and Conservation.* Junk, The Hague.

Defran, R. H. and Pryor, K. (1980) 'The behaviour and training of cetaceans in captivity', in *Cetacean Behaviour: Mechanisms and Functions*, Herman, M. L. (ed.), John Wiley, New York, pp. 319–362.

de Waal, F. B. M. (1977) The organisation of agonistic relations within two captive groups of Java monkeys (*Macaca fascicularis*). *Z. Tierpsychol.* **44**, 225–282.

de Waal, F. B. M. and van Roosmalen, A. (1979) Reconciliation and consolation among chimpanzees. *Behav. Ecol. Sociobiol.* **5**, 55–66.

de Waal, F. B. M. and Hoekstra, J. A. (1980) Contexts and predictability of aggression in Chimpanzees. *Anim. Behav.* **28**, 929–937.

Dewsbury, D. A. (1972) Patterns of copulatory behaviour in male mammals. *Quart. Rev. Biol.* **47**, 1–33.

Dewsbury, D. A. (1982) Dominance rank, copulatory behaviour and differential reproduction. *Quart. Rev. Biol.* **57**, 135–159.

Dewsbury, D. A. and Baumgartner, D. J. (1981) Studies of sperm competition in two species of muroid rodents. *Behav. Ecol. Sociobiol.* **9**, 121–133.

Diamond, J. M. (1982) Big bang reproduction and ageing in male marsupial mice. *Nature* **298**, 115–116.

Dittus, W. P. J. (1977) The social regulation of population density and age-sex distribution in the toque monkey *Macaca sinica*. *Behaviour* **63**, 281–322.

Dittus, W. P. J. (1979) The evolution of behaviours regulating density and age-specific sex ratios in a primate population. *Behaviour* **69**, 265–302.

Dixon, A. K. and Mackintosh, J. H. (1971) Effect of female urine on the social behaviour of adult male mice. *Anim. Behav.* **19**, 138–140.

Dixon, A. K. and Mackintosh, J. H. (1976) Olfactory mechanisms affording protection from attack to juvenile mice (*Mus musculus* L.). *Z. Tierpsychol.* **41**, 225–234.

Dixson, A. F. (1977) Observations on the displays, menstrual cycles and sexual behaviour of the 'Black ape' of Celebes (*Macaca nigra*). *J. Zool., Lond.* **182**, 63–84.

Dixson, A. F. (1981) *The Natural History of the Gorilla.* Weidenfeld and Nicholson, London.

Dixson, A. F. (1983) Observations on the evolution and behavioural significance of 'sexual skin' in female primates. *Advances in the Study of Behaviour* **13**, 63–106.

Dobroruka, L. J. (1960) Einige Beobachtungen an Ameisenigeln *Echidna aculeata* Shaw (1872). *Z. Tierpsychol.* **17**, 178–181.

Dolhinow, P. J. (1972) 'The North Indian langur', in *Primate Patterns*, Dolhinow, P. J. (ed.), Holt Reinhart and Winston, New York, pp. 181–238.

Doty, R. L. (1976) *Mammalian Olfaction, Reproductive Processes and Behaviour.* Academic Press, New York.

Douglas-Hamilton, I. (1973) On the ecology and behaviour of the Lake Manyara elephants. *E. Afr. Wildl. J.* **11**, 401–403.

Douglas-Hamilton, I. and Douglas-Hamilton, O. (1975) *Among the Elephants.* Viking, New York.

Downhower, J. F. and Armitage, K. B. (1981) Dispersal of yearling yellow bellied marmots (*Marmota flaviventris*). *Anim. Behav.* **29**, 1064–1069.

Drickamer, L. C. (1974) A ten year summary of reproductive data for free ranging *Macaca mulatta*. *Folia Primatol.* **21**, 61–80.

Dunbar, R. I. M. (1979*a*) Structure of gelada baboon reproductive units. I. Stability of social relationships. *Behaviour* **69**, 72–87.

Dunbar, R. I. M. (1979*b*) 'Population demography, social organization, and mating strategies', in *Primate Ecology and Human Origins*, Bernstein, I. S. and Smith, E. O. (eds.), Garland, New York, pp. 65–88.

Dunbar, R. I. M. (1980a) Determinants and evolutionary consequences of dominance among female gelada baboons. *Behav. Ecol. Sociobiol.* **7**, 253–265.

Dunbar, R. I. M. (1980b) Demographic and life history variables of a population of Gelada baboons (*Theropithecus gelada*). *J. Anim. Ecol.* **49**, 485–506.

Dunbar, R. I. M. (1982a) Structure of social relationships in a captive Gelada group: a test of some hypotheses derived from studied of a wild population. *Primates* **23**, 89–94.

Dunbar, R. I. M. (1982b) 'Intraspecific variations in mating strategy', in *Perspectives in Ethology*, **5**, Klopfer, P. and Bateson, P. P. S. (eds.), pp. 385–43.

Dunbar, R. I. M. and Dunbar, E. P. (1975) 'Social dynamics of Gelada baboons', in *Contributions to Primatology*, **6**, Karger, Basel.

Dunbar, R. I. M. and Dunbar, E. P. (1980) The pairbond in Klipspringer. *Anim. Behav.* **28**, 219–229.

Dunbar, R. I. M. and Dunbar, E. P. (1981) The grouping behaviour of male walia ibex with special reference to the rut. *Af. J. Ecol.* **19**, 251–263.

Dunford, C. (1977) Social system of round tailed ground squirrels. *Anim. Behav.* **25**, 885–906.

Eaton, R. L. (1970) Group interactions spacing and territoriality in cheetah. *Z. Tierpsychol.* **27**, 492–504.

Eaton, R. L. (1974) *The Cheetah: The Biology, Ecology and Behaviour of an Endangered Species.* Van Nostrand Reinhold, New York.

Ehret, G. (1980) Development of sound communication in mammals. *Advances in the Study of Behaviour* **11**, 179–225.

Einon, D., Morgan, M. and Kibbler, C. C. (1978) Brief periods of socialization and later behaviour in the rat. *Dev. Psychobiol* **11**, 213–225.

Eisenberg, J. F. (1966) The social organisation of mammals. *Handbuch der Zoologie* **10**, 1–92.

Eisenberg, J. F. (1977) 'The evolution of the reproductive unit in the class Mammalia', in *Reproductive Behaviour and Evolution*, Rosenberg, J. S. and Komisaruk, B. R. (eds.), Plenum Press, New York, pp. 39–71.

Eisenberg, J. F. (1981) *The Mammalian Radiations. An analysis of trends in evolution, adaptation and behaviour.* Athlone Press, London.

Eisenberg, J. F. and Golani, I. (1977) 'Communication in Metatheria', in *How Animals Communicate*, Sebeok, T. A. (ed.), Indiana University Press, Bloomington.

Eisenberg, J. F. and Kleiman, D. G. (1972) Olfactory communication in mammals. *Ann. Rev. Ecol. System.* **3**, 1–32.

Eisenberg, J. F., Collins, L. R. and Wemmer, L. (1975) Communication in the tasmanian devil *Sarcophilus harrisii* and a survey of auditory communication in the Marsupialia. *Z. Tierpsychol.* **37**, 379–399.

Eisenberg, J. F., McKay, G. M. and Jainudeen, M. R. (1971) Reproductive behaviour of the Asiatic Elephant (*Elephas maximus maximus* L.). *Behaviour* **38**, 193–225.

Eisenberg, J. F., Muckenhirn, N. A. and Rudran, R. (1972) The relation between ecology and social structure in Primates. *Science, Wash.* **176**, 863–874.

Elliot, L. (1978) Social behaviour and foraging ecology of the eastern chipmunk (*Tamias striatus*) in the Adirondack mountains. *Smithsonian Contrib. Zool.* **265**, 1–107.

Elwood, R. W. (1975) Paternal and maternal behaviour in the Mongolian gerbil. *Anim. Behav.* **23**, 766–772.

Elwood, R. W. (1977) Changes in the responses of male and female gerbils (*Meriones unguiculatus*) towards test pups during the pregnancy of the female. *Anim. Behav.* **25**, 46–51.

Epple, G. (1974a) 'Pheromones in Primate reproduction and social behaviour', in *Reproductive Behaviour*, Montagna, W. and Sadler, W. A. (eds.), Plenum, New York, pp. 131–155.

Epple, G. (1974b) Olfactory communication in South American primates. *Ann. N.Y. Acad. Science* **237**, 261–278.

Epple, G. (1978a) 'Notes on the establishment and maintenance of the pair bond in *Saguinus fuscicollis*, in *The Biology and Conservation of the Callitrichidae*, Kleiman, D. G. (ed.), Smithsonian Institution, Washington.

220 SOCIAL BEHAVIOUR IN MAMMALS

Epple, G. (1978b) Reproductive and social behaviour of marmosets with special reference to captive breeding. *Prim. med.* **10**, 50–62.

Epple, G. (1979) Gonadal control of male scent in the tamarin *Saguinus fuscicollis* (Callitrichidae, Primates).

Erlinge, S. (1968) Territoriality of the otter *Lutra lutra* L. *Oikos* **19**, 81–98.

Erlinge, S. (1974) Distribution, territoriality and numbers of the weasel (*Mustela nivalis*) in relation to prey abundance. *Oikos* **25**, 308–314.

Erlinge, S. (1977a) Spacing strategy in stoat *Mustela erminea*. *Oikos* **28**.

Erlinge, S. (1979b) Agonistic behaviour dominance in the stoats *Mustela erminea* L. Z. *Tierpsychol.* **44**, 375–388.

Erlinge, S. (1979a) Adaptive significance of sexual dimorphism in weasels. *Oikos* 33, 233–245.

Erlinge, S. (1979b) Food preference, optimal diet and reproductive output in stoats *Mustela erminea* in Sweden. *Oikos* **36**, 303–315.

Estes, R. D. (1967) The comparative behaviour of Grant's and Thomson's gazelles. *J. Mamm.* **48**, 189–209.

Estes, R. D. (1969) Territorial behaviour of the Wildebeest (*Connochaetes taurinus* Burchell). *Z. Tierpsychol* **26**, 284–370.

Estes, R. D. and Estes, R. K. (1979) The birth and survival of wildebeest calves. *Z. Tierpsychol.* **50**, 45–95.

Evans, S. (1983) The pair bond of the common marmoset, *Callithrix jacchus jacchus*: an experimental investigation. *Anim. Behav.* **31**, 651–658.

Evans, S. and Poole, T. B. (1983) Pair bond formation and breeding success in the common marmoset *Callithrix jacchus jacchus*. *Int. J. Primatol.* **4**, 83–97.

Evans, W. and Bastian, J. (1969) 'Marine mammal communications: social and ecological factors', in *The Biology of Marine Mammals*, Andersen, H. T. (ed.), Academic Press, New York.

Ewer, R. F. (1963) The behaviour of the meerkat *Suricata suricatta* Schreber. *Z. Tierpsychol.* **20**, 570–607.

Ewer, R. F. (1968) *The Ethology of Mammals*. Plenum, New York.

Ewer, R. F. (1971) The biology and behaviour of a free living population of black rats (*Rattus rattus*). *Animal Behaviour Monographs* **4**(3), 125–174.

Ewer, R. F. (1973) *The Carnivores*. Cornell University Press, Ithaca, New York.

Fagen, R. (1981) *Animal Play Behaviour*. Oxford University Press, Oxford.

Fanning, F. D. (1982) 'Reproduction, growth and development in *Ningai* sp. (Dasyuridae, Marsupialia) from the Northern Territory', in *Carnivorous Marsupials*, Archer, M. (ed.), Roy. Zool. Soc. New South Wales, Sydney.

Farentinos, R. C. (1971) Some observations on the play behaviour of the Steller sea lion (*Eumetopias jubata*). *Z. Tierpsychol.* **28**, 428–438.

Farentinos, R. C. (1974) Social communication of the tassel eared squirrel (*Sciurus albertii*) a descriptive analysis. *Z. Tierpsychol.* **34**, 441–458.

Fedigan, L. (1972) Social and solitary play in a colony of vervet monkeys *Cercopithecus aethiops*. *Primates* **13**, 347–364.

Feist, J. D. and McCullough, D. R. (1976) Behaviour patterns and communication in feral horses. *Z. Tierpsychol.* **41**, 337–371.

Ferguson, J. W. H., Nel, J. A. J. and de Wet, J. (1983) Social organization and movement patterns of Black backed jackals, *Canis mesomelas*, in South Africa. *J. Zool., Lond.* **199**, 487–502.

Fleay, D. (1944) *We Breed the Platypus*. Robertson and Mullens, Melbourne.

Floody, O. R. and Arnold, P. (1975) Uganda kob (*Adenota kob thomasi*) territoriality and the spatial distributions of sexual and agonistic behaviours at a territorial ground. *Z. Tierpsychol.* **37**, 192–212.

Fogden, S. C. L. (1968) Suckling behaviour in the Grey seal (*Halichoerus grypus*) and the Northern Elephant seal (*Mirounga angustirostris*). *J. Zool., Lond.* **154**, 415–420.

Fogden, S. C. L. (1971) Mother-young behaviour at Grey seal breeding beaches. *J. Zool., Lond.* **164**, 61–92.

Fossey, D. (1972) Vocalizations of the mountain gorilla (*Gorilla gorilla beringei*). *Anim. Behav.* **22**, 568–581.

Fossey, D. and Harcourt, A. H. (1977) 'Feeding ecology of free ranging mountain gorilla (*Gorilla gorilla beringei*)', in *Primate Ecology*, Clutton-Brock, T. H. (ed.), Academic Press, London.

Fourie, P. B. (1977) Acoustic communication in the rock Hyrax (*Procavia capensis*). *Z. Tierpsychol.* **44**, 194–219.

Fox, M. W. (1975) 'Evolution of social behaviour in canids', in *The Wild Canids*, Fox, M. W. (ed.), van Nostrand Reinhold, New York, pp. 429–460.

Fox, M. W. and Cohen, J. A. (1977) 'Canid communication', in *How Animals Communicate*, Sebeok, T. A. (ed.), Indiana University Press, Bloomington, pp. 728–748.

Frame, L. H., Malcolm, J. R., Frame, G. W. and van Lawick, H. (1979) Social organisation of African wild dogs (*Lycaon pictus*) on the Serengeti plains, Tanzania 1967–1978. *Z. Tierpsychol.* **50**, 225–249.

Gadgil, M. and Bossert, W. H. (1970) Life historical consequences of natural selection. *American Naturalist* **104**, 1–24.

Galdikas, B. M. F. (1981) 'Orang utan reproduction in the wild', in *Reproductive Biology of the Great Apes*, Graham, C. E. (ed.), Academic Press, New York, pp. 281–300.

Galdikas, B. M. F. (1982) Wild orang utan birth at Tanjung Puting reserve. *Primates* **23**, 500–510.

Galdikas-Brindamoor, B. and Brindamoor, R. (1975) Orang utans, Indonesia's people of the forest. *Nat. Geographic.* **148**, 444–473.

Galef, B. G. Jr. (1981) 'The ecology of weaning, parasitism and the achievement of independence by altrical mammals', in *Parental Behaviour in Mammals*, Gubernick, D. J. and Klopfer, P. H. (eds.), Plenum, New York, pp. 211–241.

Gallup, G. G. (1979) Self awareness in Primates. *American Scientist* **67**, 417–421.

Gautier, J. P. and Gautier, A. (1977) 'Communication in old world monkeys', in *How Animals Communicate*, Sebeok, T. A. (ed.), Indiana University Press, New York, pp. 890–964.

Geist, V. (1966) The evolution of horn-like organs. *Behaviour* **27**, 175–215.

Geist, V. (1974) On the relationship of social evolution and ecology in ungulates. *Am. Zool.* **14**, 205–220.

Gentry, R. L. (1974) The development of social behaviour through play in the Steller sea lion. *Amer. Zool.* **14**, 391–403.

Gerell, R. (1970) Home ranges and movements of the mink *Mustela vison* Schreber in southern Sweden. *Oikos* **21**, 160–173.

Gibson, R. M. and Guinness, F. E. (1980) Differential reproduction among red deer stags on Rhum. *J. Anim. Ecol.* **49**, 199–208.

Gittleman, J. L. and Harvey, P. H. (1982) Carnivore home-range size, metabolic needs and ecology. *Behav. Ecol. Sociobiol.* **10**, 57–63.

Gleason, K. K. and Reynierse, J. H. (1969) The behavioural significance of pheromones in vertebrates. *Psychological Bulletin* **71**, 58–73.

Goddard, J. (1966) Mating and courtship of the black rhinoceros (*Diceros bicornis* L.). *E. African Wildl. J.* **4**, 69–76.

Goddard, J. (1967) Home range, behaviour and recruitment rates of two black rhinoceros populations. *E. African Wildl. J.* **5**, 133–151.

Godfrey, J. (1958) The origin of sexual isolation between bank voles. *Proc. Roy. Phys. Soc. Edinburgh* **27**, 47–55.

Golani, I. (1976) 'Homeostatic motor processes in mammalian interactions: a choreography of display', in *Perspectives in Ethology*, **2**, Bateson, P. P. G. and Klopfer, P. H. (eds.), Plenum, New York.

Golani, I. and Keller, A. (1975) 'A longitudinal field study of the behaviour of a pair of golden jackals', in *The Wild Canids*, Fox, M. W. (ed.), van Nostrand Reinhold, New York, pp. 303–335.

Goldman, L. and Swanson, H. H. (1975) Developmental changes in pre-adult behaviour in confined colonies of golden hamsters. *Dev. Psychobiol.* **8**, 137–150.

Goodall, J. (1965) 'Chimpanzees of the Gombe reserve', in *Primate Behaviour: Field Studies of Monkeys and Apes*, De Vore, I. (ed.) Holt Reinhart and Winston, New York.

Goodall, J. van L. (1967) 'Mother-offspring relationships in free ranging chimpanzees', in *Primate Ethology*, Morris, D. (ed.), pp. 287–346.

Goodall, J. van L. (1968a) The behaviour of free living chimpanzees in the Gombe Stream reserve. *Animal Behaviour Monographs* **1**(3), 161–311.

Goodall, J. van L. (1968b) 'A preliminary report on expressive movements and communication in the Gombe stream chimpanzees', in *Primate Patterns*, Dolhinow, P. (ed.), Hold Reinhart and Winston, New York, pp. 25–84.

Goodall, J. van L. (1975) 'Chimpanzees of Gombe National Park: thirteen years of research', in *Hominisation und Verhalten*, Eibl-Eibesfeldt, I. (ed.), Gustav Fischer Verlag, Stuttgart, pp. 56–100.

Goodall, J. van L. (1977) Infant killing and cannibalism in free-living chimpanzees. *Folia. Primat.* **28**, 259–282.

Gorman, M. L. and Mills, M. G. L. (1984) Scent marking strategies in hyaenas (Mammalia). *J. Zool., Lond.* **202**, 535–547.

Gosling, L. M. (1972) The construction of antorbital gland mating sites by male Oribi (*Ourebia ourebia* Zimmerman 1783). *Z. Tierpsychol.* **30**, 271–276.

Gosling, L. M. (1974) 'The social behaviour of Coke's hartebeest *Alcelaphus busephalus cokei*,' in *The Behaviour of Ungulates and its Relation to Management*, Geist, V. and Walther, F. R. (eds.), Morges, IUCN.

Gosling, L. M. (1981) Demarkation in a Gerenuk territory: an economic approach. *Z. Tierpsychol.* **56**, 305–322.

Gosling, L. M. (1983) A reassessment of the function of scent marking in territories. *Z. Tierpsychol.* **60**, 89–118.

Gosling, L. M. and Petrie, M. (1981) 'The economics of social organization,' in *Physiological Ecology: An Evolutionary Approach to Resource Use*, Townsend, C. R. and Calow, P. (eds.), Blackwell, Oxford.

Goss-Custard, J. D., Dunbar, R. I. M. and Aldrich-Blake, F. P. G. (1972) Survival, mating and rearing strategies in the evolution of primate social structure. *Folia. primatol.* **17**, 1–19.

Gossow, H. (1970) Vergleichende Verhaltensstudien an Marderartigen I. Uber Lautausserungen und zum Beuteverhalten. *Z. Tierpsychol.* **27**, 405–480.

Gould, E. (1978) The behaviour of the moonrat, *Echinosorex gymnurus* (Erinaceidae) and the pentail shrew *Ptilocercus lowi* (Tupaiidae) with comments on the behaviour of the Insectivora. *Z. Tierpsychol.* **48**, 1–27.

Gould, S. J. (1966) Allometry and size in ontogeny and phylogeny. *Biol. Rev.* **41**, 587–640.

Grafen, A. (1979) The Hawk-dove game played between relatives. *Anim. Behav.* **27**, (3), 905–907.

Grafen, A. (1982) How not to measure inclusive fitness. *Nature* **298**, 425–426.

Graham, C. E. (ed.) (1981) *Reproductive Biology of the Great Apes.* Academic Press, New York.

Grant, E. G. and Mackintosh, J. F. (1963) A comparison of social postures of some common laboratory rodents. *Behaviour* **21**, 246–259.

Grau, H. J. (1982) Kin recognition in white footed deermice *Peromyscus leucopus*. *Anim. Behav.* **30**, 497–505.

Greenwood, P. J. (1980) Mating systems, philopatry and dispersal in birds and mammals. *Anim. Behav.* **28**, 1140–1162.

Griffiths, M. (1968) *Echidnas*. Pergamon Press, New York.

Griffiths, M. (1978) *The Biology of Monotremes*. Academic Press, New York.

Grundlach, H. (1968) Brutforsorge, Brutpflege, Verhaltensontogenese und Tagesperiodik beim Europaischen Wildschwein (*Sus scrofa* L.). *Z. Tierpsychol* **25**, 955–995.

Gubernick, D. J. (1980) Maternal 'imprinting' or maternal labelling in goats? *Anim. Behav.* **28**, 124–129.

Gubernick, D. J. (1981) 'Parent and infant attachment in mammals,' in *Parental Care in Mammals*, Gubernick, D. J. and Klopfer, P. H. (eds.), Plenum, New York, pp. 243–305

Gubernick, D. J. and Klopfer, P. H. (eds.) *Parental Care in Mammals*. Plenum, New York and London.

Guiler, R. E. (1970*a*) Observations on the Tasmanian devil, *Sarcophilus harrisii* (Marsupialia : Dasyuridae) I. Numbers, home range, movements and food in two populations. *Australian J. Zool.* **18**, 49–62.

Guiler, R. E. (1970*b*) Observations on the Tasmanian devil *Sarcophilus harrisii* (Marsupialia : Dasyuridae) II. Reproduction, breeding and growth of pouch young. *Australian J. Zool.* **18**, 63–70.

Guiness, F. E., Hall, M. J. and Cockerill, R. A. (1979). Mother-offspring association in Red deer (*Cervus elaphus* L.) on Rhum. *Anim. Behav.* **27**, 536–544.

Guyot, G. W., Bennett, T. L. and Cross, H. A. (1980) The effects of social isolation on the behaviour of juvenile domestic cats. *Dev. Psychobiol.* **13**, 317–329.

Hadidian, J. (1980) Yawning in an old world monkey (*Macaca nigra*) (Primates: Cercopithecidae). *Behaviour* **75**, 133–147.

Haimoff, E. (1981) Video analysis of Siamang (*Hylobates syndactylus*) songs. *Behaviour* **78**, 128–151.

Hall, K. R. L. (1965) Behaviour and ecology of the wild patas monkey in Uganda. *J. Zool., Lond.* **148**, 15–87.

Hall, K. R. L. and De Vore, I. (1965) 'Baboon social behaviour,' in *Primate Behaviour. Field Studies of Monkey and Apes,* De Vore, I. (ed.), Holt Reinhart and Winston, New York, pp. 53–110.

Halliday, T. R. (1978) 'Sexual selection and mate choice,' in *Behavioural Ecology: an Evolutionary Approach*, Krebs J. R., and Davies, N. B. (eds.), Blackwell, Oxford, pp. 180–213.

Hamilton, W. D. (1964) The genetical evolution of social behaviour. *J. Theor. Biol.* **7**, 1–16.

Hamburg, D. A. and McCown, E. R. (eds.) (1979) *The Great Apes.* Benjamin/Cummings, California.

Hamilton, W. D. (1971) Geometry for the selfish herd. *J. Theor. Biol.* **31**, 295–311.

Hamilton, W. J. III, Busse, C. and Smith, K. S. (1982) Adoption of infant orphan chacma baboons. *Anim. Behav.* **30**, 29–34.

Harcourt, A. H. (1978) Strategies of emigration and transfer by primates with particular reference to gorillas. *Z. Tierpsychol.* **48**, 401–420.

Harcourt, A. H. (1979) Social relationships between adult male and female mountain gorillas in the wild. *Anim. Behav.* **27**, 325–342.

Harcourt, A. H., Stewart, K. S. and Fossey, D. (1976) Male emigration and female transfer in wild mountain gorillas. *Nature* **263**, 226–227.

Harcourt, A. H., Fossey, D., Stewart, K. J. and Watts, D. O. (1980) Reproduction in wild gorillas and some comparisons with chimpanzees. *J. Reprod. Fert. Suppl.* **28**, 59–70.

Harlow, H. F. and Harlow, M. K. (1966) Learning to love. *American Scientist*, **54**, 224–272.

Harper, L. V. (1981) 'Offspring effects on parents', in *Parental Care in Mammals*, Gubernick, D. J. and Klopfer, P. H. (eds.), Plenum, New York, pp. 117–177.

Harrington, F. H. and Mech, L. D. (1979) Wolf howling and its role in territory maintenance. *Behaviour* **68**, 207–249.

Harrington, J. E. (1976) Recognition of territorial boundaries by olfactory cues in mice (*Mus musculus* L.). *Z. Tierpsychol.* **41**, 295–306.

Harrington, J. E. (1976) Discrimination between individuals by scent in *Lemur fulvus. Anim. Behav.* **24**, 207–212.

Harvey, P. H. and Greenwood, P. J. (1978) 'Anti predator defense strategies, some evolutionary problems', in *Behavioural Ecology: an Evolutionary Approach*, Krebs, J. R. and Davies, N. B. (eds.), Blackwell, London, pp. 129–151.

Hartman, D. S. (1979) Ecology and behaviour of the manatee (*Trichecus manatus*) in Florida. *Spec. Pubs* No. **5**, Am. Soc. Mammalogists.

Haskins, R. (1979) A causal analysis of kitten vocalization: an observational and experimental study. *Anim. Behav.* **27**, 726–736.

Hausfater, G. (1975) Dominance and reproduction in baboons (*Papio cynocephalus*). *Contrib. Primatology* **7**, 1–150.

Hausfater, G. and Vogel, C. (1982) 'Infanticide in Langur monkeys (genus *Presbytis*): Recent research and a review of hypotheses', in *Advanced Views in Primate Biology*, Chiarelli, A. B. and Coruccini, R. S. (eds.), Springer Verlag, Berlin, pp. 160–176.

Healey, M. C. (1967) Aggression and self regulation of population size in deermice. *Ecology* **48**, 377–392.

Hendrichs, H. (1975a) Observations on a population of Bohor Reedbuck *Redunca redunca* (Pallas 1767). *Z. Tierpsychol.* **38**, 44–54.

Hendrichs, H. (1975b) Changes in a population of Dikdik *Madoqua (Rhynchotragus) kirkii* (Gunther 1880). *Z. Tierpsychol.* **38**, 55–69.

Henry, J. D. and Herrero, S. M. (1974) Social play in the American Black bear: its similarity to Canid social play and an examination of its identifying characteristics. *Amer. Zool.* **14**, 371–389.

Henwood, K. and Fabrick, A. (1979) A quantitative analysis of the dawn chorus: Temporal selection for communicatory optimization. *Amer. Nat.* **114**, 260–274.

Herman, L. M. (1980) *Cetacean Behaviour: Mechanisms and Functions*. John Wiley, New York.

Herman, L. M. and Tavolga, W. N. (1980) 'The communications systems of cetaceans', in *Cetacean Behaviour: Mechanisms and Functions*, Herman, L. M. (ed.), John Wiley & Co, New York, pp. 149–210.

Herter, K. (1959) *Iltisse und Frettchen*. A. Ziemsen Verlag, Wittenberg-Lutherstadt.

Hill, H. L. and Bekoff, M. (1977) The variability of some motor components of social play and agonistic behaviour in infant eastern coyotes *Canis latrans* var. *Anim. Behav.* **25**, 907–909.

Hinde, R. A. (ed.) (1972) *Non-verbal communication*. Cambridge University Press, London.

Hinde, R. A. (1981) Animal signals: ethological and games theory approaches are not incompatible. *Anim. Behav.* **29**, 535–542.

Hinde, R. A. and Spencer-Booth, Y. (1979) 'The effect of social companions on mother-infant relations in Rhesus Monkeys', in *Primate Ethology*, Morris, D. (ed.), pp. 267–286.

Hladik, C. M. (1977) 'A comparative study of the feeding strategies of two sympatric species of leaf monkeys, *Presbytis senex* and *Presbytis entellus*', in *Primate Ecology*, Clutton-Brock, T. H. (ed.), Academic Press, London.

Hladik, C. M. and Charles-Dominique, P. (1974) 'The behaviour and ecology of the sportive lemur (*Lepilemur mustelinus*) in relation to its dietary peculiarities', in *Prosimian Biology*, Martin, R. D., Doyle, G. A. and Walker, A. C. (eds.), Duckworth, London, pp. 23–37.

Hodgdon, H. E. and Larson, J. S. (1973) Some sexual differences in behaviour within a colony of marked beavers *Castor canadensis*. *Anim. Behav.* **21**, 147–152.

Hoeck, H. N. (1982) Population dynamics, dispersal and genetic isolation in two species of *Hyrax* (*Heterohyrax brucei* and *Procavia johsoni*) on habitat islands in the Serengeti. *Z. Tierpsychol.* **59**, 177–210.

Hoeck, H., Klein, H. and Hoeck, P. (1982) Flexible social organizations in *Hyrax*. *Z. Tierpsychol.* **59**, 265–298.

Hofer, M. A. (1981) 'Parental contributions to the development of their offspring', in *Parental Care in Mammals*, Gubernick, D. J. and Klopfer, P. H. (eds.), Plenum, New York, pp. 77–115.

Hogarth, P. J. (1978) *Biology of Reproduction*. Blackie, Glasgow.

Hoogland, J. L. (1979) The effects of colony size on individual alertness of Prairie dogs (Sciuridae: *Cynomys* sp.). *Anim. Behav.* **27**, 394–407.

Horn, H. S. (1978) 'Optimal tactics of reproduction and life history', in *Behavioural Ecology: an Evolutionary Approach*, Krebs, J. R. and Davies, N. B. (eds.), Blackwell, Oxford, pp. 411–429.

Horr, D. A. (1977) 'Orang-utan maturation: growing up in a female world', in *Primate Biosocial Development and Ecological Determinants*, Chevalier-Skolnikoff, S. and Poirier, F. E. (eds), Garland, New York, pp. 259–322.

Hrdy, S. B. (1974) Male: male competition and infanticide among langurs (*Presbytis entellus*) of Abu, Rajasthan. *Folia Primatol.* **22**, 19–58.

Hrdy, S. B. (1976) Care and exploitation of primate infants by conspecifics other than the mother. *Advances in the Study of Behaviour*, **6**, 101–158.

Hrdy, S. B. (1977) *The langurs of Abu, female and male strategies in reproduction*. Harvard University Press, Cambridge, Mass.

Huff, J. N. and Price, E. O. (1968) Vocalizations of the least weasel *Mustela nivalis*. *J. Mammal.* **49**, 548–550.

Humphreys, A. P. and Einon, D. F. (1981) Play as a reinforcer for maze learning in juvenile rats. *Anim. Behav.* **29**, 259–270.

Hunsaker, D. II (1977) *The Biology of Marsupials*. Academic Press, New York.

Hunsaker, D. II and Shupe, D. (1977) 'The Behaviour of New World marsupials', in *The Biology of Marsupials*, Hunsaker, D. II (ed.), Academic Press, New York.

Hutson, G. D. (1982) An analysis of offensive and defensive threat displays in *Dasyuroides byrnei* (Dasyuridae, Marsupialia), in *Carnivorous Marsupials* Archer, M. (ed.), Royal Zoological Society of New South Wales, Sydney, pp. 345–363.

Huxley, J. (1966) A discussion of ritualization of behaviour in animals and men. *Phil. Trans. Roy. Soc. Lond.* **251**, 249–271.

Izawa, K. (1980) Social behaviour of the wild black-capped capuchin (*Cebus apella*). *Primates* **21**, 443–467.

Jarman, P. J. (1974) Social organization of antelopes in relation to their ecology. *Behaviour* **48**, 215–267.

Jarvis, J. U. M. and Sale, J. B. (1971) Burrowing and burrow patterns of East African Mole rats, *Tachyoryctes splendens*. *J. Zool., Lond.* **163**, 451–479.

Jarvis, J. U. M. (1981) Eusociality in a mammal: cooperative breeding in naked male-rat colonies. *Science* **212**, 571–573.

Jay, P. C. (ed.) (1968) *Primates. Studies in Adaptation and Variability*. Holt Reinhart and Winston, New York, pp. 1–529.

Jewell, P. A. (1966) The concept of home range in mammals. *Symp. zool. Soc. Lond.* **18**, 85–107.

Johns, D. W. and Armitage, K. B. (1979) Behavioural ecology of yellow bellied marmots. *Behav. Ecol. Sociobiol.* **5**, 133–157.

Johnsingh, A. J. T. (1982) Reproductive and social behaviour of the Dhole (*Cuon alpinus*) (Canidae). *J. Zool., Lond.* **198**, 443–463.

Johnson, R. P. (1973) Scent marking in mammals. *Anim. Behav.* **21**, 521–535.

Jolly, A. (1966) *Lemur Behaviour*. University of Chicago Press, Chicago.

Jolly, A. (1972) *The Evolution of Primate Behaviour*. Macmillan, New York.

Jones, R. B. and Nowell, N. W. (1973) Aversive and aggression-promoting properties of urine from dominant and subordinate mice. *Anim. Learn. Behav.* **3**, 207–210.

Jones, R. B. and Nowell, N. W. (1974) The urinary aversive pheromone of mice: species strain and grouping effects. *Anim. Behav.* **22**, 187–191.

Jouventin, P. and Cornet, A. (1980) The sociobiology of pinnipeds. *Advances in the study of Behaviour* **11**, 121–141.

Kareem, A. M. and Barnard, C. J. (1982) The importance of kinship and familiarity in social interactions between mice. *Anim. Behav.* **30**, 594–601.

Kaufmann, J. H. (1962) Ecology and social behaviour of the coati (*Nasua narica*) Barro Colorado Island, Panama. *Univ. Calif. Publ. Zool.* **60**, 95–222.

Kaufmann, J. H. (1974a) Social ecology of the whiptail wallaby *Macropus parryi* in northeastern New South Wales. *Anim. Behav.* **22**, 281–369.

Kaufmann, J. H. (1974b) The ecology and evolution of social organization in the kangaroo family (Macropodidae). *Amer. Zool.* **14**, 51–62.

Kawai, M. (ed.) (1979) *Ecological and sociological studies of Gelada baboons.* Contributions to Primatology 16, Kodansha, Tokyo and Karger, Basel.

Kawamichi, T. (1976) Hay territory and dominance rank of pikas. *J. Mammal.* **57**, 133–148.

Kawamichi, T. and Kawamichi, M. (1979) Spatial organization and territory in tree shrews (*Tupaia glis*). *Anim. Behav.* **27**, 381–393.

Kawamichi, T. and Kawamichi, M. (1982) Social system and independence of offspring in tree shrews. *Primates*, **23**, 189–205.

Kawamura, S. (1958) Matriarchial social ranks in the Minoo-B troop: a study of the rank system in Japanese monkeys. *Primates* **1**, 149–156.

Keverne, E. B. (1976) Sexual receptivity and attractiveness in the female Rhesus monkey. *Advances in the Study of Behaviour* **7**, 155–200.

Keverne, E. B. (1978) 'Olfactory cues in mammalian sexual behaviour', in *Biological Determinants of Sexual Behaviour*, Hutchinson, J. B. (ed.), Wiley, New York, pp. 727–763.

Kiley, M. (1972) The vocalizations of ungulates their causation and function. *Z. Tierpsychol.* **31**, 171–222.

Kiley, M. (1976) The tail movements of ungulates, canids and felids with particular reference to their causation and function as displays. *Behaviour* **56**, 69–115.

Kiley-Worthington, M. (1965) The waterbuck (*Kobus defassa* Ruppell 1835 and *K. elipsiprymnus* Ogilby 1833) in East Africa: spatial distribution. A study of sexual behaviour. *Mammalia* **29**, 177–204.

Kiley-Worthington, M. (1978) The causation, evolution and function of the visual displays of the eland (*Taurotragus oryx*). *Behaviour* **66**, 179–222.

King, C. M. (1975) The home range of the weasel (*Mustela nivalis*) in an English woodland. *J. Anim. Ecol.* **44**, 639–668.

King, J. A. (1955) Social behaviour, social organization and population dynamics in a black-tailed prairie dog town in the Black Hills of South Dakota. *Contrib. Lab. Vertebr. Biol. Univ. Mich.* **67**, pp. 1–123.

King, J. A. (1958) Maternal behaviour and behavioural development in the subspecies of *Peromyscus maniculatus. J. Mammal* **39**, 177–190.

King, J. A. (1963) 'Maternal behaviour in *Peromyscus*', in *Maternal Behaviour in Mammals*, Rheingold, H. L. (ed.), John Wiley & Sons, New York, pp. 58–93.

King's College Sociobiology Group (eds.) (1982) *Current Problems in Sociobiology.* Cambridge University Press, Cambridge.

Kinzey, W. G. (1977) 'Diet and feeding behaviour of *Callicebus torquatus*', in *Primate Ecology*, Clutton-Brock, T. H. (ed.), Academic Press, London.

Kinzey, W. G., Rosengerger, A. L., Heisler, P. S., Prowse, D. L. and Trilling, J. S. (1977) A preliminary field investigation of the yellow handed titi monkey *Callicebus torquatus torquatus* in Northern Peru. *Primates* **18**, 159–181.

Kitchen, D. W. (1974) Social behaviour and ecology of the pronghorn. *Wildl. Monogr.* **38**, 1–96.

Kleiman, D. G. (1966) Scent marking in Canidae. *Symp. zool Soc. Lond.* **18**, 167–177.

Kleiman, D. (1972) Maternal behaviour of the green acouchi (*Myoprocta pratti* Pocock): a south American caviomorph rodent. *Behaviour* **43**, 48–84.

Kleiman, D. G. (1974) 'Patterns of behaviour in Hystricomorph rodents', in *Biology of Hystricomorph Rodents. Symp. zool. Soc. Lond.* **34**, 171–209.

Kleiman, D. G. (1977) Monogamy in mammals. *Q. Rev. Biol.* **52**, 39–69.

Kleiman, D. G. (1979) Parent-offspring conflict and sibling competition in a monogamous primate. *Am. Nat.* **114**, 753–759.

Kleiman, D. G. and Eisenberg, J. F. (1973) Comparisons of canid and felid social systems from an evolutionary perspective. *Anim. Behav.* **21**, 637–659.

Kleiman, D. G. and Malcolm, J. R. (1981) 'The evolution of male parental investment in mammals', in *Parental Care in Mammals*, Gubernick, D. J. and Klopfer, P. H. (eds.), Plenum Press, New York, pp. 347–387.

Klingel, H. (1974) A comparison of the social behaviour of the Equidae. *IUCN pubs* **24**(1), 124–132.

Klingel, H. (1977*a*) Observations on the social organization and behaviour of African and Asiatic wild asses (*Equus africanus* and *E. hemionus*). *Z. Tierpsychol.* **44**, 323–331.

Klingel, H. (1977*b*) 'Communication in Perissodactyla', in *How Animals Communicate*, Sebeok, T. A. (ed.), Indiana University Press, Bloomington.

Klopfer, P. H. (1977) 'Communication in prosimians', in *How Animals Communicate*, Sebeok, T. A. (ed.), Indiana University Press, Bloomington, pp. 841–850.

Klopfer, P. H. and Boskoff, U. J. (1979) 'Maternal behaviour of Prosimians,' in *The Study of Prosimian Behaviour*, Doyle, G. A. and Martin, R. D. (eds.), Academic Press, New York, pp. 123–154.

Klopfer, P. and Klopfer, M. (1977) Compensatory responses of goat mothers to their impaired young. *Anim. Behav.* **25**, 286–291.

Koford, C. B. (1957) The vicuna and the puma. *Ecol. Monogr.* **27**, 153–219.

Kolata, C. B. (1976) Primate behaviour: sex and the dominant male. *Science* **191**, 55–56.

Krebs, J. R. and Davies, N. B. (eds.) (1978) *Behavioural Ecology: an Evolutionary Approach.* Blackwell, Oxford.

Kruuk, H. (1972) *The Spotted Hyaena: A Study in Predation and Social Behaviour.* University of Chicago Press, Chicago.

Kruuk, H. (1977) Spatial organization and territorial behaviour of the European badger *Meles meles. J. Zool., Lond.* **184**, 1–19.

Kummer, H. (1968) Social organization of hamadryas baboons, a field study. *Bibliotheca Primatol.* **6**, 1–189.

Kummer, H., Gotz, W. and Angst, W. (1974) Triadic differentiation: an inhibitory process protecting pair bonds in baboons. *Behaviour* **49**, 62.

Kurland, J. A. (1977) Kin selection in the Japanese monkey. *Contrib. Primatol.* **12**, 1–145.

Kuroda, S. (1979) Grouping of the pygmy chimpanzees. *Primates* **20**, 181–197.

Lagerspetz, K. (1964) Studies on the aggressive behaviour of mice. *Ann. Acad. Fenn. B.* **131**, 1–131.

Lamprecht, J. (1979) Field observations on the behaviour and social system of the bat eared fox (*Otocyon megalotis* Desmarest). *Z. Tierpsychol.* **49**, 260–284.

Lancaster, J. (1971) Play-mothering: the relations between juvenile females and young infants among free ranging vervet monkeys (*Cercopithecus aethiops*). *Folia Primatol.* **15**, 161–182.

Langaman, V. A. (1977) Cow-calf relationships in giraffe (*Giraffa camelopardalis giraffa*). *Z. Tierpsychol.* **48**, 264–286.

Lauer, C. (1980) Seasonal variability in spatial defence by free-ranging rhesus monkeys (*Macaca mulatta*) *Anim. Behav.* **28**, 476–482.

Le Boeuf, B. J. (1971) The aggression of the breeding bulls. *Natural History* **80** (2), 82–94.

Le Boeuf, B. J. (1974) Male-male competition and reproductive success in elephant seals. *Amer. Zool.* **14**, 163–176.

Le Boeuf, B. J. and Peterson, R. S. (1969) Social status and mating activity in elephant seals. *Science* **163**, 91–93.

Le Boeuf, B. J. and Petrinovich, L. F. (1974) Dialects of Northern elephant seals *Mirounga angustirostris* origin and reliability. *Anim. Behav.* **22**, 656–663.

Le Boeuf, B. J., Whiting, R. J. and Gantt, R. F. (1972) Northern elephant seals females and their young. *Behaviour* **43**, 121–156.

Lee, A. K., Woolley, P. and Braithwaite, R. W. (1982) 'Life history strategies of dasyurid marsupials, in *Carnivorous Marsupials*, Archer, M. (ed.), Roy. Zool. Soc. New South Wales, Sydney, pp. 1–11.

Lee, P. C. and Oliver, J. I. (1979) Competition, dominance and the acquisition of rank in Juvenile yellow baboons (*Papio cynocephalus*). *Anim. Behav.* **27**, 576–585.

Lee, S. Van der and Boot, L. M. (1956) Spontaneous pseudopregnancy in mice II. *Acta. Physiol. Pharmacol. Neerl.* **5**, 213–215.

Leen, N. and Novick, A. (1969) *The World of Bats*. Holt Rinehart and Winston, New York.

Lehman, M. N. and Adams, D. B. (1977) A statistical and motivational analysis of social behaviours of the male laboratory rat. *Behaviour* **61**, 238–275.

Lehner, P. N. (1978) Coyote vocalizations: a lexicon and comparisons with other canids. *Anim. Behav.* **26**, 712–723.

Le Magnen, J. (1950) L'odeur des pheromones sexuelles. *C. R. Acad. Sci. Ser. D.* **230**, 1367–1369.

Leon, M. (1978) Filial responsiveness to olfactory cues in the laboratory rat. *Advances in the Study of Behaviour* **8**, 117–153.

Leresche, L. A. (1976) Dyadic play in hamadryas baboons. *Behaviour* **57**, 190–205.

Leuthold, W. (1966) Variations in territorial behaviour of Uganda Kob *Adenota kob thomasi* (Neumann 1896). E. J. Brill, Leiden.

Leuthold, W. (1977) *African ungulates. A comparative review of their Ethology and Behavioural Ecology*. Springer-Verlag, Berlin.

Leuthold, W. (1978) On social organisation and behaviour of the Gerenuk, *Litocranius walleri* (Brooke 1878). *Z. Tierpsychol.* **47**, 194–216.

Levine, L. (1967) Sexual selection in mice IV. Experimental demonstration of selective fertilisation. *Amer. Nat.* **101**, 289–294.

Lewis, D. B. and Gower, D. M. (1980) *Biology of Communication*. Blackie, Glasgow.

Leyhausen, P. (1965) The communal organization of solitary mammals. *Symp. zool. Soc. Lond.* **14**, 249–263.

Leyhausen, P. (1979) *The Behaviour of Cats*. Garland Press, New York.

Lillehei, R. A. and Snowdon, C. T. (1978) Individual and situational differences in the vocalizations of young stumptail macaques (*Macaca arctoides*). *Behaviour* **65**, 270–281.

Lindburg, D. G. (1971) 'The Rhesus monkey in North India an ecological and behavioural study. V. Characteristics of a study population,' in *Primate Behaviour*: Vol. 2. *Developments in Field and Laboratory Research*. Rosenblum, L. A. (ed.) Academic Press, New York, pp. 1–106.

Lloyd, J. A. and Christian, J. J. (1969) Reproductive activity of individual females in three experimental freely growing populations of house mice (*Mus musculus*). *J. Mammal.* **50**, 49–59.

Lockie, J. D. (1966) Territory in small carnivores. *Symp. zool. Soc. Lond.* 18 143–165.

Lorenz, K. Z. (1943) Die angeborenen Formen Möglicher Erfahrung. *Z. Tierpsychol.* **5**, 235–409.

Lorenz, K. Z. (1966) *On Aggression*. Methuen, London.

Loudon, A. S. I., McNeilly, A. S. and Milne, J. A. (1983) Nutrition and lactational control of fertility in red deer. *Nature* **302**, 145–147.

Lott, D. F. (1979) Dominance relations and breeding rate in mature male American bison. *Z. Tierpsychol.* **49**, 418–432.

Lovecky, D. V., Estep, D. Q. and Dewsbury, D. A. (1979) Copulatory behaviour of cotton mice and their reciprocal hybrids with white-footed mice. *Anim. Behav.* **27**, 371–375.

Macdonald, D. W. (1979a) The flexible social system of the golden jackal *Canis aureus*. *Behav. Ecol. Sociobiol.* **5**, 17–38.

Macdonald, D. W. (1979b) Some observations and field experiments on urine marking behaviour of the red fox *Vulpes vulpes* L. *Z. Tierpsychol.* **51**, 1–22.

Macdonald, D. W. (1979c) 'Helpers' in fox society. *Nature* **282**, 69–71.

Mace, G. and Eisenberg, J. F. (1982) Competition, niche specialisation and the evolution of brain size in the genus *Peromyscus*. *Biol. J. Linn. Soc.* **17**, 243–257.

Mackinnon, J. R. (1974) The behaviour and ecology of wild orangutans (*Pongo pygmaeus*). *Anim.Behav.* **22**, 3–74.

Mackintosh, J. H. and Grant, E. C. (1966) The effect of olfactory stimuli on the aggressive behaviour of the laboratory mouse. *Z. Tierpsychol.* **23**, 584–587.

Mackintosh, J. H. (1970) Territory formation by laboratory mice. *Anim. Behav.* **18**, 177–183.

Mackintosh, J. (1973) Factors affecting the recognition of territory boundaries by mice (*Mus musculus*). *Anim. Behav.* **21**, 464–470.

Madsen, C. J. and Herman, L. M. (1980) 'Social and ecological correlates of cetacean vision and visual appearances,' in *Cetacean Behaviour: Mechanisms and Functions* Herman, L. M. (ed.), John Wiley & Sons, New York, pp. 101–147.

Majerus, M. E. N., O'Donald, P. and Weir, J. (1982) Female mating preference is genetic. *Nature* **300**, 521–523.

Malcolm, J. R. and Marten, K. (1982) Natural selection and the communal rearing of pups in African wild dogs (*Lycaon pictus*). *Behav. Ecol. Sociobiol.* **10**, 1–13.

Maple, T. (1980) *Orang utan Behaviour*. Van Nostrand Reinhold, New York.

Marler, P. (1966) Studies of fighting in chaffinches (3), Proximity as a cause of aggression. *Br. J. Anim. Behav.* **4**, 23–30.

Marler, P. (1970) Vocalizations of East African monkeys I. Red Colobus. *Folia Primatol.* **13**, 81–91.

Marler, P. (1976) 'Social organization, communication and graded signals: the chimpanzee and the gorilla', in *Growing points in Ethology*, Bateson, P. P. G. and Hinde, R. A. (eds.), Cambridge University Press, Cambridge, pp. 239–280.

Marler, P. (1977) 'The evolution of communication', in *How Animals Communicate*, Sebeok, T. A. (ed.), Indiana University Press, Bloomington, pp. 45–70.

Marler, P. and Tenaza, R. (1977) 'Signalling behaviour of apes with special reference to vocalization', in *How Animals Communicate*, Sebeok, T. A. (ed.) Indiana University Press, Bloomington, pp. 965–1033.

Marler, P. and Vandenbergh (eds.) (1979) *Handbook of Behavioural Neurobiology* Vol. 3. *Social Behaviour and Communication*. Plenum Press, New York.

Marsh, C. W. (1979) Comparative aspects of social organization in the Tana River Red colobus, *Colobus badius rufomitratus*. *Z. Tierpsychol.* **51**, 337–362.

Marten, K. and Marler, P. (1977) Sound transmission and its significance for animal vocalization I. Temperate habitats. *Behav. Ecol. Sociobiol.* **2**, 271–290.

Martin, R. D. (1968) Reproduction and ontogeny in tree shrews (*Tupaia belangeri*) with reference to their general behaviour and taxonomic relationships. *Z. Tierpsychol.* **25**, 409–495.

Martin, R. D. (1981) Field studies of primate behaviour. *Symp. zool. Soc. Lond.* **46**, 287–336.

Martin, R. D., Doyle, G. A. and Walker, A. C. (eds.) (1974) *Prosimian Biology*. Duckworth, London.

Martinez, D. R. and Klinghammer, E. (1978) A partial ethogram of the killer whale (*Orcinus orca* L.). *Carnivore* **3**, 13–27.

Mason, W. A. (1966) Social organisation of the South American monkey *Callicebus moloch* a preliminary report. *Tulane Studies in Zoology* **13**, 23–28.

Mason, W. A. (1968) Use of space by *Callicebus* groups,' in *Primates, Studies in Adaptation and Variability* Jay, P. C. (ed.), Holt Rinehart and Winston, New York, pp. 200–216.

Mason, W. A. (1974a) 'Differential grouping patterns in two species of South American monkey,' in *Ethology and Psychiatry*, White, N. F. (ed.), University Toronto Press, Toronto, pp. 153–170.

Mason, W. A. (1974b) Comparative studies of social behaviour in *Callicebus* and Saimiri-behaviour of male-female pairs. *Folia Primatol.* **22**, 1–8.

Massey, A. (1977) Agonistic aids and kinship in a group of pigtail macaques. *Behav. Ecol. Sociobiol.* **20**, 31–40.

Maynard-Smith, J. (1974) The theory of games and the evolution of animal conflict. *J. theor. Biol.* **47**, 209–221.

Maynard-Smith, J. (1976) Evolution and theory of games. *Am. Sci.* **64**, 41–45.

Maynard-Smith, J. and Parker, G. A. (1976) The logic of assymetric contests. *Anim. Behav.* **24**, 159–175.

Maynard-Smith, J. and Price, G. R. (1973) The logic of animal conflict. *Nature* **246**, 15–18.

McCann, T. S. (1982) Aggressive and maternal activities of female Southern Elephant seals (*Mirounga leonina*). *Anim. Behav.* **30**, 268–276.

McClean, I. G. (1982) The association of female kin in the Arctic ground squirrel *Spermophilus parryii*. *Behav. Ecol. Sociobiol.* **10**, 91–99.

McClintock, M. K. and Adler, N. T. (1978) The role of the female during copulation in wild and domestic Norway rats (*Rattus norvegicus*). *Behaviour* **67**, 67–96.

McCracken, S. F. and Bradbury, J. W. (1981) Social organization and kinship in the polygynous bat *Phyllostomus hastatus*. *Behav. Ecol. Sociobiol.* **8**, 11–34.

McKay, G. M. (1973) Behaviour and ecology of the Asiatic elephant in Southeastern Ceylon. *Smithsonian. Contrib. Zool.* **125**, Smithsonian Institution, Washington.

McKenna, J. J. (1979) The evolution of allomothering behaviour among colobine monkeys: function and opportunisms in evolution. *American Anthropologist* **81**, 818–840.

McKenna, J. J. (1981) 'Primate infant caregiving behaviour, origins, consequences and variability with emphasis on the common Indian langur monkey', in *Parental Care in Mammals*, Gubernick, D. J. and Klopfer, P. H. (eds.), Plenum Press, New York, pp. 381–416.

McLean, I. G. (1982) The association of female kin in the arctic ground squirrel *Spermophilus parryi*. *Behav. Ecol. Sociobiol.* **10**, 91–99.

McNab, B. V. (1963) Bioenergetics and home range size. *Amer. Nat.* **97**, 133–140.

Mech, L. D. (1970) *The Wolf.* Natural History Press, New York.

Medjo, D. C. and Mech, L. D. (1976) Reproductive activity in nine and ten month old wolves. *J. Mammal.* **57**, 406–408.

Melton, D. A. (1976) The biology of aardvarks (Tubulidentata Orycteropodidae). *Mammal Review* **6**, 75–88.

Mendelssohn, H. (1965) Breeding the Syrian hyrax *Procavia capensis syriaca* Schreber 1784. *Int. Zoo. Yearb.* **5**, 116–125.

Michael, R. and Keverne, E. B. (1970) Primate sex pheromones of vaginal origin. *Nature* **225**, 84–85.

Miller, E. H. (1975) Walrus ethology I. The social role of tusks and applications of multidimensional scaling. *Canadian J. Zool.* **53**, 590–613.

Mills, M. G. L. (1982) The mating system of the brown hyaena, *Hyaena brunnea* in the southern Kalahari. *Behav. Ecol. Sociobiol.* **10**, 131–136.

Mills, M. G. L. (1983) Behavioural mechanisms in territory and group maintenance of the brown hyaena *Hyaena brunnea* in the southern Kalahari. *Anim. Behav.* 503–510.

Mitani, J. C. and Rodman, P. S. (1979) Territoriality: Relation of ranging pattern and home range size to defendability, with an analysis of territoriality among primate species. *Behavioural Ecology and Sociobiology* **5**, 241–251.

Mitchell, G. D. (1969) Paternalistic behaviour in primates. *Psychol. Bull.* **71**, 399–417.

Mitchell, G. (1979) *Behavioural Sex Differences is Non-human Primates.* van Nostrand Reinhold, New York.

Moehlman, P. D. (1979) Jackal helpers and pup survival. *Nature* **277**, 382–383.

Montgomerie, R. D. (1981) Why do jackals help their parents? *Nature* **289**, 824–825.

Montgomery, G. G. and Lubin, Y. D. (1977) 'Prey influences on movement of Neotropical anteaters', in *Proceedings of the 1975 Predator Symposium*, Phillips, R. and Tonkel, C. (eds.), University of Montana Press, Missoula, pp. 103–131.

Montgomery, G. G. and Lubin, Y. D. (1978) Impact of anteaters (*Tamandua* and *Cyclopes*, Edentata: Myrmecophagidae) on arboreal ant populations. *American Society of*

Mammalogists, Abstr. III, p. 56, *Abstracts of Technical Papers*, 58th Annual Meeting.

Montgomery, G. G. and Sunquist, M. E. (1974) Contact-distress calls of young sloths. *J. Mammal.* **55**, 211–213.

Montgomery, G. G. and Sunquist, M. E. (1975) 'Impact of sloths on Neotropical energy flow and nutrient cycling', in *Tropical Ecosystems: Trends in Terrestrial and Aquatic Research*, Golley, F. B. and Medina, E. (eds.), Springer, New York, pp. 69–98.

Montgomery, G. G. and Sunquist, M. E. (1978) 'Habitat selection and use by two toed and three toed sloths', in *The Ecology of Arboreal Folivores*, Montgomery, G. G. (ed.), Smithsonian Institution, Washington, D.C., pp. 329–359.

Morris, D. (ed.) (1967) *Primate Ethology*. Weidenfeld & Nicholson, London.

Moss, C. J. (1983) Oestrus behaviour and female choice in the African elephant. *Behaviour* **86**, 167–196.

Moss, C. J. and Poole, J. H. (1983) 'Relationships and social structure of African elephants', in *Primate Social Relationships*, Hinde, R. A. (ed.), Blackwell, Oxford, pp. 315–325.

Moyer, K. E. (1976) *The Psychobiology of Aggression*. Harper and Row, New York.

Muller, H. (1970) Beitrage zur Biologie des Hermelins *Mustela erminea* Linne 1758. *Saugetierkdl, Mittlg*. **18**, 293–380.

Muller-Schwarze, D. (1974) 'Olfactory recognition of species, groups, individuals and physiological states among mammals', in *Pheromones*, Birch, M. C. (ed.) Elsevier, Netherlands, pp. 316–326.

Muller-Schwarze, D. (ed.) (1978) Evolution of play behaviour. *Benchmark Papers in Animal Behaviour*, Vol. 10, Dowden Hutchinson & Ross, Stroudsburg, Pa.

Muller-Schwarze, D., Stagge, B. and Muller-Schwarze, C. (1982) Play behaviour persistence, decrease and energetic compensation during food shortage in deer fawns. *Science* **215**, 85–87.

Myers, K. and Schneider, E. C. (1964) Observations on reproduction, mortality and behaviour in a small, free living population of wild rabbits. *CSIRO Wildl. Res.* **9**, 138–143.

Mykytowycz, R. (1958) Social behaviour of an experimental colony of wild rabbits *Oryctolagus cuniculus* (L) I. Establishment of the colony. *CSIRO Wildl. Res.* **3**, 7–25.

Mykytowycz, R. (1959) Social behaviour of an experimental colony of wild rabbits *Oryctolagus cuniculus* (L) II. First breeding season. *CSIRO Wildl. Res.* **4**, 1–13.

Mykytowycz, R. (1960) Social behaviour of an experimental colony of wild rabbits *Oryctolagus cuniculus* (L) III. Second breeding season. *CSIRO Wildl. Res.* **5**, 1–20.

Mykytowycz, R. (1968) Territorial marking by rabbits. *Scient. Am.* **218**, 116–126.

Mykytowycz, R. (1970) 'The role of skin glands in mammalian communication', in *Communication by Chemical Signals*: 1, Johnston, J. W., Moulton, D. G. and Turk, A. (eds.), Appleton-Century-Crofts, New York, pp. 327–360.

Mykytowycz, R. and Dudzincki, M. L. (1972) Aggressive and protective behaviour of adult rabbits *Oryctolagus cuniculus* L. towards juveniles. *Behaviour* **43**, 97–120.

Mykytowycz, R. and Hesterman, E. R. (1975) An experimental study of aggression in captive European rabbits *Oryctolagus cuniculus* (L). *Behaviour* **52**, 104–123.

Nagel, U. (1971) Social organization in a baboon hybrid zone. *Proc. 3rd Int. Congr. Primat. Zurich* (1970) Vol. 3, 48–57.

Nash, L. T. (1978) The development of mother-infant relationships in wild baboons *Papio anubis*. *Anim. Behav.* **26**, 746–759.

Neal, E. (1970) The banded mongoose *Mungos mungo* Gmelin. *E. Afr. Wildl. J.* **8**, 63–71.

Nelson, J. E. (1965) Behaviour of Australian Pteropodidae (Megachiroptera). *Anim. Behav.* **13**, 544–557.

Neyman, P. (1978) 'Aspects of the ecology and social organization of free ranging cotton top tamarins (*Saguinus oedipus*) and the conservation status of this species', in *The Biology and Conservation of the Callitrichidae*, Kleiman, D. G. (ed.), Smithsonian Institution Press, Washington, pp. 39–71.

Nicholas, J. D., Conley, W., Batt, B. and Tipton, A. R. (1976) Temporarily dynamic reproductive strategies and the concept of r and K selection. *Am. Nat.* **110**, 995–1005.

Niemitz, C. (1979) 'Outline of the behaviour of *Tarsius bancanus*', in *The Study of Prosimian*

Behaviour, Doyle, G. A. and Martin, R. D. (eds.), Academic Press, New York, pp. 631–660.

Nishida, T. (1968) The social group of wild chimpanzees in the Mahali mountains. *Primates* 9, 167–224.

Noirot, E. (1969) Serial order of maternal responses in mice. *Anim. Behav.* 17, 547–550.

Norris, K. S. (ed.) (1966) *Whales, Dolphins and Porpoises*. University of California Press, Berkeley.

Norris, K. S. and Dohl, T. P. (1980) 'The structure and functions of cetacean schools', in, *Cetacean Behaviour: Mechanisms and Function*, Herman, L. M. (ed.), John Wiley, New York, pp. 211–262.

Novicki, S. and Armitage, K. B. (1979) Behaviour of juvenile yellow-backed marmots: play and social integration. *Z. Tierpsychol.* 51, 85–105.

Nudds, T. D. (1978) Convergence of group size strategies by mammalian social carnivores. *Amer. Nat.* 112, 957–960.

Nyby, J., Wysocki, C. J., Whitney, G. and Dizinno, G. (1977) Pheromonal regulation of male mouse ultrasonic courtship (*Mus musculus*). *Anim. Behav.* 25, 333–341.

Oates, J. F. (1977) The social life of a black and white colobus monkey, *Colobus guereza*. *Z. Tierpsychol.* 45, 1–60.

O'Donald, P. (1983) 'Sexual selection by female choice', in *Mate Choice*, Bateson, P. (ed.), Cambridge University Press, Cambridge.

Oppenheimer, J. R. (1977) 'Communication in New World monkeys', in *How Animals Communicate*, Sebeok, T. A. (ed.), Indiana University Press, Bloomington, pp. 851–889.

Oglesby, J. M., Lanier, D. L. and Dewsbury, D. A. (1981) The role of prolonged copulatory behaviour on facilitating reproductive success in male Syrian golden hamsters (*Mesocricetus auratus*) in a competitive mating situation. *Behav. Ecol. Sociobiol.* 8, 47–54.

Ohsawa, H. (1979) 1. The local Gelada population and environment of the Gich area. 2. Herd dynamics, in *Ecological and Sociological Studies of Gelada Baboons*, Kawai, M. (ed.), *Contributions to Primatology* 16, 4–75. Karger, Basel.

Ohsumi, S. (1971) Some investigations on the school structure of sperm whales. *Sci. Rep. Whales Res. Inst.* 23, 1–25.

Owen-Smith, N. (1975) The social ethology of the white rhinoceros *Ceratotherium simum* Burchell 1817. *Z. Tierpsychol.* 38, 337–384.

Owens, D. D. and Owens, M. J. (1979a) Notes on the social organization and behaviour in brown hyaenas (*Hyaena brunnea*). *J. Mammal.* 60, 405–408.

Owens, D. D. and Owens, M. J. (1979b) Communal denning and class associations in brown hyaenas (*Hyaena brunnea* Thunberg) of the central Kalahari desert. *Afr. J. Ecol.* 17, 35–44.

Owens, M. J. and Owens, D. D. (1978) Feeding ecology and its influence on social organization of brown hyaenas (*Hyaena brunnea* Thunberg) of the Central Kalahari desert. *E. Afr. Wildl. J.* 16, 113–135.

Owens, N. W. (1975) Social play behaviour in free-living baboons, *Papio anubis*. *Anim. Behav.* 23, 387–408.

Owens, N. W. (1976) The development of socio sexual behaviour in free living baboons, *Papio anubis*. *Behaviour* 57, 241–259.

Packer, C. (1975) Male transfer in olive baboons. *Nature* 255, 219–220.

Packer, C. (1977) Reciprocal altruism in *Papio anubis*. *Nature* 265, 441–443.

Packer, C. (1979a) Male dominance and reproductive activity in *Papio anubis*. *Anim. Behav.* 27, 37–45.

Packer, C. (1979b) Inter troop transfer and inbreeding avoidance in *Papio anubis*. *Anim. Behav.* 27, 1–36.

Packer, C. (1980) Male care and exploitation of infants in *Papio anubis*. *Anim. Behav.* 28, 512–520.

Packer, C. and Pusey, A. E. (1982) Cooperation and competition within coalitions of male lions: kin selection or game theory? *Nature* 296, 740–742.

Packer, C. and Pusey, A. E. (1983) Adaptations of female lions to infanticide by incoming males. *Amer. Nat.* **121**, 716–728.

Pages, E. (1965) Notes sur les pangolins de Gabon. *Biol. Gabonica* **1**, 209–338.

Pages, E. (1970) Sur l'écologie et les adaptations de l'orycterope et des pangolins sympatriques du Gabon. *Biol. Gabonica* **6**, 27–92.

Pages, E. (1972*a*) Comportement maternel et developpement du jeune, chez un pangolin arboricole (*M. tricuspis*). *Biol. Gabonica* **8**, 63–120.

Pages, E. (1972*b*) Comportement aggressif et sexual chez les pangolins arboricoles (*Manis tricuspis* et *M. longicaudata*). *Biol. Gabonica* **8**, 1–62.

Pages, E. (1976) Etude eco-ethologique de *Manis tricuspis* par radio tracking. *Mammalia* **39**, 613–641.

Pariente, G. (1979) 'The role of vision in prosimian behaviour', in *The Study of Prosimian Behaviour*, Doyle, G. A. and Martin, R. D. (eds.), Academic Press, New York, pp. 411–459.

Payne, A. P. and Swanson, H. (1970) Agonistic behaviour between pairs of hamsters of the same and opposite sex in a neutral observation area. *Behaviour* **36**, 259–269.

Payne, R. S. and McVay, S. (1971) Songs of humpback whales. *Science* **173**, 585–597.

Peters, R. P. and Mech. L. D. (1975) Scent marking in wolves. *Amer. Sci.* **63**, 628–637.

Peterson, R. S. and Bartholomew, G. A. (1967) The natural history and behaviour of the California sea lion. *Am. Soc. Mammal. Spec. Publ.* **1**, 1–79.

Petrinovich, L. (1974) Individual recoginition of pup vocalization by Northern elephant seal mothers. *Z. Tierpsychol.* **34**, 308–312.

Petter, J-J and Charles-Dominique, P. (1979) 'Vocal communication in prosimians', in *The Study of Prosimian Behaviour*, Doyle, G. A. and Martin, R. D. (eds.) Academic Press, New York, pp. 247–304.

Pianka, C. R. (1970) On *r*- and *K*- selection. *Amer. Nat.* **104**, 592–597.

Platt, W. J. (1976) The social organization and territoriality of short tailed shrew (*Blarina brevicauda*) populations in old field habitats.

Poduschka, W. (1977) 'Insectivore communication', in *How Animals Communicate*, Sebeok, T. A. (ed.), Indiana University Press, Bloomington, pp. 600–633.

Poindron, P. and Le Neindre, P. (1980) Endocrine and sensory regulation of maternal behaviour in the ewe. *Advances in the Study of Behaviour* **11**, 75–119.

Poirier, F. E. and Smith, E. O. (1974) Socializing functions of primate play behaviour. *Amer. Zool.* **14**, 275–287.

Pollock, J. I. (1979) 'Spatial distribution and ranging behaviour in lemurs', in *The Study of Prosimian Behaviour*, Doyle, G. A. and Martin, R. D. (eds.), Academic Press, New York, pp. 359–407.

Poole, J. H. and Moss, C. J. (1981) Musth in the African elephant *Loxodonta africana*. *Nature* **292**, 830–831.

Poole, T. B. (1966) Aggressive play in polecats. *Symp. zool. Soc. Lond.* **18**, 23–44.

Poole, T. B. (1967) Aspects of aggressive behaviour in polecats. *Z. Tierpsychol.* **24**, 351–369.

Poole, T. B. (1972) Dyadic interactions between pairs of male polecats (*Mustela furo* and *Mustela furo × Mustela putorius* hybrids) under standardised environmental conditions in the breeding season. *Z. Tierpsychol.* **30**, 45–58.

Poole, T. B. (1973) The aggressive behaviour of individual male polecats (*Mustela putorius, M. furo* and hybrids) towards familiar and unfamiliar opponents. *J. Zool., Lond.* **170**, 395–414.

Poole, T. B. (1974*a*) The effects of oestrous condition and familiarity on the sexual behaviour of polecats (*Mustela putorius* and *M. furo × M. putorius* hybrids). *J. Zool., Lond.* **172**, 357–362.

Poole, T. B. (1974*b*) Detailed analysis of fighting in polecats (Mustelidae) using cine film. *J. Zool., Lond.* **173**, 369–393.

Poole, T. B. (1978*a*) An analysis of social play in polecats (Mustelidae) with comments on the evolutionary history of the open mouth play face. *Anim. Behav.* **26**, 36–49.

Poole, T. B. (1978*b*) 'A behavioural investigation of 'pair bond' maintenance in *Callithrix jacchus jacchus*', in *Biology and Behaviour of Marmosets*, Rothe, H. Wolters, H. J. and Hearn, J. P. (eds.), Eigenverlag Hartmut Rothe, Gottingen.

Poole, T. B. and Fish, J. (1975) An investigation of playful behaviour in *Rattus norvegicus* and *Mus musculus* (Mammalia). *J. Zool., Lond.* **175**, 61–71.

Poole, T. B. and Fish, J. (1976) An investigation of individual, age and sexual differences in the play of *Rattus norvegicus*. *J. Zool., Lond.* **179**, 249–260.

Poole, T. B. and Morgan, H. D. R. (1973) Differences in aggressive behaviour between male mice (*Mus musculus* L.) in colonies of different sizes. *Anim. Behav.* **21**, 788–795.

Poole, T. B. and Morgan, H. D. R. (1975) Aggressive behaviour of male mice (*Mus musculus*) towards familiar and unfamiliar opponents. *Anim. Behav.* **23**, 470–479.

Poole, T. B. and Morgan, H. D. R. (1976) Social and territorial behaviour of laboratory mice (*Mus musculus*) in small complex areas. *Anim. Behav.* **24**, 476–480.

Porter, F. L. (1979) Social behaviour in the leaf nosed bat (*Carollia perspicillata*). *Z. Tierpsychol.* **49**, 406–417.

Porter, R. H. and Wyrick, M. (1979) Sibling recognition in spiny mice (*Acomys cahirinus*): influence of age and isolation. *Anim. Behav.* **27**, 761–766.

Powell, R. A. (1979) Mustelid spacing patterns: variations on a theme by *Mustela*. *Z. Tierpsychol.* **50**, 153–165.

Pratt, D. M. and Anderson, V. H. (1979) Giraffe cow-calf relationships and social development of the calf in the Serengeti. *Z. Tierpsychol.* **51**, 233–251.

Price, E. O. (1980) Sexual behaviour and reproductive composition in male wild and domestic Norway rats. *Anim. Behav.* **28**, 657–667.

Pruscha, H. and Maurus, M. (1976) The communicative function of some agonistic behaviour patterns in squirrel monkeys: the relevance of social contact. *Behav. Ecol. Sociobiol.* **1**, 185–214.

Pruitt, C. H. and Burghardt, G. M. (1977) 'Communication in terrestrial carnivores: Mustelidae, Procyonidae and Ursidae', in *How Animals Communicate*, Sebeok, T. A. (ed.), Indian University Press, Bloomington, pp. 767–793.

Pusey, A. E. (1980) Inbreeding avoidance in chimpanzees. *Anim. Behav.* **28**, 543–552.

Ralls, K. (1976) Mammals in which females are larger than males. *Quart. Rev. Biol.* **51**, 245–276.

Ralls, K. (1977) Sexual dimorphism in mammals: avian models and unanswered questions. *American Naturalist* **111**, 917–938.

Rasa, O. A. E. (1971) Social interaction and object manipulation in weaned pups of the Northern elephant seal *Mirounga angustirostris*. *Z. Tierpsychol.* **29**, 82–102.

Rasa, O. A. E. (1973*a*) Marking behaviour and its social significance in the African dwarf mongoose *Helogale undulata rufula*. *Z. Tierpsychol.* **32**, 293–318.

Rasa, O. A. E. (1973*b*) Intrafamilial sexual repression in the dwarf mongoose *Helogale parvula*. *Naturwissenschaften* **6**, 303–304.

Rasa, O. A. E. (1977) The ethology and sociology of the dwarf mongoose (*Helogale undulata rufula*). *Z. Tierpsychol.* **43**, 337–406.

Rasa, O. A. E. (1979) The effects of crowding on the social relationships and behaviour of the dwarf mongoose (*Helogale undulata rufa*). *Z. Tierpsychol.* **49**, 317–319.

Rasmussen, D. R. (1979) Correlates of patterns of range use of a troop of yellow baboons (*Papio cynocephalus*) 1. Sleeping sites, impregnable females, births and male emigrations and immigrations. *Anim. Behav.* **27**, 1098–1112.

Rathbun, G. B. (1979) The social structure and ecology of elephant shrews. *Z. Tierpsychol. Suppl.* **20**, 1–76.

Redican, W. K. (1975) 'Facial expressions in non-human primates', in *Primate Behaviour*, Vol. 4: *Developments in field and laboratory research*, Rosenblum, L. A. (ed.), Academic Press, New York.

Reimer, J. D. and Petras, M. (1967) Breeding structure of the house mouse (*Mus musculus*) in a population cage *J. Mammal.* **48**, 88–99.

Reynolds, V. and Reynolds, F. (1965) 'Chimpanzees in the Budongo forest', in *Primate Behaviour Field Studies of Monkeys and Apes*, De Vore, I. (ed.), Holt Rinehart and Winston, New York, pp. 368–424.

Rheingold, H. L. (ed.) (1963) *Maternal Behaviour in Mammals*. John Wiley & Sons, New York.

Richards, S. M. (1974) The concept of dominance and methods of assessment. *Anim. Behav.* **22**, 914–930.

Ridgeway, S. H. and Benirschke, K. (eds.) (1977) *Breeding Dolphins: Present Status, suggestions for the future*. US Marine Mammal Commission Report MMC-76/0, Washington.

Rijksen, H. D. (1978) *A field study on Sumatran orang utans*. Veenman and Zonen, Wageningen.

Robinson, J. G. (1979*a*) Vocal regulation of use of space by groups of titi monkeys *Callicebus moloch*. *Behav. Ecol. Sociobiol.* **5**, 1–15.

Robinson, J. G. (1979*b*) An analysis of the organization of vocal communication in the titi monkey *Callicebus moloch*. *Z. Tierpsychol.* **49**, 381–405.

Robinson, J. G. (1982) Intrasexual competition and mate choice in primates. *Amer. J. Primatol.* Suppl. **1**, 131–144.

Rodman, P. S. (1973) 'Population composition and adaptive organization among orang-utans of the Kutai reserve', in *Comparative Ecology and Behaviour of Primates*, Crook, J. H. and Michael, R. P. (eds.), Academic Press, London, pp. 171–209.

Rodman, P. G. (1981) Inclusive fitness and group size with a reconsideration of group sizes in lions and wolves. *Amer. Nat.* **118**, 275–283.

Rood, J. P. (1980) Mating relationships and breeding suppression in the dwarf mongoose. *Anim. Behav.* **28**, 143–150.

Rood, J. P. (1972) Ecological and behavioural comparisons of three genera of Argentine cavies. *Anim. Behav. Monographs* **5** (1), 1–83.

Rosenblatt, J. S. and Siegel, H. I. (1981) 'Factor governing the onset and maintenance of maternal behaviour among non-primate mammals. The role of hormonal and non-hormonal factors', in *Parental Care in Mammals*, Gubernick, D. J. and Klopfer, P. H. (eds.), Plenum Press, New York, pp. 14–76.

Rosenblum, L. A. and Swartz, K. B. (1981) 'The social context of parental behaviour. A perspective on primate socialisation', in *Parental Care in Mammals*, Gubernick, D. J. and Klopfer, P. H. (eds.), Plenum Press, New York, pp. 417–454.

Rothe, H. (1975) Some aspects of sexuality and reproduction in groups of captive marmosets *Callithrix jacchus*. *Z. Tierpsychol.* **37**, 255–273.

Rothman, R. J. and Mech, L. D. (1979) Scent marking in lone wolves and newly formed pairs. *Anim. Behav.* **27**, 750–760.

Rowell, T. E. (1960) On the retrieving of young and other behaviour in lactating golden hamsters. *Proc. zool Soc. Lond.* **135**, 265–282.

Rowell, T. E. (1962) Agonistic noises of the rhesus monkey (*Macaca mulatta*). *Symp. zool. Soc. Lond.* **8**, 91–96.

Rowell, T. E. (1966*a*) Forest living baboons in Uganda. *J. Zool., Lond.* **149**, 344–364.

Rowell, T. E. (1972) *Social Behaviour of Monkeys*. Penguin Books, London.

Rowell, T. E. and Hinde, R. A. (1962) Vocal communication by the rhesus monkey (*Macaca mulatta*). *Proc. zool. Soc. Lond.* **138**, 279–294.

Rowell, T. E. (1974) The concept of social dominance. *Behav. Biol.* **11**, 131–154.

Rowell, T. and Dixson, A. F. (1975) Changes in social organization during the breeding season of wild talapoin monkeys. *J. Reprod. Fert.* **43**, 419–434.

Rudnai, J. (1973) Reproductive biology of lions (*Panthera leo massaica* Neumann) in Nairobi National Park. *E. Afr. Wildl. J.* **11**, 241–253.

Rylands, A. B. (1981) Preliminary field observations on the marmoset *Callithrix humeralifer intermedius* (Hershkovitz 1977) at Dardanelos, Rio Aripuana, Mato Grosso. *Primates* **22**, 46–59.

Saayman, G. S. and Tayler, C. K. (1979) The socioecology of humpback dolphins (*Sousa* sp.), in *Behaviour of Marine Mammals*, Winn, H. E. and Bori, L. O. (eds.) Plenum Press, New York.

Sandegren, F. E. (1976) Courtship display, agonistic behaviour and social dynamics in the Steller sea lion (*Eumetopias jubatus*). *Behaviour* **57**, 157–172.

Sachs, B. D. and Barfield, R. J. (1976) Functional analysis of masculine copulatory behaviour in the rat. *Advances in the Study of Behaviour* **7**, 91–154.

Schaller, G. B. (1963) *The Mountain gorilla: Ecology and Behaviour*. University of Chicago Press, Chicago.

Schaller, G. B. (1967) *The Deer and the Tiger: a Study of Wildlife in India*. University of Chicago Press, Chicago.

Schaller, G. B. (1972) *The Serengeti Lion*. University of Chicago Press, Chicago.

Schenckel, R. (1947) Expression studies of wolves. *Behaviour* **1**, 81–129.

Schilling, A. (1979) 'Olfactory communication in prosimians', in *The study of Prosimian Behaviour*, Doyle, G. A. and Martin, R. D. (eds.), Academic Press, New York, pp. 461–538.

Schneirla, T. C., Rosenblatt, J. S. and Tobach, E. (1963) 'Maternal behaviour in the cat', in *Maternal Behaviour in Mammals*, Rheingold, H. L. (ed.), John Wiley, New York, pp. 122–168.

Schurmann, C. (1982) 'Mating behaviour in wild orang utans', in *The Orangutan, Its Biology and Conservation*, de Boer, L. E. M. (ed.), Junk, The Hague.

Schultze-Westrum, T. (1965) Innerartliche Verstandigung durch Dufte beim Gleitbeutler *Petaurus breviceps papuanus* (Thomas) (Marsupialia, Phalangeriidae). *Z. versl. Physiol.* **50**, 151–220.

Schultze-Westrum, T. (1969) 'Social communication by chemical signals in flying phalangers', in *Olfaction and Taste*, Pfaffmann, C. (ed.), Rockefeller University Press, New York, pp. 268–272.

Scott, J. P. and Fuller, J. L. (1965) *Genetics and the Social Behaviour of the Dog*. University of Chicago Press, Chicago.

Sebeok, T. (ed.) (1977) *How Animals Communicate*. Indiana University Press, Bloomington.

Seidensticker, J. C. IV, Hornocker, M. C., Wiles, M. V. and Messick, J. P. (1973) Mountain lion social organization in the Idaho Primitive area. *Wildlife Monogr.* **35**, 1–60.

Selander, R. U. (1970) Behaviour and genetic variation in natural populations. *Amer. Zool.* **10**, 53–66.

Settle, G. A. (1977) The quiddity of tiger quolls. *Aus. Nat. Hist.* **19**, 166–169.

Settle, G. A. and Croft, D. B. (1982) 'Maternal behaviour of *Antechinus stuartii* (Dasyuridae, Marsupiallia) in captivity', in *Carnivorous Marsupials*, Archer, M. (ed.), Royal Zoological Society of New South Wales, Sydney, pp. 365–381.

Seyfarth, R. M. (1976) Social relationships among adult female baboons. *Anim. Behav.* **24**, 917–938.

Seyfarth, R. M. (1980) The distribution of grooming and related behaviours among adult female vervet monkeys. *Anim. Behav.* **28**, 798–813.

Seyfarth, R. M. and Cheney, D. L. (1984) Grooming, alliances and reciprocal altruism in vervet monkeys. *Nature* **308**, 541–542.

Seyfarth, R. M., Cheney, D. L. and Marler, P. (1980) Vervet monkey alarm calls: semantic communication in a free-ranging primate. *Anim. Behav.* **28**, 1070–1094.

Sherman, P. W. (1977) Nepotism and the evolution of alarm calls. *Science* **197**, 1246–1253.

Shillito-Walser, E. (1977) Maternal behaviour in mammals. *Symp. zool. Soc. Lond.* No **41**, 313–331.

Simons, P. E. (1974) *Adult-young Relationships. The Social Primates*. Harper and Row, New York.

Simpson, H. J. A., Simpson, A. E., Hooley, J. and Zunz, H. (1981) Infant-related influences in birth intervals in rhesus monkeys. *Nature* **290**, 49–51.

Sinclair, A. R. E. (1977) *The African Buffalo*. University of Chicago Press, Chicago.

Slater, P. J. B. (1978) *Sex hormones and behaviour*. Edward Arnold, Southampton, England.

Slijper, E. J. (1962) *Whales*. Hutchinson, London.

Smith, P. K. (1982) Does animal play matter? Functional and evolutionary aspects of animal and human play. *The Behavioural and Brain Sciences* **5**, 139–184.

Smith, E. O. and Pfeffer-Smith, P. G. (1982) Triadic interactions in captive barbary macaques (*Macaca sylvanus* Linnaeus 1758): 'Agonistic Buffering'? *Amer. J. Primatol.* **2**, 99–107.

Smith, W. J. (1968) 'Message meaning analysis', in *Animal Communication*, Sebeok, T. A. (ed.), Indiana University Press, Bloomington, pp. 44–60.

Smythe, N. (1978) The natural history of the central American agouti (*Dasyprocta punctata*). *Smithsonian Contrib. Zool.* **257**, 1–52.

Snowdon, C. T. and Cleveland, J. (1980) Individual recognition of contact calls by pygmy marmosets. *Anim. Behav.* **28**, 717–727.

Snowdon, C. T. (1978) Marmosets as models of speech and language disorders. *Prim. Med.* **10**, 225–231.

Snowdon, C. T. and Hodun, A. (1979) Monkeys vary call structure according to distance between conspecifics. *Bull Psychom. Soc.* **14**, 230.

Somers, P. (1973) Dialects in Southern Rocky Mountain pikas, *Ochotona princeps* (Lagomorpha). *Anim. Behav.* **21**, 124–137.

Sorenson, M. W. (1970) Behaviour of tree shrews. *Primate Behaviour* **1**, 141–193.

Southern, H. N. (1948) Sexual and aggressive behaviour in the wild rabbit. *Behaviour* **1**, 173–194.

Southwick, C. H., Siddiqui, M. F., Farooqui, M. Y. and Pal, B. L. (1974) 'Xenophobia among free ranging rhesus groups in India', in *Primate Aggression, Territoriality and Xenophobia, a Comparative Perspective*, Holloway, R. L. (ed.), Academic Press, New York.

Sparks, J. (1967) 'Allogrooming in primates: a review', in *Primate Ethology*, Morris, D. (ed.), Weidenfeld and Nicholson, London.

Spencer-Booth, Y. (1970) The relationships between mammalian young and conspecifics other than mother and peers: a review. *Advances in the Study of Behaviour* **3**, 119–194.

Stammbach, E. (1978) On social differentiation in groups of captive female hamadryas baboons. *Behaviour* **67**, 322–338.

Steel, E. (1980) Changes in female attractivity and proceptivity throughout the oestrous cycle of the Syrian hamster *Mesocricetus auratus*. *Anim. Behav.* **28**, 256–265.

Steiner, A. L. (1971) Play activity of Columbian ground squirrel, *Z. Tierpsychol.* **28**, 247–261.

Steiniger, B. (1976) Beitrage zum Verhalten und zur soziologie des Bisams (*Ondatra zibethicus* L.). *Z. Tierpsychol.* **41**, 55–79.

Sternglanz, S. H., Gray, J. L. and Murkami, M. (1977) Adult preferences for infantile facial features: an ethological approach. *Anim. Behav.* **25**, 108–115.

Stevenson, M. F. and Poole, T. B. (1976) An ethogram of the common marmoset *Callithrix jacchus jacchus*: general behavioural repertoire. *Anim. Behav.* **24**, 428–451.

Stevenson, M. F. and Poole, T. B. (1982) Playful interactions in family groups of the common marmoset (*Callithrix jacchus jacchus*). *Anim. Behav.* **30**, 886–900.

Stevenson, M. F. and Rylands, A. (in press) 'The marmoset monkeys: genus *Callithrix*', in *Ecology and Behaviour of Neotropical Primates*, Vol. 2: Academia Brasileira de Biencas, Rio de Janeiro.

Stoddart, E. (1977) 'Breeding and behaviour of Australian bandicoots', in *The Biology of Marsupials*, Stonehouse, B. and Gilmore, D. (eds.), Macmillan, London, pp. 179–192.

Stoddart, D. M. (1976) *Mammalian odours and pheromones.* Edward Arnold, London.

Stoddart, D. M. (ed.) (1980) Olfaction in Mammals. *Symp. zool. Soc. Lond.* **45**.

Stonehouse, B. and Gilmore, D. (eds.) (1977) *The Biology of Marsupials.* Macmillan, London.

Strahan, R. and Thomas, D. E. (1975) Courtship in the platypus *Ornithorhynchus anatinus. Aust. Zool.* **18**, 165–178.

Struhsaker, T. T. (1971) Social behaviour of mother and infant vervet monkeys (*Cercopithecus aethiops*). *Anim. Behav.* **19**, 233–250.

Struhsaker, T. T. (1975) *The Red Colobus Monkey.* Chicago University Press, Chicago.

Struhsaker, T. T. (1977) Infanticide and social organization in the red tail monkey, *Cercopithecus ascanius schmidti*, in the Kibale forest, Uganda. *Z. Tierpsychol.* **4**, 75–84.

Struhsaker, T. and Gartlan, J. S. (1970) Observations on the ecology and ethology of the patas monkeys *Erythrocebus patas* in the Waza reserve, Cameroon. *J. Zool. Lond.* **161**, 49–63.

Srikosamatara, S. (1982) 'Ecology of the pileated gibbon in southeast Thailand', in *The Lesser Apes Evolutionary and Behavioural Biology*, Preuschoft, H., Chivers, D. J., Brockelman, W. Y. and Creed, N. (eds.), University of Edinburgh Press, Edinburgh.

Suarez, B. and Ackerman, D. R. (1971) Social dominance and reproductive behaviour in male rhesus monkeys. *A. J. Phys. Anthropol.* **35**, 219–222.

Sugiyama, Y. (1960) On the division of a natural troop of Japanese monkeys at Takasakiyama. *Primates* **2**, 109–148.

Sugiyama, Y. (1976) Life history of male Japanese macaques. *Advances in the Study of Behaviour* **7**, 255–284.

Sugiyama, Y. and Ohsawa, H. (1982) Population dynamics of Japanese macaques at Ryozenyama: III female desertion of the troop. *Primates* **23**, 31–44.

Suomi, S. J. and Harlow, H. F. (1972) Social rehabilitation of isolate-reared monkeys. *Developmental Psychology* **6**, 487–495.

Sussman, R. W. (1975) 'A preliminary study of the behaviour and ecology of *Lemur fulvus rufus* Audebert 1800', in *Lemur Biology*, Tattersall, I. and Sussman, R. W. Plenum Press, New York, pp. 237–258.

Sussman, R. W. (ed) (1979) *Primate Ecology: Problem Orientated Field Studies.* John Wiley, New York.

Sutcliffe, A. G. and Poole, T. B. (1978) Scent marking and associated behaviour in captive common marmosets *Callithrix jacchus jacchus* with a description of the histology of the scent glands. *J. Zool., Lond.* **185**, 41–56.

Suttie, J. M. (1980) The effect of antler removal on dominance and fighting behaviour in farmed Red deer stags. *J. Zool. Lond.* **190**, 217–224.

Svare, B. B. (1981) 'Maternal aggression in mammals', in *Parental Care in Mammals*, Gubernick, D. J. and Klopfer, P. H. (eds.), Plenum Press, New York, pp. 179–210.

Symons, D. (1978) *Play and Aggression: A study of rhesus monkeys.* Columbia University Press, New York.

Takahata, Y. (1982) Social relations between adult males and females of Japanese monkeys in the Arashiyama B troop. *Primates* **23**, 1–23.

Tayler, C. K. and Saayman, G. S. (1972) The social organization and behaviour of dolphins *Tursiops aduncus* and baboons *Papio ursinus*. Some comparisons and assessments. *Ann. Cape Prov. Mus. Nat. Hist.* **9**, 11–49.

Thoman, E. B. and Levine, S. (1970) Hormonal and Behavioural changes in the rat mother as a function of early experience treatments of the offspring. *Physiology and Behaviour*, **5**, 1417–1421.

Thomas, J. A. and Birney, E. C. (1979) Parental care and mating system of the prairie vole, *Microtus ochrogaster. Behav. Ecol. Sociobiol.* **5**, 171–186.

Trillmich, F. (1981) Mutual mother-pup recognition in Galapagos fur seals and sea lions, cues used and functional significance. *Behaviour* **78**, 21–42.

Trivers, R. L. (1972) 'Parental investment and sexual selection', in *Sexual selection and the Descent of Man 1871–1971*, Campbell, B. (ed.), Aldine Press, Chicago, pp. 136–179.

Trivers, R. (1974) Parent-offspring conflict. *Amer. Zool.* **14**, 249–264.

Trivers, R. L. and Willard, D. E. (1973) Natural selection and parental ability to vary the sex ratio of offspring. *Science* **179**, 90–92.

Tutin, C. E. G. (1979a) Responses of Chimpanzees to copulation with special reference to interference by immature individuals. *Anim. Behav.* **27**, 845–854.

Tutin, C. E. G. (1979b) Mating patterns and reproductive strategies in a community of wild chimpanzees (*Pan troglodytes schweinfurthii*). *Behav. Ecol. Sociobiol.* **6**, 29–38.

Tutin, C. E. G. (1980) Reproductive behaviour of wild chimpanzees in the Gombe National Park, Tanzania, *J. Reprod. Fert. Suppl.* **28**, 43–57.

Tutin, C. E. G. and McGinnis, P.R. (1981) 'Chimpanzee reproduction in the wild', in *Reproductive Biology of the Great Apes*, Graham, C. E. (ed.), Academic Press, New York, pp. 239–264.

Tuttle, R. H. (ed.) (1975) *Socioecology and Psychology of Primates*. Mouton, The Hague.

Tyack, P. (1981) Interactions between singing Hawaiian humpback whales and conspecifics nearby. *Behav. Ecol. Sociobiol.* **8**, 105–116.

Tyler, S. J. (1972) The behaviour and social organization of the New Forest ponies. *Animal Behav. Monographs* **5** (2), 85–196.

Tyndale-Biscoe, H. (1973) *Life of Marsupials*. Edward Arnold, London.

van Hoof, J. A. R. A. M. (1962) Facial expressions in higher primates. *Symp. zool. Soc. Lond.* **8**, 47–125.

van Hoof, J. A. R. A. M. (1967) 'The facial expressions of the catarrhine monkeys and apes', in *Primate Ethology*, Morris, D. (ed.), Weidenfeld & Nicholson, London, pp. 7–68.

van Hoof, J. A. R. A. M. (1970) A component analysis of the structure of the social behaviour of a semi-captive chimpanzee group. *Experientia* **26**, 549–550.

van Horn, R. and Gray Eaton, G. (1979) 'Reproductive physiology and behaviour of prosimians', in *The Study of Prosimian Behaviour*, Doyle, G. A. and Martin, R. D. (eds.), Academic Press, New York, pp. 79–122.

van Lawick, H. (1974) *Solo, the Story of an African Wild Dog*. Houghton Mifflin, Boston, MA.

Vehrencamp, S. L. (1983) A model for the evolution of despotic versus egalitarian societies. *Anim. Behav.* **31**, 667–682.

Vehrencamp, S. L. Stiles, F. G. and Bradbury, J. W. (1977) Observations on the foraging behaviour and avian prey of the neotropical carnivorous bat *Vampyrum spectrum. J. Mammal.* **58**, 469–479.

Verberne, G. (1976) Chemocommunication among domestic cats mediated in the olfactory and vomeronasal senses, II. The relation between the function of Jacobson's organ (Vomero nasal organ) and flehmen behaviour. *Z. Tierpsychol.* **42**, 113–128.

Verberne, G. and de Boer, J. (1976) Chemocommunication among domestic cats mediated by the olfactory and vomeronasal senses. I. Chemocommunication *Z. Tierpsychol.* **42**, 86–109.

Verberne, G. and Leyhausen, P. (1976) Marking behaviour of some Viverridae and Felidae, time analysis of the marking patterns. *Behaviour* **58**, 192–253.

Vincent, L. E. and Bekoff, M. (1978) Quantitative analyses of the ontogeny of predatory behaviour in Coyotes (*Canis latrans*). *Anim. Behav.* **26**, 225–231.

Wade, T. D. (1978) 'The status and the ecological significance of behavioural dominance', in *Perspectives in Ethology*. 3. *Social Behaviour*, Bateson, P. P. G. and Klopfer, P. H. (eds), Plenum Press, New York, pp. 17–54.

Wade, T. D. (1978) Status and hierarchy in non human primate societies. *Perspectives in Ethology 3 (Social Behaviour)*, 109–134,

Walther, F. R. (1977) 'Artiodactyla', in *How Animals communicate*, Sebeok, T. A. (ed.), Indiana University Press, Bloomington, pp. 655–714.

Walther, F. R. (1978a) Forms of aggression in Thomson's gazelle: their situational motivation and their relative frequency in different sex, age and social classes. *Z. Tierpsychol.* **47**, 113–172.

Walther, F. R. (1978a) Mapping the structure and marking system of a territory of the Thomson's gazelle. *E. Afr. Wild. J.* **16**, 167–176.

Waring, A. and Perper, T. (1979) Parental behaviour in the Mongolian gerbil (*Meriones unguiculatus*). 1. Retrieval. *Anim. Behav.* **27**, 1091–1097.

Waring, A. and Perper, T. (1980) Parental behaviour in Mongolian gerbils (*Meriones unguiculatus*). II. Parental interactions. *Anim. Behav.* **28**, 331–340.

Waser, P. M. and Homewood, K. (1979) Cost-benefit approaches to territoriality a test with forest primates. *Behav. Ecol. Sociobiol.* **6**, 115–119.

Waser, P. M. and Waser, M. S. (1977) Experimental studies of Primate vocalization, specializations for long-distance propagation. *Z. Tierpsychol.* **43**, 231–263.

Welker, W. I. (1971) 'The ontogeny of play and explanatory behaviours: a definition of problems and a search for new conceptual solutions', in *The Ontogeny of Vertebrate Behaviour*, Moltz, H. (ed.), Academic Press, New York, pp. 171–228.

Wells, M. C. and Bekoff, M. (1981) An observational study of scent marking in coyotes, *Canis latranus. Anim. Behav.* **29**, 332–350.

Wells, R. S., Irvine, A. B. and Scott, A. D. (1980). 'The social ecology of Odontocetes', in *Cetacean Behaviour: Mechanisms and Functions*, Herman, L. M. (ed.) John Wiley, New York, pp. 263–318.

Wemmer, C. and Fleming, M. J. (1974) Ontogeny of playful contact in social mongoose, the meerkat *Suricata suricatta. Amer. Zool.* **14**, 415–426.

Wemmer, C. and Scow, K. (1977) 'Communication in the Felidae with emphasis on scent marking and contact patterns', in *How Animals Communicate*, Sebeok, T. A. (ed.), Indiana University Press, Bloomington, pp. 749–766.

West, M. (1974) Social play in the domestic cat. *Amer. Zool.* **14**, 427–436.

Wharton, C. H. (1950) Notes on the life history of the flying lemur. *J. Mammal.* **31**, 269–273.

Whittingham, D. G. and Wood, M. J. (1983) 'Reproductive physiology', in *The Mouse in Biomedical Research*, Vol. 3: Small, J. D., Foster, H. L. and Fox, J. G. (eds.) Academic Press, London, pp. 137–164.

Wickler, W. (1967) 'Socio-sexual signals and their intraspecific imitation among primates', in *Primate Ethology*, Morris, D. (ed.), Aldine, Chicago.

Wickler, W. and Seibt, U. (1983) 'Monogamy: an ambiguous concept', in *Mate Choice*, Bateson, P. (ed.), Cambridge University Press, Cambridge, pp. 33–50.

Wilson, E. O. (1975) *Sociobiology, the New Synthesis*. Belknap Press, Cambridge Mass. (Harvard University Press).

Wilson, S. C. (1974) Juvenile play of the common seal *Phoca vitulina vitulina* with comparative notes on the grey seal *Halichoerus grypus*. Behaviour **48**, 37–60.

Wilson, S. C. and Kleiman, D. G. (1974) Eliciting play: a comparative study. *Amer. Zool.* **14**, 341–370.

Winn, H. E. and Olla, B. L. (eds.) (1979) *Behaviour of marine animals: Current perspectives in research.* Vol. 3: Cetaceans, Plenum Press, New York.

Winn, H. E. and Schneider, J. (1977) 'Communication in Sireniens, Sea Otters and Pinnipeds', in *How Animal Communicate*, Sebeok, T. A. (ed.), Indiana University Press, Bloomington, pp. 809–840.

Wirtz, P. (1981) Terrestrial defence and territory takeover by satellite males in the waterbuck *Kobus ellipsiprymnus* (Bovidae). *Behav. Ecol. Sociobiol.* **8**, 161–162.

Wiseman, G. L. and Hendrickson, G. O. (1950) Notes on the life history and ecology of the opossum in southeast Iowa. *J. Mammal.* **31**, 331–337.

Wittenberger, J. F. (1979) 'The evolution of mating systems in birds and mammals', in *Handbook of Behavioural Neurobiology*, Vol. 3, pp. 271–349.

Wolfe, L. D. (1981) Display behaviour of three troops of Japanese monkeys (*Macaca fuscata*). *Primates* **22**, 24–32.

Woodward, S. L. (1979) The social systems of feral asses (*Equus asinus*). *Z. Tierpsychol.* **49**, 304–316.

Woolpy, J. H. and Eckstrand, I. (1979) 'Wolf pack genetics, a computer simulation with theory', in *The Behaviour and Ecology of Wolves*, Klinghammer, E. (ed.), Garland, New York, pp. 206–224.

Wrangham, R. W. (1979) On the evolution of ape social systems. *Social Science Information* **18**, 335–368.

Wrangham, R. W. (1980) An ecological model of female-bonded primate groups. *Behaviour* **75**, 262–300.

Wrangham, R. W. and Smuts, B. B. (1980) Sex differences in behavioural ecology of chimpanzees in the Gombe National Park, Tanzania. *J. Reprod. Fert.* Suppl. **28**, 13–31.

Wu, M. H., Holmes, W. G., Medina, S. R. and Sackett, G. P. (1980) Kin preference in *Macaca nemestrina*. *Nature* **285**, 225–227.

Index

Terms marked * are defined in the glossary (pp. 208 – 11)